201 All-Occasion Ornaments

in Plastic Canvas

Edited by
Laura Scott

HOUSE of
WHITE
BIRCHES

PUBLISHERS
SINCE 1947

201 All-Occasion Ornaments in Plastic Canvas

Editor: Laura Scott
Associate Editor: Cathy Reef
Design Associate: Vicki Blizzard
Technical Editor: June Sprunger
Book and Cover Design: Jessi Butler
Copy Editor: Mary Martin
Publications Coordinator: Tanya Turner

Photography: Tammy Christian, Jeff Chilcote, Kelly Heydinger, Justin P. Wiard
Photography Assistant: Linda Quinlan

Production Coordinator: Brenda Gallmeyer
Graphic Arts Supervisor: Ronda Bechinski
Graphic Artist: Cherie Pendley
Production Assistants: Janet Bowers, Marj Morgan
Traffic Coordinator: Sandra Beres
Technical Artists: Leslie Brandt, Julie Catey, Chad Summers

Publishers: Carl H. Muselman, Arthur K. Muselman
Chief Executive Officer: John Robinson
Marketing Director: Scott Moss
Book Marketing Manager: Craig Scott
Product Development Director: Vivian Rothe
Publishing Services Manager: Brenda R. Wendling

Printed in the United States of America
First Printing: 2002
Library of Congress Number: 00-112319
ISBN: 1-882138-81-3

A NOTE FROM
The Editor

Dear Crafters,

An ornament is, in many ways, the ideal plastic canvas project!

Not only are ornaments small and usually fairly easy to stitch, but they are so useful! Ornaments make wonderful commemorative gifts for many special occasions—birthdays, office parties, weddings, baby showers, anniversaries, graduations, holidays and Christmas. Because they are so small, gift ornaments don't need to match a certain decor.

Ornaments are also guaranteed moneymakers at bazaars. Who can resist a cute ornament to hang up in their home? Again, because they are small, you can whip up a dozen in no time at all.

Now some may think that ornaments are only for hanging on a tree. I use ornaments for many other purposes, and in a variety of places! You can hang them in a window, hang them off your car's rearview mirror, tie them to a gift package, make them into magnets and plant pokes, attach them to your child's school bag, use them as luggage-identifiers, string them together into a mobile—just to name a few!

One final bonus for making ornaments is that they are wonderful scrap users. You can finally work your way through that box of plastic canvas scraps and partial skeins of yarn!

I'm sure your reasons and uses for the delightful ornaments in this vibrant and fun collection will be equally clever and wonderful!

Warm regards,

Laura Scott

We hope you enjoy stitching and sharing each of these merry projects with friends and family for many years.

Welcome   Welcome   Welcome   Welcome   Welcome   Welcome   Welcome

Contents

Contents   Contents   Contents   Contents   Contents   Contents   Contents

August

October

December

September

November

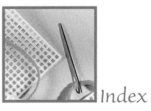

Index

WELCOME
Little Star

Design by Susan Leinberger

Celebrate the arrival of the newest member of your family with this keepsake star ornament framing Baby's first photo!

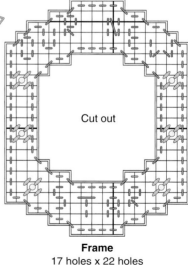

Skill Level: Beginner

Finished Size

5½ inches W x 5½ inches H

Materials

- ¼ sheet 7-count plastic canvas
- 1 Uniek QuickShape plastic canvas star
- Uniek Needloft plastic canvas yarn as listed in color key
- Uniek Needloft metallic craft cord as listed in color key
- #16 tapestry needle
- 1 yard ⅝-inch-wide white picot-edge satin ribbon
- Photo
- Hot-glue gun

Instructions

1. Cut plastic canvas according to graphs, cutting away gray area on star. From two loops at top of star, cut only top loop from star, leaving bottom loop intact.

2. Stitch pieces following graph, working uncoded areas on frame with white Continental Stitches.

3. Overcast frame edges with white. Overcast edges indicated on star with solid silver.

4. Work embroidery on frame with 1 ply yarn.

5. Cut photo to fit frame; center and glue behind opening on frame back.

6. Center and glue frame over unstitched area on star.

7. Cut one 10-inch length white satin ribbon and thread through loop at top of star; knot ends. Glue ends to loop.

8. Cut remaining ribbon in half. Place both lengths together and tie in a bow. Trim tails as desired. Glue bow over knot and plastic hanging loop. ✄

COLOR KEY	
Plastic Canvas Yarn	**Yards**
☐ Pink #07	1
▨ Sail blue #35	2
Uncoded areas are white #41 Continental Stitches	4
✎ White #41 Overcasting	
✎ Sail blue #35 Backstitch	
✎ Lilac #45 Backstitch	1
○ Baby yellow #21 French Knot	1
Metallic Craft Cord	
☐ Solid silver #55021	3
Color numbers given are for Uniek Needloft plastic canvas yarn and metallic craft cord.	

Our New Star
Cut 1
Cut away gray areas

Frame
17 holes x 22 holes
Cut 1

Cut out

Skill Level: Beginner

Finished Sizes

Hope star: 3⅞ inches W x 5½ inches H

Wish star: 3¼ inches W x 5¾ inches H

Materials

- ⅓ sheet 7-count plastic canvas
- Coats & Clark Red Heart Classic worsted weight yarn Art. E267 as listed in color key
- ⅛-inch-wide Plastic Canvas 7 Metallic Needlepoint Yarn by Rainbow Gallery as listed in color key
- ¹⁄₁₆-inch-wide Plastic Canvas 10 Metallic Needlepoint Yarn by Rainbow Gallery as listed in color key
- #16 tapestry needle
- 12 inches gold glitter stem from Designs by Joan Green
- Pencil
- Fabric glue

Instructions

1. Cut plastic canvas according to graphs.

2. Work uncoded background on hope star with amethyst Continental Stitches and uncoded background on wish star with skipper blue Continental Stitches. Overcast with gold ⅛-inch-wide metallic needlepoint yarn.

3. When background stitching and Overcasting are completed, work embroidery with gold ¹⁄₁₆-inch-wide metallic needlepoint yarn.

4. Using photo as a guide, cut glitter stem in half and coil each length around pencil. Glue stems to center bottom backside of stars.

5. For each star, cut a 6-inch to 7-inch length of gold ¹⁄₁₆-inch-wide metallic needlepoint yarn. Glue ends to top backside of star, forming a loop for hanging. ✄

As you start the new year, be sure to face it with plenty of wishes and lots of hope to make those wishes come true!

COLOR KEY

Worsted Weight Yarn	Yards
Uncoded background on hope star is amethyst #588 Continental Stitches	5
Uncoded background on wish star is skipper blue #848 Continental Stitches	5
⅛-Inch Metallic Needlepoint Yarn	
⁄ Gold #PC1 Overcasting	5
¹⁄₁₆-Inch Metallic Needlepoint Yarn	
⁄ Gold #PM51 Backstitch and Straight Stitch	5
○ Gold #PM51 French Knot	

Color numbers given are for Coats & Clark Red Heart Classic worsted weight yarn Art. E267 and Rainbow Gallery Plastic Canvas 7 and Plastic Canvas 10 Metallic Needlepoint yarns.

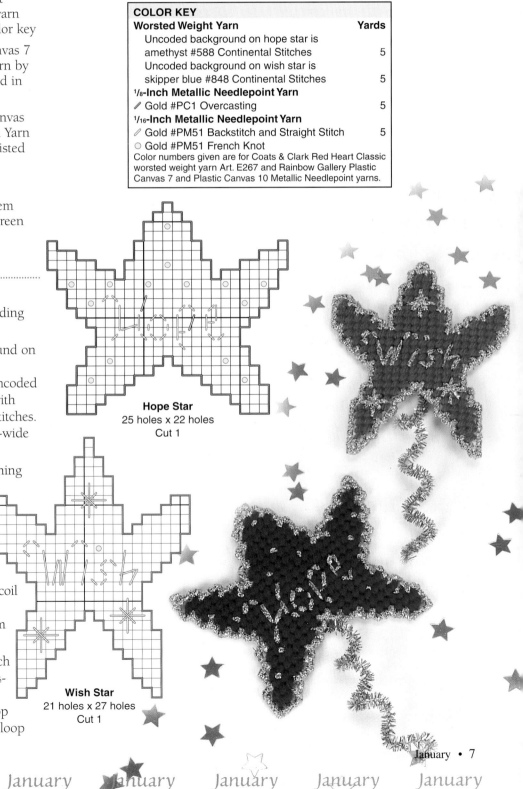

Hope Star
25 holes x 22 holes
Cut 1

Wish Star
21 holes x 27 holes
Cut 1

SPARKLING
Snowflakes

Designs by Ruby Thacker

Strands of silver thread and accents of faceted stones make this set of three snowflakes sparkle and shine with pristine beauty!

Skill Level: Intermediate

Finished Sizes

Large snowflake: 4½ inches W x 5¾ inches H

Medium snowflake: 3¾ inches W x 4½ inches H

Small snowflake: 3¼ inches W x 4 inches H

Materials

- 3 Uniek QuickShape plastic canvas hexagons
- Caron International Christmas Glitter worsted weight yarn Article 1285 as listed in color key
- #16 tapestry needle
- Crystal #006 acrylic faceted stones from The Beadery:

  6 (10mm x 5mm) navettes

  12 (15mm x 7mm) navettes

  1 (13mm) round

  12 (7mm) rounds

- 3 small suction cups
- Jewel glue

COLOR KEY
SMALL SNOWFLAKE

Worsted Weight Yarn	Yards
☐ Christmas glitter white #7501	3
● Attach round faceted stone	
● Attach navette faceted stone	

Color numbers given are for Caron International Christmas Glitter worsted weight yarn Article 1285.

COLOR KEY
MEDIUM SNOWFLAKE

Worsted Weight Yarn	Yards
☐ Christmas glitter white #7501	4
● Attach navette faceted stone	

Color number given is for Caron International Christmas Glitter worsted weight yarn Article 1285.

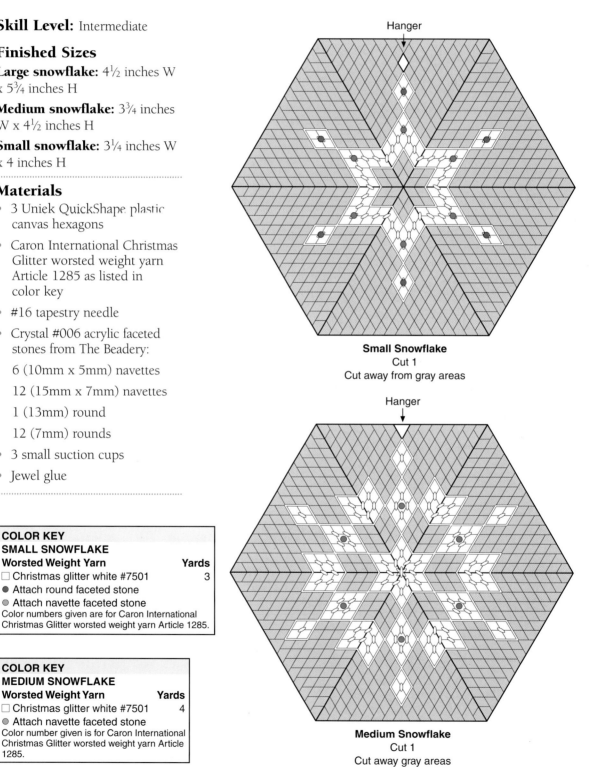

Small Snowflake
Cut 1
Cut away from gray areas

Medium Snowflake
Cut 1
Cut away gray areas

Instructions

1. Cut plastic canvas according to graphs, cutting away gray areas. Do not cut away hanging loop at top of large snowflake.

2. Stitch and Overcast pieces following graphs.

3. Using photo as a guide and jewel glue through step 4, glue six 10mm x 5mm navette stones and six 7mm round stones to large snowflake where indicated on graph.

4. Glue six 15mm x 7mm navette stones and six 7mm round stones to small snowflake; glue six 15mm x 7mm navette stones to medium snowflake where indicated on graphs. Glue 13mm round stone to center of medium snowflake.

5. Insert hook of suction cup into hanging loop of large snowflake and into holes indicated for hangers on medium and small snowflakes. ✄

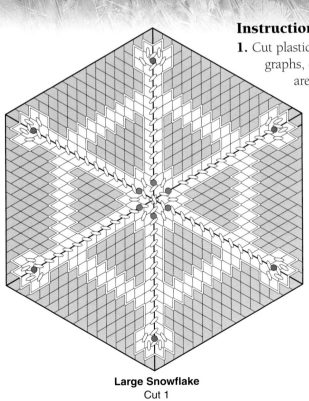

Large Snowflake
Cut 1
Cut away gray areas

CLOWNING
Around

Design by Lee Lindeman

Start the new year with lots of fun and laughter! Hang this whimsical ornament in your kitchen to remind the whole family to enjoy each day!

Skill Level: Beginner

Finished Size

3⅝ inches W x 6 inches H

Materials

- ⅓ sheet 7-count plastic canvas
- Coats & Clark Red Heart Classic worsted weight yarn Art. E267 as listed in color key
- Coats & Clark Red Heart Super Saver worsted weight yarn Art. E300 as listed in color key
- 6-strand embroidery floss as listed in color key
- #16 tapestry needle
- 6 inches ¼-inch-wide yellow satin ribbon
- Small amount red felt or synthetic suede
- ½-inch-wide gold star
- 5 (15mm) Christmas balls in assorted colors
- 10 inches thin wire
- Thin gold cord
- Small amount fiberfill
- Tacky craft glue or hot-glue gun

Instructions

1. Cut plastic canvas according to graphs.

2. Cut a ⅜-inch circle for nose and a narrow ½-inch-wide smiling mouth from red felt or synthetic suede.

3. Stitch pieces following graphs, working uncoded areas with

Clowning Around Front
23 holes x 29 holes
Cut 1

Clowning Around Back
23 holes x 29 holes
Cut 1

COLOR KEY

Worsted Weight Yarn	Yards
■ Orange #245	3
□ White #311	1
■ Black #312	2
□ Bright yellow #324	5
■ Hot red #390	6
■ Grenadine #730	1
Uncoded areas are baby pink #724 Continental Stitches	2
╱ Baby pink #724 Whipstitching	
● Orange #245 Turkey Loop Stitches	
6-Strand Embroidery Floss	
● Black French Knot	1

Color numbers given are for Coats & Clark Red Heart Classic worsted weight yarn Art. E267 and Super Saver worsted weight yarn Art. E300.

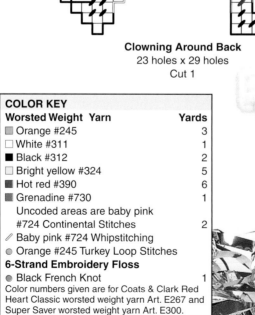

SKI
Sweater

Design by Lynne L. Langer

Remember those cold, snowy winter days and bundling up in your favorite warm sweater with this cute ornament!

Skill Level: Beginner

Finished Size

4⅞ inches W x 3⅛ inches H

Materials

- ¼ sheet 7-count plastic canvas
- Worsted weight yarn as listed in color key
- Metallic craft cord as listed in color key
- #16 tapestry needle
- Ornament hook

Instructions

1. Cut plastic canvas according to graph.

2. Stitch pieces following graph, working uncoded areas with light blue Continental Stitches and working royal blue stitches over bottom and sleeve edges with a double strand.

3. Overcast front and back pieces between dots at neck and wrists. Whipstitch wrong sides together along all remaining edges except bottom edge.

4. Insert ornament hook in top center hole of sweater back. ✂

COLOR KEY	
Worsted Weight Yarn	**Yards**
☐ Light blue	5
◼ Royal blue	3
☐ White	1
◼ Black	1
Uncoded areas are light blue Continental Stitches	
Metallic Craft Cord	
☐ Silver	1

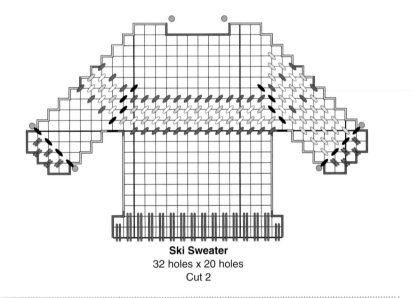

Ski Sweater
32 holes x 20 holes
Cut 2

CLOWNING
Around

baby pink Continental Stitches.

4. When background stitching is completed, work black floss French Knots on head front for eyes and orange Turkey Loop Stitches on head front and back for hair.

5. Whipstitch wrong sides together following graphs, filling

body with a small amount of fiberfill before closing. Cut Turkey Loop Stitches and unravel; trim as desired.

6. Glue gold star to tip of hat. Tie yellow ribbon in a bow and glue under face for bow tie. Glue nose and mouth to face.

7. Using photo as a guide through step 8, for balloons, thread five Christmas balls onto

middle of thin wire. Twist ends of wire together, to make wire stiff.

8. For hanger, cut a 10-inch length of thin gold cord. Thread ends of cord through hole of one balloon; knot and glue to secure. Glue balloons together with a small amount of glue, bringing hanging loop up through center of balloons. Glue end of wire into hand on yellow arm. ✂

HAPPY BIRTHDAY
Cake & Clown

Designs by Mary T. Cosgrove

Either of these ornaments makes delightful gift tags! Tie them onto packages with brightly colored ribbon for extra fun!

Skill Level: Beginner

Finished Sizes

Cake: 4¾ inches W x 5 inches H

Clown: 5⅜ inches W x 5¼ inches H

Materials

- ½ sheet Uniek QuickCount 7-count plastic canvas
- Uniek Needloft plastic canvas yarn as listed in color key
- #16 tapestry needle
- Nylon thread

Instructions

1. Cut plastic canvas according to graphs.

2. Stitch and Overcast pieces following graphs, working uncoded area on cake with cinnamon Continental Stitches.

3. When background stitching is completed, work Backstitches, Straight Stitches and French Knots.

4. For hangers, cut desired length of nylon thread. For cake, thread ends through yarn on backside of two outside candle flames. Tie ends in a knot, trim excess. Repeat for clown, attaching ends to back of hat pompom and yellow balloon. ✂

COLOR KEY	
CLOWN	
Plastic Canvas Yarn	**Yards**
■ Christmas red #02	3
□ White #41	2
□ Yellow #57	2
■ Bright orange #58	2
■ Bright blue #60	2
■ Bright pink #62	1
■ Bright purple #64	2
✏ Black #00 Backstitch, Straight Stitch and Overcasting	2
✏ Bright purple #64 Backstitch	
● Christmas red #02 French Knot	
○ White #41 French Knot	
Color numbers given are for Uniek Needloft plastic canvas yarn.	

COLOR KEY	
CAKE	
Plastic Canvas Yarn	**Yards**
□ White #41	3
■ Bright blue #60	1
■ Bright pink #62	4
□ Bright yellow #63	1
Uncoded areas are cinnamon #14 Continental Stitches	7
✏ Cinnamon #14 Overcasting	
✏ White #41 Backstitch and Straight Stitch	
Color numbers given are for Uniek Needloft plastic canvas yarn.	

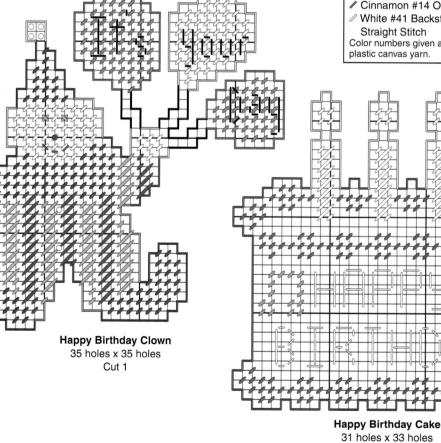

Happy Birthday Clown
35 holes x 35 holes
Cut 1

Happy Birthday Cake
31 holes x 33 holes
Cut 1

BALLOON
Trio

Design by Nancy Marshall

Nothing adds cheer like colorful balloons! Stitch this uplifting project for birthdays, or to cheer a shut-in!

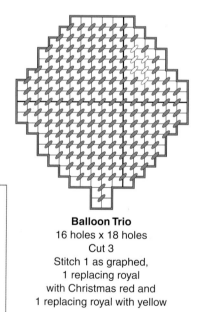

Skill Level: Beginner

Finished Size

3⅝ inches W x 5½ inches H

Materials

- ¼ sheet Uniek QuickCount 7-count plastic canvas
- Uniek Needloft plastic canvas yarn as listed in color key
- #16 tapestry needle
- 11 assorted sequins
- 3 (6-inch) lengths Wire Art gray plastic-coated wire from Duncan Enterprises
- Wire cutters
- Pliers
- ¼-inch-diameter metal or wooden rod
- Nylon monofilament
- Tacky craft glue

Instructions

1. Cut three balloons from plastic canvas according to graph.

2. Stitch one balloon with royal and white as graphed and one each replacing royal with Christmas red and yellow. Overcast with adjacent colors.

3. Leaving 2 inches of each length of wire straight, wrap wire around rod to make coil.

4. For each balloon, using pliers, wrap straight end of one length around neck of balloon, twisting wire around itself on backside to secure. Pull coil to extend length.

5. Using photo as a guide, glue balloons together, then glue sequins on balloons as desired.

6. Thread desired length of nylon monofilament through a center top hole of top balloon. Tie ends together in a knot to form a loop for hanging. ✄

Celebrate!
Just for Fun

Festival of
Sleep Day is
Jan. 3

National
Popcorn Day
is Jan. 19

Balloon Trio
16 holes x 18 holes
Cut 3
Stitch 1 as graphed,
1 replacing royal
with Christmas red and
1 replacing royal with yellow

COLOR KEY	
Plastic Canvas Yarn	**Yards**
Christmas red #02	4
■ Royal #32	4
□ White #41	1
Yellow #57	4
Color numbers given are for Uniek Needloft plastic canvas yarn.	

Skill Level: Beginner

Finished Size

2⅞ inches W x 3¼ inches H

Materials

- ½ sheet 7-count plastic canvas
- Worsted weight yarn as listed in color key
- Darice metallic cord as listed in color key
- #16 tapestry needle
- 16 (12mm) dogwood flower beads in coordinating colors from The Beadery
- 16 (3mm) round gold beads
- 4 (3mm) round black beads
- Sewing needle and gold and black sewing thread
- Thin gold cord

BLUEBELL &
Rosebud Angels

Designs by Alida Macor

Stitch a diminutive guardian angel as a gift for a favorite little girl! Tell her to think of your love every time she sees it!

Instructions

1. Cut plastic canvas according to graphs.

2. Stitch bluebell pieces as graphed. Stitch rosebud pieces replacing light blue with white, rust with yellow and white/gold with pink/silver.

3. Following graphs through step 4, Attach beads for eyes to head fronts with sewing needle and black sewing thread. Place gold beads in center of flowers and attach with sewing needle and gold sewing thread.

4. Overcast bottom edges of angels' robes from dot to dot. Whipstitch wrong sides of corresponding pieces together along remaining edges.

5. For each angel, attach desired length of thin gold cord through top center hole of head with a Lark's Head Knot. Tie ends together in a knot to form a loop for hanging. ✂

COLOR KEY	
Worsted Weight Yarn	**Yards**
☐ Light blue	5
White	5
■ Rust	2
Yellow	2
☐ Peach	2
▨ Green	1
Metallic Cord	
Pink/silver #34021-117	2
☐ White/gold #34021-149	2
● Attach black bead	
● Attach flower and gold bead	
Color numbers given are for Darice metallic cord.	

Angel Back
19 holes x 19 holes
Cut 1 for each angel
Stitch as graphed for bluebell
For rosebud, replace light blue
with white, rust with yellow and
white/gold with pink/silver

Angel Front
19 holes x 19 holes
Cut 1 for each angel
Stitch as graphed for bluebell
For rosebud, replace light blue
with white, rust with yellow and
white/gold with pink/silver

TOOTH
Fairy

Design by Janna Britton

As soon as your child's first tooth begins to wiggle, hang this sweet tooth fairy ornament close to her bed to watch for the momentous occasion!

Skill Level: Intermediate

Finished Size
4¾ inches W x 5⅜ inches H

Materials
- ¼ sheet Uniek QuickCount clear 7-count plastic canvas
- Small amount white 7-count plastic canvas
- Small amount clear 10-count plastic canvas
- Uniek Needloft plastic canvas yarn as listed in color key
- DMC 6-strand embroidery floss as listed in color key
- ¼-inch-wide satin ribbon as listed in color key
- 1 yard platinum #101 Kreinik Heavy (#32) Braid
- #16 tapestry needle
- 44 inches 1¼-inch-wide pre-gathered white nylon lace
- 4½ inches 2½-inch-wide iridescent white #29 Ballet #28-9119 wire-edge ribbon from Offray
- DecoArt Americana Baby pink #DA31 acrylic paint
- Iridescent glitter paint
- ½-inch-wide flat paintbrush
- 6 inches silver tinsel stem
- 7 inches 4mm round transparent crystal bead-on-a-string
- 2 (15mm) crystal acrylic faceted stars from The Beadery
- Dark brown Lil' Loopies small loopy textured doll hair from One & Only Creations
- Sewing needle and pink sewing thread

- Silver metallic thread
- 8-ounce cup
- ⅓ cup water
- Paper towels
- Low-temperature glue gun

Cutting & Stitching
1. Cut body pieces and purse from clear 7-count plastic canvas, tooth from white 7-count plastic canvas and face from 10-count clear plastic canvas according to graphs.

2. Following graphs through step 4, stitch fairy bodies with plastic canvas yarn, reversing one for fairy back and stitching entire head on back with brown Continental Stitches. Whipstitch wrong sides together.

3. Stitch and Overcast face with embroidery floss, then work rose Backstitches for mouth and very dark beige brown

French Knots for eyes with 6-plies.

4. Stitch and Overcast purse with silver metallic ribbon. Stitch tooth with white ribbon; do not Overcast.

Hair
1. Glue face to front of head on fairy.

2. Wrap 1 strand hair around index finger six to 10 times; glue to head, beginning at front bottom edge and working up around face and down other side.

3. Continue working rows on back of head, covering brown stitching.

Crown & Wand
1. Using photo as a guide through step 2, for crown, cut a 4-inch length of silver tinsel stem. Twist 4½-inch length pearl strand around stem. Wrap around head, overlapping ends. Glue in place.

2. For wand, matching edges, glue backs of crystal faceted stars together over one end of remaining silver tinsel stem. Wrap remaining pearl strand around stem, trimming as necessary to fit. Glue to back of top hand.

Skirt
1. For skirt, pour water into cup and squirt a 2-inch stream of baby pink

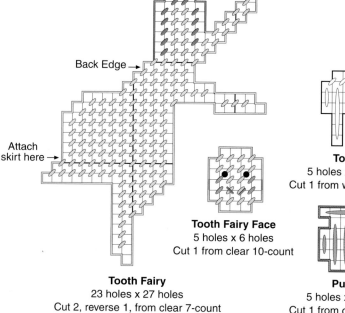

Back Edge →

Attach skirt here →

Tooth Fairy
23 holes x 27 holes
Cut 2, reverse 1, from clear 7-count

Tooth Fairy Face
5 holes x 6 holes
Cut 1 from clear 10-count

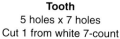

Tooth
5 holes x 7 holes
Cut 1 from white 7-count

Purse
5 holes x 6 holes
Cut 1 from clear 7-count

paint into water; mix well.

2. Place lace trim in paint water and stir well. Remove from paint water and blot on paper towels. Hang to dry.

3. Paint lace with iridescent glitter paint. Allow to dry.

4. Using sewing needle and pink sewing thread through step 5, hand-gather lace as needed for more ruffle.

5. Begin tacking lace to bottom backside of fairy where indicated on graph. Moving upward for each layer, tack skirt around fairy in four layers, making each layer ¼ inch to ½ inch apart and ending lace on backside.

Wings

1. Fold ribbon in half with wire edges at top and bottom. Using pattern given, cut scallops along top edge, cutting away wire. Cut ribbon down fold to wire edge. Do not cut wire.

2. Fold wire in half. Gather ribbon, sliding on wire, then twist ends together snuggly, forming wings.

3. Using photo as a guide, tack center of wings to back edge of fairy with sewing needle and pink sewing thread.

Final Assembly

1. Use photo as a guide throughout assembly. Tie a knot in center of silver heavy (#32) braid, leaving a ¾-inch loop. Wrap tails of braid around neck of purse, tying in a knot on front. Tie a knot in both ends; trim excess.

2. Slip loop over lower arm to elbow joint. Glue purse to skirt.

3. Glue tooth to front of bottom hand.

4. Cut two 7½-inch lengths of silver metallic thread. Place lengths together and thread through top of head. Tie ends together in a knot to form a loop for hanging; trim excess. ✄

Scallop Edge

Fold

Wings
Cut 1 from
iridescent white
wire-edge ribbon

Wire Edge

COLOR KEY	
Plastic Canvas Yarn	**Yards**
☐ Pink #07	6
■ Brown #15	2
☐ Flesh tone #56	2
6-Strand Embroidery Floss	
■ Light cranberry #604	1
☐ Light tawny #951	2
╱ Rose #335 Backstitch	1
● Very dark beige brown #838 French Knot	1
¼-Inch-Wide Satin Ribbon	
■ Silver metallic	1
☐ White	1
Color numbers given are for Uniek Needloft plastic canvas yarn and DMC 6-strand embroidery floss.	

CELEBRATION
Balloons

Design by Janelle Giese

Start a boy's or girl's birthday with a festive touch with this cheery celebration ornament!

Skill Level: Beginner

Finished Size

4¾ inches W x 5¾ inches H

Materials

- ¼ sheet Uniek QuickCount 7-count plastic canvas
- Uniek Needloft plastic canvas yarn as listed in color key
- DMC #5 pearl cotton as listed in color key
- DMC #8 pearl cotton as listed in color key
- #16 tapestry needle
- 6 (4-inch) lengths 30-gauge white covered stem wire
- Thick white glue

Cutting & Stitching

1. Cut plastic canvas according to graphs.

2. Stitch and Overcast banner following graph, working uncoded background with white Continental Stitches.

3. When background stitching and Overcasting are completed, work embroidery with #5 pearl cotton, wrapping pearl cotton around needle twice for French Knot.

4. Stitch and Overcast balloons following graph, working uncoded area with yellow Continental Stitches.

5. For embroidery, use full strand of black yarn to work two Straight Stitches for each pupil on yellow balloon and one Straight Stitch for each pupil on royal and Christmas red balloons.

6. Use 1 ply white to Straight Stitch eye highlights on yellow balloon, coming up through black yarn Straight Stitches and going down over intersection as indicated.

7. Use 1 ply to work all white and yellow Straight Stitches. Use black #8 pearl cotton to work Backstitches and Straight Stitches outlining balloons.

8. Use black #5 pearl cotton for all remaining embroidery.

Assembly

1. For hanger, cut a 7-inch length of black #8 pearl cotton. Thread ends from front to back through holes indicated on graph. Knot ends on backside so loop extends 3 inches above top of ornament; trim ends as needed. To secure, glue knot to backside.

2. Using photo as a guide through step 3, for balloon strings, bend three lengths of wire serpentine style. Glue one length to backside of each balloon at neck. Allow to dry.

3. Tie each remaining length of wire into a tiny bow and glue to front of balloons at necks. Glue banner over strings. Allow to dry. ✂

COLOR KEY	
Plastic Canvas Yarn	**Yards**
■ Black #00	1
■ Christmas red #02	3
☐ Tangerine #11	2
☐ Moss #25	1
■ Royal #32	2
☐ White #41	4
Uncoded background on banner is white #41 Continental Stitches	
Uncoded areas on balloons are yellow #57 Continental Stitches	4
╱ Black #00 Straight Stitch	
╱ White #41 Straight Stitch	
╱ Yellow #57 Straight Stitch and Overcasting	
#5 Pearl Cotton	
╱ Black #310 Backstitch and Straight Stitch	3
● Black #310 French Knot	
#8 Pearl Cotton	
╱ Black #310 Backstitch and Straight Stitch	1
● Attach hanger	
Color numbers given are for Uniek Needloft plastic canvas yarn and DMC pearl cotton.	

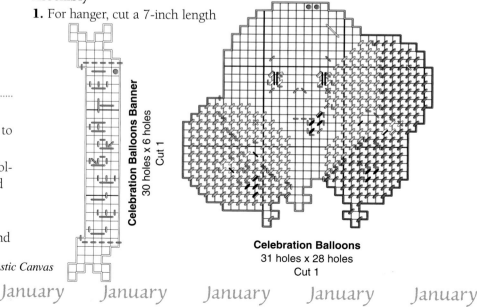

Celebration Balloons Banner
30 holes x 6 holes
Cut 1

Celebration Balloons
31 holes x 28 holes
Cut 1

BIRTHDAY
Cake

Design by Janna Britton

Create a memory and keepsake by giving this ornament to a special friend on her birthday!

Skill Level: Intermediate

Finished Size

3¼ inches H x 3 inches in diameter, including candles

Materials

- ¼ sheet Uniek QuickCount 7-count plastic canvas
- 2 (3-inch) Uniek QuickShape plastic canvas radial circles
- Uniek Needloft plastic canvas yarn as listed in color key
- DMC #3 pearl cotton as listed in color key
- #16 tapestry needle
- 4¼-inch Kreative Kanvas non-woven fabric-covered plastic core circle from Kunin Felt
- 12-inch white iridescent glitter stem
- Small amount yellow felt
- 10 inches monofilament line
- Low-temperature glue gun

Cutting & Stitching

1. Cut plastic canvas according to graphs, cutting away gray area from cake top. Do not cut cake base.

2. Cut 4½-inch non-woven fabric-covered plastic core circle to fit cake base. Set aside.

3. Using white through step 4, Straight Stitch around cake top circle from the first outside row of holes to the fourth row of holes, using two stitches per hole as necessary in the fourth row of holes.

4. Now Straight Stitch from the fourth row of holes to the four center holes. *Note: There should be six stitches in each section.*

5. When background stitching is completed, work Lazy Daisy Stitches and French Knots following cake top graph.

6. Stitch base and side following graphs, overlapping where indicated on side before stitching and working uncoded area on side with white Continental Stitches.

7. When background stitching is completed, work embroidery with yarn and pearl cotton.

Assembly

1. Use photo as a guide throughout assembly. Using white, Whipstitch cake top to cake side with white, then work French Knots around Whipstitched edge.

2. Using pearl cotton through

Continued on page 21

COLOR KEY	
Plastic Canvas Yarn	**Yards**
☐ White #41	20
Uncoded area on side is white #41 Continental Stitches	
◐ Pink #07 French Knot	2
○ Yellow #57 French Knot	2
◑ Fern #23 French Knot	2
⬮ Fern #23 Lazy Daizy Stitch	
#3 Pearl Cotton	
✎ Medium pink #776 Backstitch	3
● Medium pink #776 French Knot	
Color numbers given are for Uniek Needloft plastic canvas yarn and DMC #3 pearl cotton.	

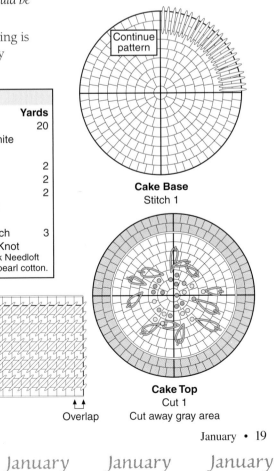

Continue pattern

Cake Base
Stitch 1

Cake Top
Cut 1
Cut away gray area

Cake Side
50 holes x 11 holes
Cut 1

↑↑
Overlap

↑↑
Overlap

CHERUB
Valentine

Design by Janelle Giese

Your extra effort in stitching this exquisite ornament is sure to be appreciated and cherished for many years to come!

Skill Level: Advanced

Finished Size
5⅞ inches W x 5⅞ inches H

Materials
- ½ sheet 7-count plastic canvas
- Coats & Clark Red Heart Classic worsted weight yarn Art. E267 as listed in color key
- DMC #5 pearl cotton as listed in color key
- DMC #8 pearl cotton as listed in color key
- #16 tapestry needle
- Hot-glue gun

Instructions

1. Cut plastic canvas according to graph.

2. Continental Stitch piece following graph, working uncoded areas on cherub with sea coral Continental Stitches and uncoded area on heart with pale rose Continental Stitches. Overcast following graph.

3. When background stitching and Overcasting are completed, use 2 plies light coral rose to Backstitch lips. Work medium beige brown and black pearl cot-

ton embroidery. Work letters on heart with very dark garnet, wrapping pearl cotton one time for French Knot.

4. Work orange Straight Stitches for flower centers. Using 2 plies white yarn, work Straight Stitches along each side of orange stitches, and French Knots for baby's breath, wrapping pearl cotton one time around needle.

5. For each eye, use 2 plies white to work Straight Stitch over sea coral Continental Stitch where indicated on graph. Use 2 plies light periwinkle to work a Pin Stitch, bringing needle up, around white stitch, then back down through same hole (Fig. 1).

Fig. 1

6. Using black pearl cotton throughout, work Straight Stitch in same direction as white Straight Stitch, then work a Pin Stitch, bringing needle up and around black and periwinkle stitches, then down through same hole (Fig. 2).

Fig. 2

7. Using 2 plies white, come up in hole indicated and down through center of pupil (Fig. 3).

Fig. 3

8. Use a full strand light clay to Straight Stitch eyelid (Fig. 3).

9. For hanger, thread a 7-inch length of medium beige brown pearl cotton from front to back through holes indicated on graph. Tie ends together in a knot, forming a 3-inch to 3¼-inch loop. Trim ends and glue knot to backside. ✄

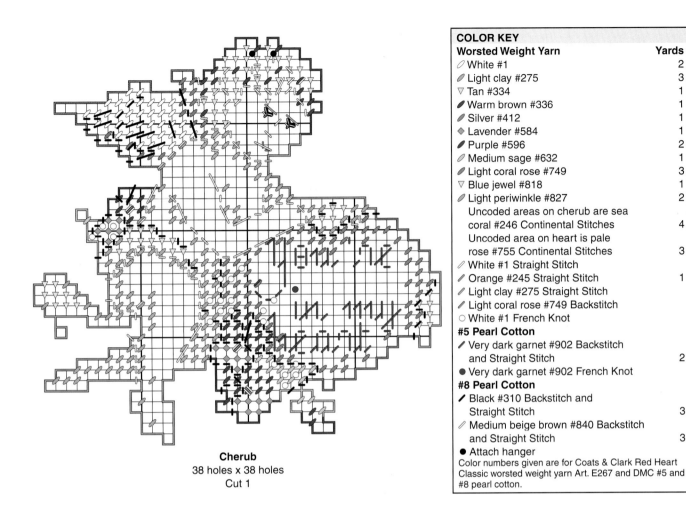

Cherub
38 holes x 38 holes
Cut 1

BIRTHDAY
Cake

Continued from page 19

step 3, work a wave around French Knots along top edge, going up and around one French Knot, then down and around the French Knot next to it. Continue wrapping around each knot, alternating over and under each knot around cake.

3. Work a second wave around French Knots, going on opposite side of knots than in previous wave.

4. Using white, center and tack cake to base, then work French Knots around bottom edge of cake side.

5. Glue nonwoven fabric-covered plastic core circle to bottom of base.

6. For candles, cut glitter stem into six 1½-inch lengths; insert as desired into cake top. Cut six small flames from yellow felt; glue one to tip of each candle.

7. For hanger, cut desired length of monofilament. Thread ends through top edges on opposite sides of cake; knot and trim excess. ✂

Celebrate!
Just for Fun

Kite Flying Day is Feb. 8

Do a Grouch a Favor Day is Feb. 16

YES

CONVERSATION
Cuties

Designs by Vicki Blizzard

Delight a friend with one of these adorable valentine sweeties! Any or all of them are sure to make him or her feel special!

Skill Level: Beginner

Finished Sizes

Bunny: 3½ inches W x 5¼ inches H

Pig: 3½ inches W x 4¼ inches H

Bear: 3½ inches W x 4 inches H

Materials

- 1 sheet 7-count plastic canvas
- Coats & Clark Red Heart Classic worsted weight yarn Art. E267 as listed in color key
- 1 yard star yellow #9100 Kreinik Fine (#8) Braid
- #16 tapestry needle
- 5mm round black cabochon from The Beadery
- 6 (4mm) round black cabochons from The Beadery
- 10 (5mm) round light rose AB Austrian crystal heat-set rhinestones from Creative Crystals Co.
- BeJeweler heat-set tool from Creative Crystals Co.
- Jewel glue
- Hot-glue gun

Cutting & Stitching

1. Cut plastic canvas according to graphs (this page and page 24).

2. Continental Stitch and Overcast large bear heart with lily pink, pig heart with mist green, and bunny heart with maize.

3. Stitch and Overcast remaining pieces following graphs, reversing one pig ear before stitching. Work one mini heart with maize as graphed, one with lily pink

and one with mist; Overcast with adjacent colors.

4. When background stitching and Overcasting are completed, work French Knots on bear's feet with 4 plies eggshell. Work messages on hearts and all other Backstitches and Straight Stitches with two plies yarn.

Assembly

1. Use photo as guide throughout assembly. With heat-set tool, attach one light rose crystal rhinestone to top of bunny's muzzle for nose. Attach one rhinestone to center of each flower.

2. Using jewel glue, attach 5mm black cabochon to bear's muzzle for nose.

3. Using hot glue through step 4, glue faces to back of corresponding large hearts. Glue muzzles to faces. Glue ears to pig's and bear's faces. Glue hands and hooves to sides of hearts. Glue pig's tail to back of heart.

4. Glue bear's feet to front of heart. Glue bunny's and pig's feet to back of hearts.

5. Using jewel glue, attach two 4mm cabochons to each face for eyes.

6. Wrap 1 yard white yarn around two fingers of one hand. Slide loops off fingers. Tie a 6-inch length of white yarn around center of loops. Trim loops to form a small pompom. Fluff out ends of yarn with tip of needle. Hot-glue pompom to back of

bunny's heart for tail.

7. For hangers, cut fine (#8) braid into three equal lengths. For each ornament, thread ends of one length from front to back through top two center holes of face. Tie ends in a bow to form a loop for hanging.

8. Hot-glue one flower to top of each face, then glue mini hearts and remaining flowers to front of large hearts as desired. ✄

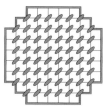

Pig & Bear Face
9 holes x 9 holes
Cut 1 for each
Stitch as graphed for pig
Stitch with warm brown for bear

Pig Snout
4 holes x 4 holes
Cut 1

Pig Leg
3 holes x 7 holes
Cut 2

Pig Ear
3 holes x 3 holes
Cut 2, reverse 1

Pig Tail
6 holes x 4 holes
Cut 1

Daisy
5 holes x 3 holes
Cut 9

Pig Hoof
3 holes x 4 holes
Cut 2

Conversation Cuties Mini Heart
5 holes x 5 holes
Cut 3
Stitch 1 as graphed,
1 with lily pink,
1 with mist green

Graphs continued on page 24

CONVERSATION
Cuties

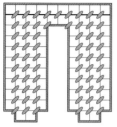

Bunny Legs
10 holes x 11 holes
Cut 1

Bunny Muzzle
7 holes x 4 holes
Cut 1

Bunny Face
9 holes x 15 holes
Cut 1

Large Bunny Heart
19 holes x 18 holes
Cut 1

Bear Ear
3 holes x 3 holes
Cut 2

Bunny Hand
5 holes x 4 holes
Cut 2

Bear Muzzle
5 holes x 4 holes
Cut 1

Bear Hand
5 holes x 3 holes
Cut 2

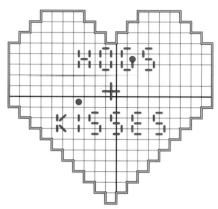

Large Pig Heart
19 holes x 18 holes
Cut 1

Large Bear Heart
19 holes x 18 holes
Cut 1

Bear Foot
4 holes x 6 holes
Cut 2

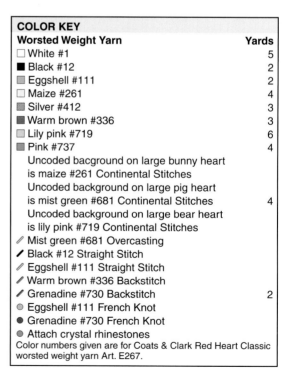

COLOR KEY

Worsted Weight Yarn	Yards
☐ White #1	5
■ Black #12	2
▨ Eggshell #111	2
☐ Maize #261	4
▨ Silver #412	3
■ Warm brown #336	3
☐ Lily pink #719	6
▨ Pink #737	4

Uncoded bacground on large bunny heart
is maize #261 Continental Stitches
Uncoded background on large pig heart
is mist green #681 Continental Stitches   4
Uncoded background on large bear heart
is lily pink #719 Continental Stitches

⁄ Mist green #681 Overcasting
⁄ Black #12 Straight Stitch
⁄ Eggshell #111 Straight Stitch
⁄ Warm brown #336 Backstitch
⁄ Grenadine #730 Backstitch   2
● Eggshell #111 French Knot
● Grenadine #730 French Knot
● Attach crystal rhinestones
Color numbers given are for Coats & Clark Red Heart Classic
worsted weight yarn Art. E267.

Skill Level: Beginner

Finished Size

3½ inches W x 4 inches H x 1 inch D

Materials

- ½ sheet 7-count plastic canvas
- Uniek Needloft plastic canvas yarn as listed in color key
- #16 tapestry needle
- 2 (5mm) black cabochons
- 4 (⅜-inch) buttons
- Nylon thread
- Thick tacky craft glue
- Hot-glue gun

Instructions

1. Cut plastic canvas according to graphs.

2. Stitch pieces following graphs, reversing one body, one head, two arms and two legs before stitching.

3. Overcast ears with maple. Whipstitch wrong sides of hearts together with burgundy.

4. Whipstitch wrong sides of head pieces together with maple, then Whipstitch again over nose area from dot to dot with black. Cut yarn and glue end securely to head with tacky glue.

5. Using maple throughout, Whipstitch wrong sides of body pieces together. Matching edges, Whipstitch wrong sides of two leg pieces and two arm pieces together. Repeat with remaining arm and leg pieces.

6. Using photo as a guide through step 8 and hot glue through step 7, glue head to body, placing the extra hole at bottom of head in the front. Glue one cabochon for eyes and one ear to each side of head.

7. Glue one arm to each side of body at shoulders. Glue one leg to bottom of body at each side, making sure all edges are even. Glue heart between hands. Glue one button to each arm and each leg.

8. Cut a 6-inch length of lavender yarn and tie in a bow around bear's neck.

9. Cut desired length of nylon thread and thread through top of bear's head. Tie ends together in a knot to form a loop for hanging. ✂

TEDDY'S Heart

Design by Terry Ricioli

Warm the heart of someone you adore with this delightful country bear, holding a sweet Valentine in her paws!

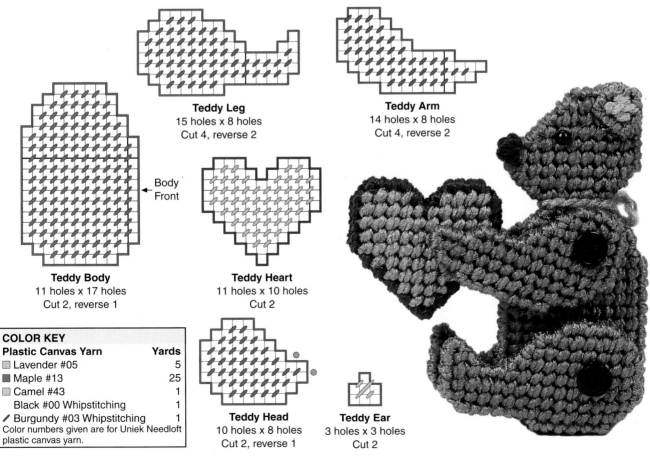

Teddy Leg
15 holes x 8 holes
Cut 4, reverse 2

Teddy Arm
14 holes x 8 holes
Cut 4, reverse 2

Teddy Body
11 holes x 17 holes
Cut 2, reverse 1

Body Front

Teddy Heart
11 holes x 10 holes
Cut 2

Teddy Head
10 holes x 8 holes
Cut 2, reverse 1

Teddy Ear
3 holes x 3 holes
Cut 2

COLOR KEY	
Plastic Canvas Yarn	**Yards**
☐ Lavender #05	5
■ Maple #13	25
☐ Camel #43	1
Black #00 Whipstitching	1
╱ Burgundy #03 Whipstitching	1
Color numbers given are for Uniek Needloft plastic canvas yarn.	

VALENTINE
Angel

Design by Nancy Marshall

Share this sweet angel with your friends or coworkers to wish them a happy Valentine's Day!

Skill Level: Beginner

Finished Size

4 inches W x 5½ inches H

Materials

- ⅓ sheet 7-count plastic canvas
- Uniek Needloft plastic canvas yarn as listed in color key
- 6-strand embroidery floss as listed in color key
- #16 tapestry needle
- 2 (6mm) black beads
- ½-inch light pink ribbon rose with leaves
- 2 inches ⅜-inch-wide white lace trim
- Light brown Lil' Loopies small loopy textured doll hair from One & Only Creations
- 4 inches gold tinsel stem
- 12mm gold heart charm
- Small amount gold fine metallic cord
- Nylon thread
- Felt in coordinating color (optional)
- Hot-glue gun

Cutting & Stitching

1. Cut plastic canvas according to graphs.

2. Stitch pieces following graphs, working uncoded areas on head, feet and hands with beige Continental Stitches.

3. When background stitching is completed, Backstitch mouth with 3 plies black embroidery floss.

Continued on page 29

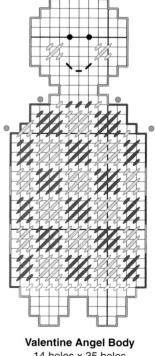

COLOR KEY

Plastic Canvas Yarn	Yards
■ Christmas red #02	4
▨ Pink #07	3
□ White #41	4
Uncoded areas are beige #40 Continental Stitches	3
⁄ Beige #40 Overcasting	
6-Strand Embroidery Floss	
⁄ Black Backstitch	1
● Attach black bead	

Color numbers given are for Uniek Needloft plastic canvas yarn.

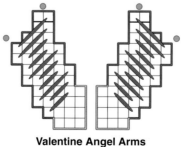

Valentine Angel Arms
7 holes x 11 holes each
Cut 1 pair

Valentine Angel Body
14 holes x 35 holes
Cut 1

Skill Level: Beginner

Finished Size

4 1/4 inches W x 3 7/8 inches H

Materials

- 1/4 sheet Uniek QuickCount 7-count plastic canvas
- Honeysuckle rayon chenille yarn by Elmore-Pisgah Inc. as listed in color key
- Kreinik 1/8-inch-wide Ribbon as listed in color key
- DMC #3 pearl cotton as listed in color key
- #16 tapestry needle

Project Note

Use a double-strand for all stitching with rayon chenille yarn.

Instructions

1. Cut plastic canvas according to graph.

2. Stitch piece following graph, working uncoded areas with honey Continental Stitches. Overcast with camel.

3. When background stitching and Overcasting are completed, work black pearl cotton embroidery, passing over each nose three times.

4. When pearl cotton embroidery is completed, work vintage red Straight Stitches.

5. For hanger, thread desired length of vintage red ribbon under two Overcast Stitches along center top edge. Double-tie ends in a bow to form a loop for hanging. ✂

BEARS
In Love

Design by Janelle Giese

Tell your sweetheart he's the one for you now and forever with this adorable pair of cuddling bears!

COLOR KEY

Rayon Chenille Yarn	Yards
■ Camel #43	12
Uncoded areas are honey #7 Continental Stitches	10
1/8-Inch-Wide Ribbon	
■ Vintage red #003V	2
╱ Vintage red #003V Straight Stitch	
#3 Pearl Cotton	
╱ Black #310 Backstitch and Straight Stitch	3

Color numbers given are for Elmore-Pisgah Honeysuckle rayon chenille yarn, Kreinik 1/8-inch-wide Ribbon and DMC #3 pearl cotton.

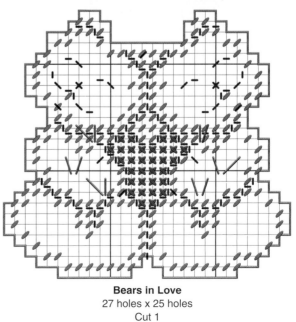

Bears in Love
27 holes x 25 holes
Cut 1

BIRDS &
The Bees

Designs by Michele Wilcox

Celebrate love with either of these colorful ornaments! Tell your sweetie to "Bee Mine" or send him or her a heart on the wings of a bluebird!

Skill Level: Beginner

Finished Sizes
Bluebird: 5 inches W x 2¾ inches H

Bee Mine Holder: 3 inches W x 3⅞ inches H

Materials
Each Ornament
- ⅓ sheet 7-count plastic canvas
- Uniek Needloft plastic canvas

yarn as listed in color key
- #3 pearl cotton as listed in color key
- #16 tapestry needle
- Hot-glue gun

Bluebird
- 18 inches ¼-inch-wide light blue satin ribbon

Bee Mine Holder
- 4 (4mm) light blue beads
- 8 inches fancy red cord

Instructions
1. Cut plastic canvas according to graphs.

2. Stitch pieces following graphs, reversing one bluebird and one wing before stitching. Work uncoded background on holder heart with red

Continental Stitches and uncoded area on bluebird with bright blue Continental Stitches.

3. When background stitching is completed, work black pearl cotton embroidery on bluebird pieces and holder hearts.

4. Following graphs throughout, Overcast hearts, wings and bees. Overcast top edges of holder pieces, then Whipstitch wrong sides together around side and bottom edges. Whipstitch wrong sides of bluebird pieces together.

5. Using black pearl cotton, attach blue beads to bees for eyes where indicated on graph.

6. Thread blue satin ribbon through hole indicated on bluebird graph; tie ends together in a knot to form a loop for hanging.

7. Using photo as a guide through step 9, glue one wing to each side of body; glue heart to one side of beak.

8. Center and glue one bee to top half of each holder side, then center and glue one heart under each bee.

9. Glue ends of fancy cord inside holder along seams. ✂

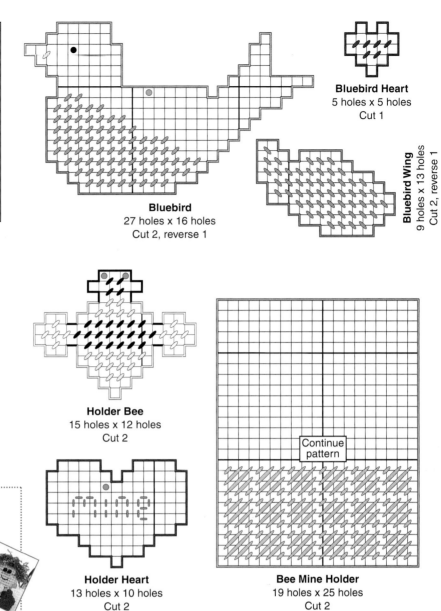

Bluebird
27 holes x 16 holes
Cut 2, reverse 1

Bluebird Heart
5 holes x 5 holes
Cut 1

Bluebird Wing
9 holes x 13 holes
Cut 2, reverse 1

Holder Bee
15 holes x 12 holes
Cut 2

Holder Heart
13 holes x 10 holes
Cut 2

Bee Mine Holder
19 holes x 25 holes
Cut 2

Continue pattern

VALENTINE
Angel

Continued from page 26

4. Following graphs throughout, Overcast wings. Overcast body, omitting shoulder areas between dots. Overcast around side and bottom edges of arms from dot to dot.

5. Place arms on body at shoulders, matching edges; Whipstitch together from dot to dot with Christmas red.

Finishing

1. For eyes, sew beads to head where indicated on graph using black embroidery floss.

2. Using photo as a guide throughout finishing, glue wings to angel back, ribbon rose to neckline on front and lace trim to bottom of skirt front over white Continental Stitches.

3. Thread gold heart charm on a 2-inch to 3-inch length of gold cord. Tie ends together at desired length, then glue to back of hands.

4. Cut seven 18-inch lengths of loopy textured doll hair. Wrap each length around a finger to make a coil. Apply a thin line of glue around edge of head. Place coils side-by-side and push a small part of each coil into glue.

5. When glue is dry, cut top of each coil. Fold some lengths at top of head to back and glue in place. Allow other lengths to stick out at sides. Trim as desired.

6. For halo, twist ends of tinsel stem together, forming a circle. Place on head.

7. Thread desired length of nylon thread through top of head. Tie ends together in a knot to form a loop for hanging.

8. If desired, cut felt to fit back of angel and glue in place. ✂

Valentine Angel Wing
11 holes x 11 holes
Cut 2

BIRTHSTONE
Heart

Design by Joan Green

Stitch a special birthday ornament accented with a heart-shaped birthstone for someone you love!

Skill Level: Beginner

Finished Size

3½ inches W x 3⅛ inches H

Materials

- Small amount 7-count plastic canvas
- Coats & Clark Red Heart Super Saver worsted weight yarn Art. E301 as listed in color key
- ⅛-inch-wide Plastic Canvas 7 Metallic Needlepoint Yarn by Rainbow Gallery as listed in color key
- 1/16-inch-wide Plastic Canvas 10 Metallic Needlepoint Yarn by Rainbow Gallery as listed in color key
- #16 tapestry needle
- 18.5mm x 18mm acrylic faceted hearts by The Beadery from Designs by Joan Green:

January and July: ruby #017

February: dark amethyst #002

March and December: turquoise #026

April: crystal #006

May: emerald #007

August: mint #013

September: dark sapphire #020

October: pink #015

November: topaz #023

- 18.5mm x 18mm heart cabochon by The Beadery from Designs by Joan Green:

June: antique white pearl #427

- Jewel glue
- Fabric glue

Instructions

1. Cut plastic canvas according to graph.

2. Stitch piece following graph, working uncoded area with black Continental Stitches. Work gold Continental Stitches in the center with ⅛-inch-wide metallic yarn. Overcast with black.

3. When background stitching and Overcasting are completed, work gold Backstitches with 1/16-inch-wide metallic yarn.

4. Glue faceted heart or heart cabochon to center of stitched heart with jewel glue.

5. Cut a 6-inch to 7-inch length of gold 1/16-inch-wide metallic yarn. Fasten ends to top center backside of ornament with fabric glue, forming a loop for hanging. ✂

COLOR KEY	
Worsted Weight Yarn	**Yards**
Uncoded area is black	
#312 Continental Stitches	8
✏ Black #312 Overcasting	
⅛-Inch Metallic Needlepoint Yarn	
☐ Gold #PC1	2
1/16-Inch Metallic Needlepoint Yarn	
✏ Gold #PM51 Backstitch	4
Color numbers given are for Coats & Clark Red Heart Super Saver worsted weight yarn Art. E301 and Rainbow Gallery Plastic Canvas 7 and Plastic Canvas 10 Metallic Needlepoint yarns.	

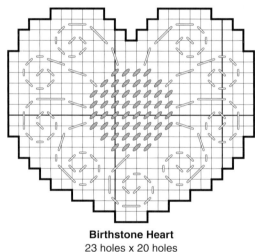

Birthstone Heart
23 holes x 20 holes
Cut 1

February   February   Febru

MINI VALENTINE
Basket

Design by Michele Wilcox

Filled with candy hearts, this darling little basket will add sweetness to any Valentine's Day.

Skill Level: Beginner

Finished Size
2½ inches W x 4¼ inches H x 2½ inch D

Materials
- ½ sheet 7-count plastic canvas
- Uniek Needloft plastic canvas yarn as listed in color key
- #16 tapestry needle
- 8 inches ½-inch-wide gold-and-white trim
- Hot-glue gun

Instructions

1. Cut plastic canvas according to graph. Cut one 3-hole by 46-hole piece for basket handle.

2. Continental Stitch and Overcast handle with eggshell. Stitch and Overcast basket following graph, working uncoded areas with eggshell Continental Stitches.

3. Fold four sides up and tack corners together at top edges with eggshell.

4. Using photo as a guide throughout, glue trim around top edge of basket. Glue handle ends inside basket. ✂

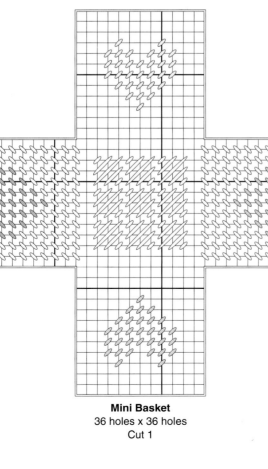

Mini Basket
36 holes x 36 holes
Cut 1

COLOR KEY	
Plastic Canvas Yarn	**Yards**
☐ Pink #07	1
☐ Moss #25	1
☐ Baby blue #36	1
☐ Eggshell #39	15
☐ Yellow #57	1
Uncoded areas are eggshell #39 Continental Stitches	
Color numbers given are for Uniek Needloft plastic canvas yarn.	

FRIENDLY
Linprechaun

Design by Janelle Giese

With a twinkle in his eye, this red-bearded Irish elf is sure to bring you lots of luck and fun!

Skill Level: Beginner

Finished Size
4 inches W x 5¼ inches H

Materials
- ¼ sheet 7-count plastic canvas
- Coats & Clark Red Heart Classic worsted weight yarn Art. E267 as listed in color key
- Kreinik 1/8-inch Ribbon as listed in color key
- DMC #5 pearl cotton as listed in color key
- DMC 6-strand embroidery floss as listed in color key
- #16 tapestry needle
- Waxed paper
- Thick white glue

Cutting & Stitching

1. Cut plastic canvas according to graphs.

2. Following graph, for each shamrock, Straight Stitch leaves, then Overcast edges. Work Cross Stitch at center last.

3. Continental Stitch and Overcast leprechaun following graph, working uncoded areas on face and hands with sea coral Continental Stitches.

4. When background stitching and Overcasting are completed, Cross Stitch cheeks using 1 strand medium salmon floss.

5. For each eye, work a Straight Stitch with a full strand true blue and one black pearl cotton Straight Stitch on each side of true blue stitch. Straight Stitch eye highlight using 2 plies white, splitting true blue stitch.

6. Work remaining black pearl cotton embroidery. Straight Stitch shamrock on hat with forest green ribbon.

7. Using a full strand yarn, work bronze Straight Stitches for

Friendly Leprechaun Shamrock
7 holes x 7 holes
Cut 3

Leprechaun
26 holes x 26 holes
Cut 1

COLOR KEY	
Worsted Weight Yarn	Ya
☐ White #1	1
■ Bronze #286	2
■ Coffee #365	2
☐ Honey gold #645	1
■ Emerald green #676	1
■ Paddy green #686	3
■ Light coral rose #749	1
Uncoded areas are sea coral #246 Continental Stitches	3
⁄ Sea coral #246 Overcasting	
⁄ White #1 Straight Stitch	
⁄ Bronze #286 Straight Stitch	1
⁄ True blue #822 Straight Stitch	2
● Medium clay #280 French Knot	
1/8-Inch Ribbon	
⁄ Green #008 Straight Stitch and Overcasting	5
#5 Pearl Cotton	
⁄ Black #310 Backstitch and Straight Stitch	
6-Strand Embroidery Floss	
✕ Medium salmon #3712 Cross Stitch	
Color numbers given are for Coats & Clark Red Heart Classic worsted weight yarn Art. E267, Kreinik 1/8-inch-wide Ribbon and DMC #5 pearl cotton and 6-strand embroidery floss.	

March   March   March   March

SHAMROCK
Suncatcher

Design by Joan Green

Pretty metallic yarn and an emerald-green cabochon make this keepsake ornament sparkle and shine in the sunlight!

Skill Level: Beginner

Finished Size

5 inches W x 5 inches H

Materials

- Small amount 7-count plastic canvas
- Coats & Clark Red Heart Super Saver worsted weight yarn Art. E300 as listed in color key
- ⅛-inch-wide Plastic Canvas 7 Metallic Needlepoint Yarn by Rainbow Gallery as listed in color key
- #16 tapestry needle
- 16mm emerald #007 round faceted stone from The Beadery
- Fabric glue
- Jewel glue

Instructions

1. Cut plastic canvas according to graph.

2. Stitch and Overcast piece following graph.

3. Using photo as a guide, glue faceted stone to center of stitched shamrock with jewel glue.

4. For hanger, cut an 8¼-inch length of gold metallic needlepoint yarn. Glue ends to top backside with fabric glue. ✂

Suncatcher
33 holes x 33 holes
Cut 1

COLOR KEY	
Worsted Weight Yarn	**Yards**
☐ Off white #3	1
▨ Grass green #687	5
⅛-Inch Metallic Needlepoint Yarn	
⟋ Gold #PC1 Overcasting	2
⟋ Forest #PC17 Overcasting	6
Color numbers given are for Coats & Clark Red Heart Super Saver worsted weight yarn Art. E300 and Rainbow Gallery Plastic Canvas 7 Metallic Needlepoint Yarn.	

Celebrate!
St. Patrick's Day is March 17

FRIENDLY
Leprechaun

eyebrows and medium clay French Knots to complete beard, wrapping yarn around needle one time.

Assembly

1. Using photo as a guide throughout assembly, thread ends

of an 8-inch length of forest green ribbon from front to back through holes indicated with blue dots on leprechaun's hands.

2. Pull center of ribbon down slightly, forming an arch. Protect leprechaun with waxed paper. Glue shamrocks to ribbon and leprechaun; allow to dry.

3. Cut ends, allowing approximately 1 inch to hang from back of hands. Secure ribbon to back

of hands at attachment point with a dab of glue.

4. For hanger, thread a length of black pearl cotton from back to front through one hole indicated with red dot on graph, then from front to back through remaining hole indicated with red dot. Tie ends together in a knot on backside so loop extends 3 inches above top edge. Trim ends; glue knot to secure. ✂

IRISH
Welcome

Designs by Vicki Blizzard

Invite one and all into your home with this festive Irish ornament! "Failte" means "welcome" in Gaelic.

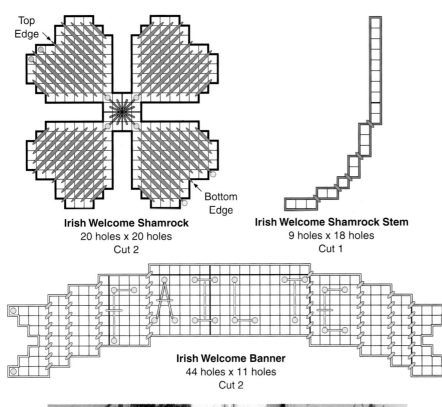

Irish Welcome Shamrock
20 holes x 20 holes
Cut 2

Irish Welcome Shamrock Stem
9 holes x 18 holes
Cut 1

Irish Welcome Banner
44 holes x 11 holes
Cut 2

Skill Level: Beginner

Finished Size
6¾ inches W x 8 inches H

Materials

- 1 sheet 7-count plastic canvas
- Uniek Needloft plastic canvas yarn as listed in color key
- Kreinik Heavy (#32) Braid as listed in color key
- Kreinik ⅛-inch metallic ribbon as listed in color key
- 2 (½-yard) lengths green #008HL Kreinik Medium (#16) Braid
- #16 tapestry needle
- 56 (4mm) round emerald AB Austrian crystal heat-set rhinestones from Creative Crystals Co.
- BeJeweler heat-set tool from Creative Crystals Co.

Instructions

1. Cut plastic canvas according to graphs.

2. Stitch and Overcast shamrock stem with holly. Stitch banner and shamrock pieces following graphs, working uncoded areas with white Continental Stitches and working holly Straight Stitches in center of shamrocks.

3. When background stitching is completed, Straight Stitch letters on banner pieces with heavy (#32) braid.

COLOR KEY	
Plastic Canvas Yarn	**Yards**
☐ Moss #25	2
■ Holly #27	9
Uncoded areas are white #41 Continental Stitches	10
⁄ White #41 Whipstitching	
⁄ Holly #27 Straight Stitch	
Heavy (#32) Braid	7
⁄ Green #008HL Straight Stitch	
⅛-Inch Metallic Braid	
⁄ Green #008HL Overcasting	3
◯ Attach hanger	
◯ Attach crystal rhinestones	
Color numbers given are for Uniek Needloft plastic canvas yarn and Kreinik Heavy (#32) Braid and ⅛-inch Ribbon.	

LUCKY
Shamrock

Design by Kathleen J. Fischer

Add extra good luck to this shamrock ornament with a shiny gold coin fastened to the center.

Skill Level: Beginner

Finished Size

3¼ inches W x 3¼ inches H

Materials

- ⅓ sheet Uniek QuickCount 7-count plastic canvas
- Worsted weight yarn as listed in color key
- ⅛-inch-wide Plastic Canvas 7 Metallic Needlepoint Yarn by Rainbow Gallery as listed in color key
- #16 tapestry needle
- ¾-inch gold la-petite button #925 from Blumenthal Lansing Co.
- Nylon thread
- Tacky craft glue

Instructions

1. Cut plastic canvas according to graphs.

2. Stitch front piece and one back piece. One back piece will remain unstitched. Overcast inside edges on front with dark green worsted weight yarn.

3. With right sides facing up, place pieces together with front piece on top, stitched back piece in the middle and unstitched back piece on the bottom. Using forest green metallic yarn, Whipstitch outside edges together through all three layers.

4. Cut desired length of nylon thread and insert through shamrock where indicated with blue dot on back graph. Tie ends together in a knot to form a loop for hanging.

5. Glue button to center front of shamrock. ✀

COLOR KEY	
Worsted Weight Yarn	**Yards**
■ Dark green	3
▨ Medium green	2
╱ Dark green Backstitch	
¹⁄₁₆-Inch Metallic Needlepoint Yarn	
╱ Forest green #PC17 Whipstitching	2
Color number given is for Rainbow Gallery Plastic Canvas 7 Metallic Needlepoint Yarn.	

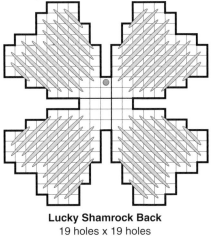

Lucky Shamrock Back
19 holes x 19 holes
Cut 2, stitch 1

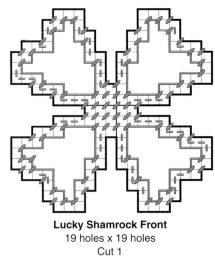

Lucky Shamrock Front
19 holes x 19 holes
Cut 1

IRISH
Welcome

4. Using green ⅛-inch ribbon, Overcast both shamrock pieces along bottom edges from dot to dot, then Whipstitch wrong sides of shamrock pieces together along remaining edges.

5. Thread ends of one length medium (#16) braid through holes indicated with pink dots on shamrock, then from front to back through two bottom center holes of one banner piece, which will now be the front piece. Tie ends in a knot on backside, making length between two pieces about 1¾ inches; cut excess.

6. Whipstitch wrong sides of banner pieces together with white, making sure to not catch medium (#16) braid in the Whipstitching so it will hang freely.

7. Thread remaining length of medium (#16) braid from back to front through center top two holes of banner, forming a 2½-inch loop. Tie ends in a bow on front.

8. Insert stem through bottom opening of shamrock.

9. Following manufacturer's instructions, attach crystal rhinestones where indicated on banner and shamrock fronts and backs. ✀

March · March March March March March March March

LITTLE
Leprechaun

Design by Lee Lindeman

Hang this delightful little leprechaun in a sunny window in your home to add sparkle and good luck to your day!

Skill Level: Intermediate

Finished Size

6 inches W x 5¼ inches H

Materials

- ⅓ sheet 7-count plastic canvas
- Coats & Clark Red Heart Classic worsted weight yarn Art. E267 as listed in color key
- 6-strand embroidery floss as listed in color key
- 2 yards ¹⁄₁₆-inch-wide gold shimmer #F4 high luster metallic Fyre Werks ribbon by Rainbow Gallery
- #16 tapestry needle
- 2 (6mm) gold jingle bells
- 1 (9mm) gold jingle bell
- 5-inch metal ring
- Brown felt
- Pinking shears
- Small amount fiberfill
- Seam sealant
- Hot-glue gun

Instructions

1. Cut plastic canvas according to graphs.

2. Cut one hat brim, one collar, two wrist cuffs and two ankle cuffs from brown felt following patterns given. Cut outside edges with pinking shears; cut out center holes and slits with regular scissors.

3. Stitch pieces following graphs, working uncoded areas with emerald green Continental Stitches.

4. When background stitching is completed, work mouth and eyes with black embroidery floss. Work lily pink French Knot for nose. Work ¼-inch to ⅜-inch orange Turkey Loop Stitches on head front and back as desired over orange Continental Stitches.

5. Whipstitch wrong sides of front and back together following graphs, stuffing with a small amount of fiberfill before closing.

6. Glue one end of gold metallic ribbon to metal ring. Keeping ribbon smooth and flat, wrap ribbon around ring, covering completely; glue end to secure.

7. Using photo as a guide through step 8, wrap hat brim, collar and cuffs around leprechaun, overlapping ends as needed; glue to secure.

8. Attach 9mm jingle bell to top of hat and one 6mm jingle bell to tip of each foot with 1 ply emerald green. Glue leprechaun to ring. If desired, make a tiny bow with gold metallic ribbon and glue to collar front below neck. Add seam sealant to ends of bow to prevent fraying.

9. Attach desired length of gold metallic ribbon to top of ring with a Lark's Head Knot. Tie ends in a bow to form a loop for hanging, adding seam sealant to ends to prevent fraying. ✄

COLOR KEY

Worsted Weight Yarn	Yards
■ Orange #245	3
▨ Lily pink #719	2
■ Grenadine #730	1
Uncoded areas are emerald green #676 Continental Stitches	11
╱ Emerald green #676 Whipstitching	
◯ Lily pink #719 French Knot	
6-Strand Embroidery Floss	
╱ Black Backstitch	1
● Black French Knot	
Color numbers given are for Coats & Clark Red Heart Classic worsted weight yarn Art. E267.	

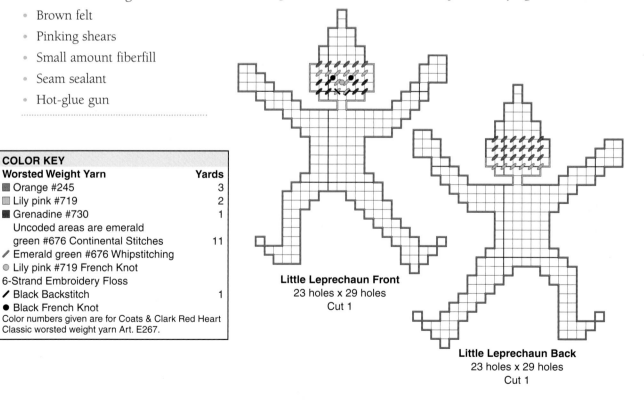

Little Leprechaun Front
23 holes x 29 holes
Cut 1

Little Leprechaun Back
23 holes x 29 holes
Cut 1

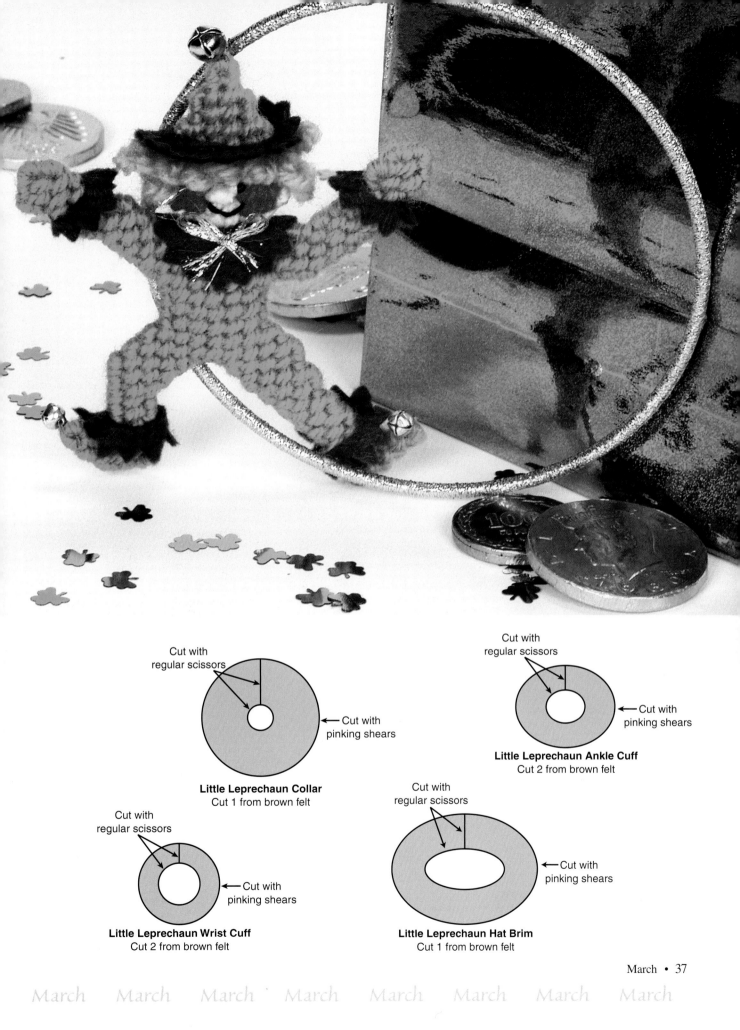

Cut with
regular scissors

←— Cut with
pinking shears

Little Leprechaun Collar
Cut 1 from brown felt

Cut with
regular scissors

←— Cut with
pinking shears

Little Leprechaun Ankle Cuff
Cut 2 from brown felt

Cut with
regular scissors

←— Cut with
pinking shears

Little Leprechaun Wrist Cuff
Cut 2 from brown felt

Cut with
regular scissors

←— Cut with
pinking shears

Little Leprechaun Hat Brim
Cut 1 from brown felt

March   March   March   March   March   March   March   March

BEE
Happy

Design by Janna Britton

Cheer an under-the-weather friend with this delightful dimensional ornament!

Materials

- ½ sheet Uniek QuickCount 7-count plastic canvas
- 2 (4-inch) Uniek QuickShape plastic canvas radial circles
- Uniek Needloft plastic canvas yarn as listed in color key
- Uniek metallic craft cord as listed in color key
- Uniek iridescent craft cord as listed in color key
- DMC 6-strand embroidery floss as listed in color key
- #16 tapestry needle
- 4½ inches ¼-inch-wide white iridescent ribbon
- 5mm movable eye
- 18 inches 15 pound clear monofilament line
- Low-temperature glue gun

Skill Level: Beginner

Finished Size

6¼ inches W x 7¼ inches H

Instructions

1. Cut plastic canvas according to graphs, cutting away gray area from radial circles.

2. Following graphs through step 5, stitch and Overcast bee and clouds.

3. Stitch rainbow and house pieces. When background stitching is completed, using white, work Straight Stitches on houses and embroider letters on rainbow front only. Work dark wedgwood Backstitches and Straight Stitches on houses.

4. Whipstitch wrong sides of rainbow pieces together with Christmas red and bright purple.

5. Whipstitch house pieces together with Christmas green, yellow and camel.

6. Using photo as a guide through step 9, fold white iridescent ribbon into two loops and glue to center back of bee's body for wings. Glue movable eye to bee's head.

7. Glue clouds to ends of rainbow front; glue bee to left of the word "HAPPY."

8. Thread monofilament down through center of rainbow and through center top hole of house; bring monofilament back up through rainbow. Tie a knot at

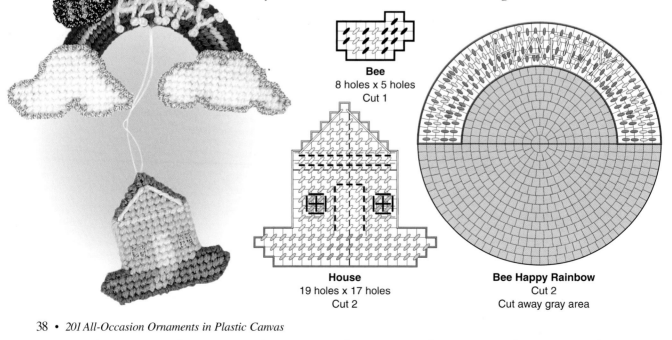

Bee
8 holes x 5 holes
Cut 1

House
19 holes x 17 holes
Cut 2

Bee Happy Rainbow
Cut 2
Cut away gray area

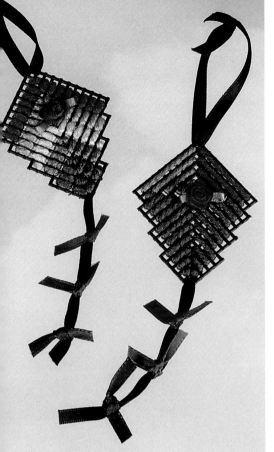

RAINBOW Kites

Designs by Ronda Bryce

With black canvas and just a few brightly colored stitches, you can have this pair of springtime kites ready to share!

Skill Level: Beginner

Finished Size

Approximately 2¼ inches W x 6¼ inches H, including tails

Materials

- Small amount black 7-count plastic canvas
- Uniek Needloft plastic canvas yarn as listed in color key
- #16 tapestry needle
- 26 inches ¼-inch-wide black satin ribbon
- ½ yard each ¼-inch-wide red, green and purple satin ribbon
- ½-inch red ribbon rose with leaves
- ½-inch purple ribbon rose with leaves
- Sewing needle with black sewing thread

Instructions

1. Cut and stitch plastic canvas according to graphs. Do not Overcast pieces.

2. For each kite tail, cut a 4-inch

to 5-inch length of black ribbon and thread ribbon through bottom hole of kite. Tack end to lower backside with sewing needle and black sewing thread.

3. Using photo as a guide through step 5, cut each length of red, green and purple ribbon in half. Tie one length of each color to each tail at regular intervals.

4. Stitch one rose to center front of each kite with sewing needle and black sewing thread.

5. Cut remaining ribbon in half. Thread one length through top hole of each kite. Tie ends together in a knot to form a loop for hanging. ✄

COLOR KEY

Plastic Canvas Yarn	Yards
■ Christmas red #02	1
■ Christmas green #28	1
■ Royal #32	1
☐ Yellow #57	1
■ Bright orange #58	1
■ Bright purple #64	1
Color numbers given are for Uniek Needloft plastic canvas yarn.	

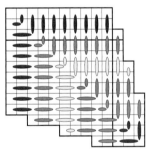

Kite A
13 holes x 13 holes
Cut 1

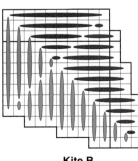

Kite B
13 holes x 13 holes
Cut 1

BEE Happy

top of rainbow, allowing house to hang approximately 1½ inches

from bottom of clouds.

9. Tie another knot at ends of monofilament to form a loop for hanging. Apply a dot of glue to monofilament at bottom of rainbow to keep line from slipping. ✄

Cloud A
18 holes x 10 holes
Cut 1

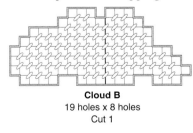

Cloud B
19 holes x 8 holes
Cut 1

PASTEL
Egg Frames

Designs by Kathleen Hurley

Show off your favorite "chicks" in this set of six pretty, pastel-colored Easter egg frames! They make delightful gifts for Grandma!

Skill Level: Beginner

Finished Size

2¾ inches W x 3 inches H

Materials

- 1 sheet 7-count plastic canvas
- Coats & Clark Red Heart Classic worsted weigh yarn Art. E267 as listed in color key
- #16 tapestry needle
- 2 yards ⅛-inch-wide white satin ribbon
- 48 inches ⅝-inch-wide white picot-edge ribbon
- Hot-glue gun

Instructions

1. Cut plastic canvas according to graphs (this page and page 42).

2. Stitch pieces following graphs, working uncoded areas with white Continental Stitches and working two stitches per hole where indicated. Overcast inside edges on front pieces with white.

3. Work all French Knots with 4 plies yarn. Work Backstitches, Straight Stitches and Lazy Daisy Stitches with 2 plies yarn.

4. Using white throughout, Overcast top edges of egg front and back pieces from dot to dot. Whipstitch wrong sides of corresponding front and back pieces together along remaining edges.

5. Cut picot-edge ribbon into six 8-inch lengths. Tie each in a bow and glue one to top front of each egg.

6. Place photos inside frames.

7. For hangers, cut ⅛-inch-wide white satin ribbon into six 12-inch lengths. For each egg, thread ends of one length through top two holes of front and back and secure with a Lark's Head Knot. Tie ends together in a knot to form a loop for hanging; trim ends close to knot. ✂

COLOR KEY	
Worsted Weight Yarn	**Yards**
▨ Sea coral #246	5
☐ Maize #261	6
▨ Light lavender #579	7
▨ Mist green #681	7
▨ Pink #737	7
☐ Blue jewel #818	8
Uncoded areas are white #1 Continental Stitches	33
╱ White #1 Overcasting and Whipstitching	
╱ Light lavender #579 Backstitch	
╱ Mist green #681 Backstitch and Straight Stitch	
╱ Pink #737 Straight Stitch	
╱ Blue jewel #818 Straight Stitch	
⟣ Mist green #681 Lazy Daisy Stitch	
⟣ Blue jewel #818 Lazy Daisy Stitch	
○ Maize #261 French Knot	
● Light lavender #579 French Knot	
Color numbers given are for Coats & Clark Red Heart Classic worsted weight yarn Art. E267.	

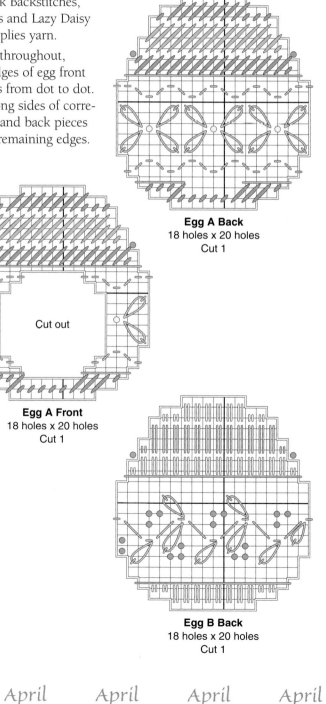

Egg A Back
18 holes x 20 holes
Cut 1

Egg A Front
18 holes x 20 holes
Cut 1

Cut out

Egg B Back
18 holes x 20 holes
Cut 1

April   April   April   April   April   April   April

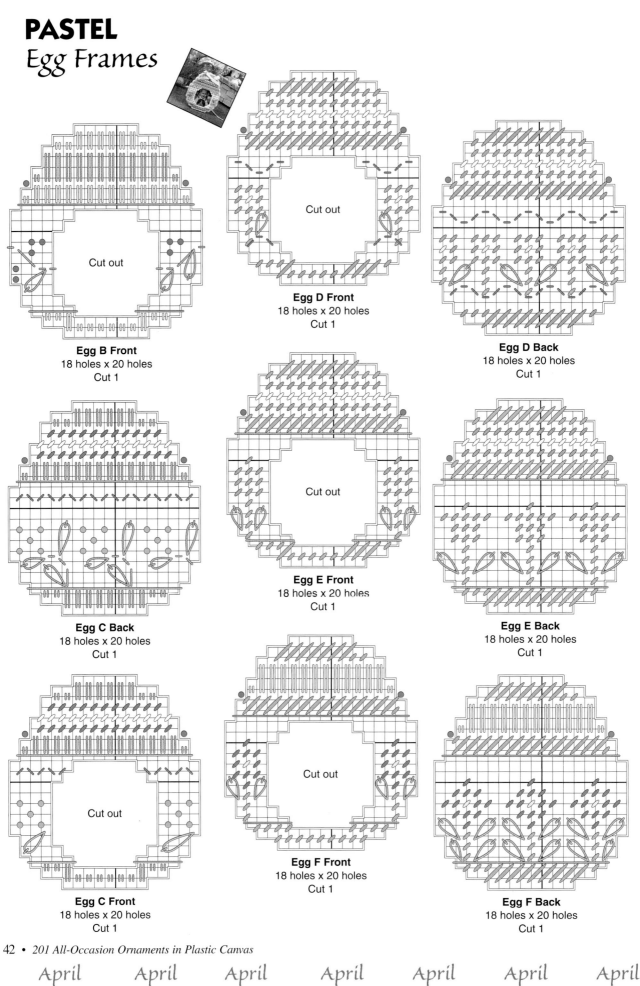

PASTEL
Egg Frames

Cut out

Egg B Front
18 holes x 20 holes
Cut 1

Cut out

Egg D Front
18 holes x 20 holes
Cut 1

Egg D Back
18 holes x 20 holes
Cut 1

Egg C Back
18 holes x 20 holes
Cut 1

Cut out

Egg E Front
18 holes x 20 holes
Cut 1

Egg E Back
18 holes x 20 holes
Cut 1

Cut out

Cut out

Egg C Front
18 holes x 20 holes
Cut 1

Cut out

Egg F Front
18 holes x 20 holes
Cut 1

Egg F Back
18 holes x 20 holes
Cut 1

April   April   April   April   April   April   April

Skill Level
Beginner

Finished Size
2¼ inches W x 3⅛ inches H, excluding lace

Materials
- ¼ sheet 7-count plastic canvas
- Worsted weight yarn as listed in color key
- Metallic craft cord as listed in color key
- #16 tapestry needle
- ½-inch to ¾-inch each gold and silver metallic ribbon rose
- 1½ yards ½-inch- to ¾-inch-wide gold metallic-and-white lace
- 1½ yards ½-inch- to ¾-inch-wide silver metallic-and-white lace
- 2 ornament hooks
- Craft glue or hot-glue gun

Instructions
1. Cut plastic canvas according to graph.

2. Stitch two crosses with gold and white as graphed. Overcast with gold. Stitch remaining two crosses, replacing gold with silver.

3. For gold-and-white cross, glue gold metallic-and-white lace

ELEGANT
Crosses

Designs by Lynne L. Langer

Add a touch of elegance and beauty to your Easter celebrations with this pair of lace-and-ribbon-rose-embellished ornaments.

around edge on backside of one cross, then glue wrong sides of crosses together. Glue gold ribbon rose to center of crossbar on one side.

4. Repeat step 3 for silver-and-white crosses, using silver metallic-and-white lace and silver ribbon rose.

5. Insert one ornament hook in a top center hole of each cross. ✂

COLOR KEY	
Worsted Weight Yarn	**Yards**
☐ White	2
Metallic Craft Cord	
▨ Gold	3
Silver	3

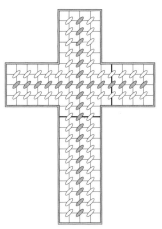

Cross
14 holes x 20 holes
Cut 4
Stitch 2 as graphed
Stitch 2, replacing gold
with silver

SPRING
Lamb

Design by Janna Britton

Adorned with a wreath of silk ribbon roses and a golden bell, this darling little lamb makes a perfect springtime ornament!

Materials

- Small amount 7-count plastic canvas
- Uniek Needloft plastic canvas yarn as listed in color key
- Jiffy mohair-look acrylic yarn from Lion Brand as listed in color key
- DMC #3 pearl cotton as listed in color key
- 6 (½-inch) ribbon roses in assorted colors with leaves
- 15mm gold cow bell
- 3-inch square antique white #379 Rainbow Plush felt from Kunin
- 9 inches 40-pound clear monofilament
- Low-temperature glue gun

Skill Level: Beginner

Finished Size

3⅛ inches W x 2½ inches H

Instructions

1. Cut plastic canvas according to graph.

2. Stitch and Overcast face area following graph. Work Straight Stitches and French Knot with medium brown pearl cotton.

3. Work French Knots for lamb's wool with fisherman yarn; Overcast legs. Do not Overcast remaining edges.

4. Using photo as a guide through step 5, glue ribbon roses to lamb so they resemble a wreath around its neck.

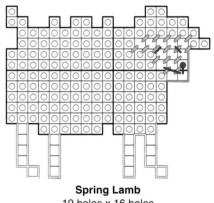

Spring Lamb
19 holes x 16 holes
Cut 1

5. Attach cowbell to lamb under face with flesh tone.

6. For hanger, attach monofilament to center top back of lamb.

7. Cut felt to fit body and head, then glue in place on backside. ✂

Celebrate!
Just for Fun

Golfer's Day
is April 10

Great Poetry
Reading Day is
April 28

BUNNY in a Basket

Design by Angie Arickx

Skill Level: Beginner

Finished Size

2 inches W x 3 inches H x 1¼ inches D

Materials

- ¼ sheet Uniek QuickCount 7-count plastic canvas
- Uniek Needloft plastic canvas yarn as listed in color key
- #16 tapestry needle
- 1½-inch pink flocked bunny
- Hot-glue gun

Instructions

1. Cut plastic canvas according to graphs.

2. Following graphs through step 4, stitch and Overcast handle. Stitch basket bottom.

3. Stitch flowers and basket sides, Overcasting flowers piece and top edges of sides while stitching.

4. Using white, Whipstitch long sides to short sides, then Whipstitch sides to bottom.

5. Using photo as a guide, glue handle ends to short sides inside basket. Glue bunny inside basket, then glue flowers behind bunny. ✄

Delight family and friends who join you for Easter Sunday brunch with one of these sweet surprises at each place setting. It makes a perfect favor!

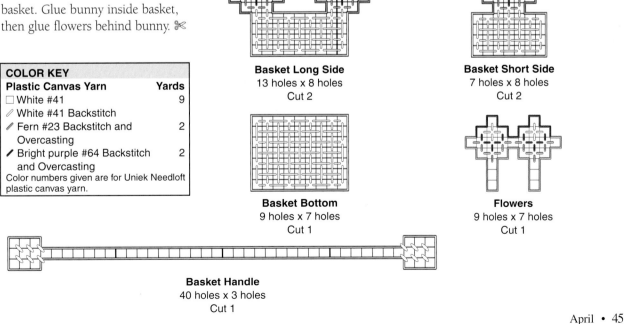

COLOR KEY	
Plastic Canvas Yarn	**Yards**
☐ White #41	9
⁄ White #41 Backstitch	
⁄ Fern #23 Backstitch and Overcasting	2
⁄ Bright purple #64 Backstitch and Overcasting	2
Color numbers given are for Uniek Needloft plastic canvas yarn.	

Basket Long Side
13 holes x 8 holes
Cut 2

Basket Short Side
7 holes x 8 holes
Cut 2

Basket Bottom
9 holes x 7 holes
Cut 1

Flowers
9 holes x 7 holes
Cut 1

Basket Handle
40 holes x 3 holes
Cut 1

April   April   April   April   April   April   April

HOLY Bible

Design by Ronda Bryce

Whether you use this ornament to hang on your car's rearview mirror, as a key chain, or simply as a household ornament, it is sure to add a touch of inspiration to your day!

Skill Level: Beginner

Finished Size

2⅛ inches W x 2¾ inches H x ¾ inches D, closed

Materials

- ¼ sheet 7-count plastic canvas
- Uniek Needloft plastic canvas yarn as listed in color key
- Nylon plastic canvas yarn as listed in color key
- Uniek Needloft metallic craft cord as listed in color key
- DMC 6-strand embroidery floss as listed in color key
- DMC 6-strand metallic embroidery floss as listed in color key
- Sewing needle and black sewing thread

Instructions

1. Cut plastic canvas according to graphs. Cut one 4-hole x 18-hole

piece for cover spine.

2. Work cover spine with black Continental Stitches. Stitch pieces following graphs, working uncoded areas on cover front and back with black Continental Stitches and uncoded areas on pages with flesh tone Continental Stitches.

3. When background stitching is completed, work black floss embroidery on back page; work gold metallic floss

embroidery on cover front only.

4. Overcast pages following graph. Using black throughout, Whipstitch left edge of cover front to one long edge of cover spine. Whipstitch right edge of cover back to remaining long edge of cover spine. Overcast all remaining cover edges.

5. Using sewing needle and black sewing thread, center and tack front page to wrong side of cover front; center and tack back page to wrong side of cover back.

6. Thread gold metallic craft cord through a top center hole of cover spine. Tie ends in a knot to form a loop for hanging. ✂

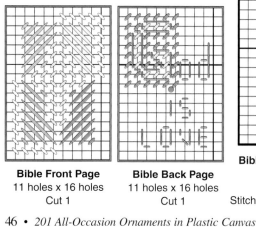

Bible Front Page
11 holes x 16 holes
Cut 1

Bible Back Page
11 holes x 16 holes
Cut 1

Bible Cover Front & Back
13 holes x 18 holes
Cut 2
Stitch embroidery on front only

COLOR KEY	
Plastic Canvas Yarn	**Yards**
☐ Baby yellow #21	1
▨ Baby blue #36	1
▨ Orchid #44	1
▨ Lilac #45	2
☐ Flesh tone #56	4
Uncoded area on cover is black #00	
Continental Stitches	12
Uncoded area on pages are flesh tone	
#56 Continental Stitches	
╱ Black Overcasting and Whipstitching	
Metallic Craft Cord	
☐ Solid gold #55020	1
╱ Gold #55001 Overcasting	4
6-Strand Embroidery Floss	
╱ Black #310 Backstitch and Straight Stitch	2
● Black #310 French Knot	
6-Strand Metallic Embroidery Floss	
╱ Gold #5282 Backstitch and Straight Stitch	1
● Gold #5282 French Knot	
Color numbers given are for Uniek Needloft plastic canvas yarn and metallic craft cord, and DMC 6-strand embroidery floss.	

April   April   April   April   April   April   April

Skill Level: Beginner

Finished Size

3½ inches W x 5¼ inches H

Materials

- ¼ sheet 7-count plastic canvas
- Acrylic plastic canvas yarn as listed in color key
- Uniek Needloft solid metallic craft cord as listed in color key
- #16 tapestry needle
- 16 inches gold lamé thread
- Assorted flowers in coordinating colors (optional)
- Hot-glue gun (optional)

Instructions

1. Cut plastic canvas according to graph.

2. Stitch and Overcast one cross as graphed. Stitch and Overcast remaining cross replacing dark turquoise with dark mauve and light turquoise with light mauve.

3. For hangers, cut gold lamé thread in half. For each cross, thread one length through top center hole. Tie ends together in a knot to form a loop for hanging.

4. Optional: Glue flowers to cross as desired. ✄

TOUCH OF
Gold Crosses

Designs by Ruby Thacker

Adorned with or without silk flowers, this lovely cross design hung in your home will be a quiet reminder of your daily walk in faith.

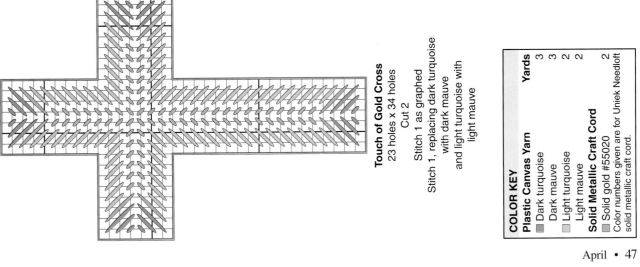

Touch of Gold Cross
23 holes x 34 holes
Cut 2
Stitch 1 as graphed
Stitch 1, replacing dark turquoise with dark mauve and light turquoise with light mauve

COLOR KEY	
Plastic Canvas Yarn	**Yards**
■ Dark turquoise	3
■ Dark mauve	3
■ Light turquoise	2
■ Light mauve	2
Solid Metallic Craft Cord	
■ Solid gold #55020	2
Color numbers given are for Uniek Needloft solid metallic craft cord.	

April   April   April   April   April   April   April

BUNNY
Buddy

Design by Susan Leinberger

Wish a friend or family member a happy Easter with this cheer-filled ornament!

Skill Level: Beginner

Finished Size

5½ inches W x 5½ inches H

Materials

- ½ sheet Uniek QuickCount 7-count plastic canvas
- Uniek Needloft plastic canvas yarn as listed in color key
- DMC #3 pearl cotton as listed in color key
- #16 tapestry needle
- 2 (½-inch) white pompoms
- 7mm pink pompom
- 2 (½-inch) pink buttons
- Hot-glue gun

Cutting & Stitching

1. Cut plastic canvas according to graphs.

2. Stitch sign and one bunny following graphs, working uncoded areas with white Continental Stitches. One bunny will remain unstitched.

3. When background stitching is completed, work letters on sign with bright purple and pink French Knots on bunny's font paws. Stitch eyes and eyebrows with black pearl cotton. Work three Turkey Loop Stitches where indicated on head for bunny's hair.

4. Overcast sign with bright purple and pink, alternating colors. When Overcasting is completed, work yellow Backstitches.

Finishing

1. For hanger, cut a 7-inch length of bright purple yarn. Thread ends from front to back through top two holes of unstitched back, then from back to front three holes down. Tie ends in a knot and glue to secure.

2. Place unstitched bunny behind

Continued on page 53

COLOR KEY	
Plastic Canvas Yarn	**Yards**
■ Pink #07	2
□ White #41	10
□ Yellow #57	7
Uncoded areas are white #41 Continental Stitches	2
✎ Bright purple #64 Backstitch, Straight Stitch and Overcasting	
⁄ Yellow #57 Backstitch	
● Pink #07 French Knot	
○ White #41 Turkey Loop Stitch	
#3 Pearl Cotton	
✎ Black #310 Backstitch and Straight Stitch	1
● Attach button	
Color numbers given are for Uniek Needloft plastic canvas yarn and DMC #3 pearl cotton.	

Sign
26 holes x 5 holes
Cut 1

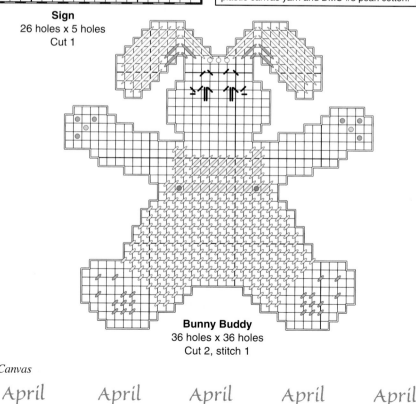

Bunny Buddy
36 holes x 36 holes
Cut 2, stitch 1

April   April   April   April   April   April   April

HAPPY Spring

Design by Janelle Giese

Celebrate spring's arrival with this happy white bunny as he nestles in a bed of lush blossoms!

Skill Level: Beginner

Finished Size

4¾ inches W x 4 inches H

Materials

- ¼ sheet Uniek QuickCount 7-count plastic canvas
- Uniek Needloft plastic canvas yarn as listed in color key
- Honeysuckle rayon chenille yarn by Elmore-Pisgah Inc. as listed in color key
- Kreinik Heavy (#32) Braid as listed in color key
- DMC #8 pearl cotton as listed in color key
- #16 tapestry needle

Project Note

Use two strands when stitching and Overcasting with chenille yarn.

Instructions

1. Cut plastic canvas according to graph.

2. Stitch and Overcast piece following graph, working uncoded areas on bunny with white chenille yarn Continental Stitches and uncoded background on sign with flesh tone Continental Stitches.

3. When background stitching and Overcasting are completed, work heavy (#32) braid Straight Stitches. Using pink yarn, work mouth, nose

and pads of feet, passing over nose and pads two times.

4. Using black pearl cotton, work message on sign and remaining detail stitching, passing over the two stitches for each eye two times.

5. For hanger, cut a 7-inch length of black pearl cotton. Thread ends through yarn on backside of stitched piece where indicated on graph. Knot ends so loop extends 3 inches above top of ornament. ✄

COLOR KEY	
Plastic Canvas Yarn	**Yards**
■ Pink #07	1
■ Fern #23	1
▨ Moss #25	1
▧ Orchid #44	2
▨ Lilac #45	3
Uncoded background on sign is flesh tone #56 Continental Stitches	1
╱ Pink #07 Straight Stitch	
Rayon Chenille Yarn	
Uncoded areas are on bunny are white #1 Continental Stitches	10
╱ White #1 Overcasting	
Heavy (#32) Braid	3
╱ Lilac #023 Straight Stitch and and Overcasting	
#8 Pearl Cotton	5
╱ Black #310 Backstitch and Straight Stitch	
● Black #310 French Knot	
● Attach hanger	
Color numbers given are for Uniek Needloft plastic canvas yarn, Elmore-Pisgah Honeysuckle rayon chenille yarn, Kreinik Heavy (#32) Braid and DMC #8 pearl cotton.	

Happy Spring
26 holes x 31 holes
Cut 1

April   April   April   April   April   April   April

PLAID
Easter Eggs

Designs by Vicki Blizzard

Quick and easy to stitch, this set of three ornaments with pretty ribbons will add springtime cheer to your home!

Skill Level: Beginner

Finished Size

2⅞ inches W x 3¼ inches H

Materials

- 1 sheet 7-count plastic canvas
- Coats & Clark Red Heart Classic worsted weight yarn Art. E267 as listed in color key
- #16 tapestry needle
- 1 yard ⅛ inch-wide white satin ribbon
- 2 yards ⅛-inch-wide light blue satin ribbon
- 1 yard ⅛-inch-wide light yellow satin ribbon
- 1 yard ⅛-inch-wide light pink satin ribbon
- 2 yards ⅛-inch-wide peach satin ribbon
- Small amount polyester fiberfill
- Hot-glue gun

Instructions

1. Cut plastic canvas according to graphs.

2. Stitch pieces following graphs. For each egg, Whipstitch wrong sides together with white, stuffing with a small amount of fiberfill before closing.

3. Using photo as a guide through step 6, cut white satin ribbon into three equal lengths. Attach one length through top hole of each ornament with a Lark's Head Knot. Tie ends together in a knot 4 inches from top of ornament to form a loop for hanging.

4. Cut one 6-inch length each of light pink and light yellow ribbon. Place remaining light pink and light yellow ribbon together and fold into soft loops; tie in center with 6-inch lengths. Trim all ends and glue to center bottom of woven ribbons egg.

5. Cut light blue ribbon into eight 9-inch lengths. Hold four pieces together as one and tie in a small bow; trim ends. Glue bow to one side of blue gingham egg. Repeat with remaining light blue ribbon, gluing to opposite side of egg.

6. Cut peach ribbon into eight 9-inch lengths. Hold lengths together and tie a knot in center. Glue knot to center top of pastel tartan egg. Trim ends. ✂

COLOR KEY	
Worsted Weight Yarn	**Yards**
☐ White #1	12
▨ Sea coral #246	3
☐ Maize #261	4
▨ Light lavender #579	3
▨ Mist green #681	3
☐ Pink #737	4
☐ Blue jewel #818	4
▨ True blue #822	3
Color numbers given are for Coats & Clark Red Heart Classic worsted weight yarn Art E267.	

Celebrate!

Just for Fun!

National Peanut Butter & Jelly Day is April 2

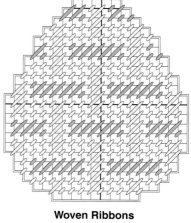

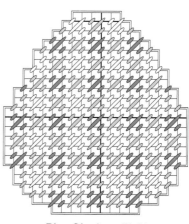

Blue Gingham Plaid
19 holes x 21 holes
Cut 2

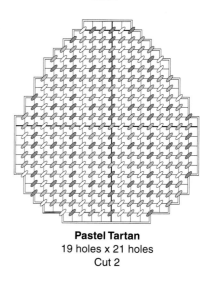

Pastel Tartan
19 holes x 21 holes
Cut 2

Woven Ribbons
19 holes x 21 holes
Cut 2

April   April   April   April   April   April   April

SPRINGTIME
Sunshine

Designs by Kathleen Hurley

Bring a touch of sunshine and cheer into your home with this set of three winsome ornaments! They're perfect for dressing up a gift basket or to use as plant pokes, too!

Skill Level: Beginner

Finished Size

Chick: 3½ inches W x 3¾ inches H

Lamb: 5½ inches W x 3¼ inches H

Goose: 4 inches W x 5¼ inches H

Materials

- 1 sheet 7-count plastic canvas
- Coats & Clark Red Heart Classic worsted weightyarn Art. E267 as listed in color key
- #16 tapestry needle
- 6 inches ⅛-inch-wide royal blue satin ribbon
- 15 inches ½-inch-wide magnetic strip
- Hot-glue gun

Instructions

1. Cut plastic canvas according to graphs.

2. Stitch and Overcast pieces following graphs, working uncoded areas with Continental Stitches in colors as follows: yellow on chick, paddy green on lamb and silver on goose.

3. When background stitching and Overcasting are completed, work all embroidery with 2 plies yarn.

4. Tie royal blue ribbon in a bow; trim ends. Glue bow to goose's hat where indicated on graph.

5. Cut magnetic strip in several lengths to fit; glue to back of stitched pieces. ✂

COLOR KEY	
LAMB	
Worsted Weight Yarn	**Yards**
☐ White #1	5
■ Nickel #401	3
▨ Pink #737	1
Uncoded area is paddy green #686 Continental Stitches	1
╱ Paddy green #686 Overcasting	
╱ Black #12 Backstitch	1
╱ Jockey red Straight Stitch	1
○ Yellow #230 French Knot	1
● Lavender #584 French Knot	1
● Grenadine #730 French Knot	1
Color numbers given are for Coats & Clark Red Heart Classic worsted weight yarn Art. E267.	

Lamb
36 holes x 21 holes
Cut 1

COLOR KEY	
CHICK	
Worsted Weight Yarn	**Yards**
■ Black #12	1
▨ Orange #245	2
▨ Lavender #584	1
▨ Emerald green #676	1
■ Grenadine #730	1
☐ Blue jewel #818	1
Uncoded areas are yellow #230 Continental Stitches	3
╱ Black #12 Backstitch	
● Black #12 French Knot	
Color numbers given are for Coats & Clark Red Heart Classic worsted weight yarn Art. E267.	

Chick
23 holes x 24 holes
Cut 1

April   April   April   April   April   April   April

Goose
25 holes x 34 holes
Cut 1

BUNNY
Buddy

Continued from page 48

stitched bunny, keeping hanging loop on the outside; Whipstitch together with adjacent colors. Be careful to not catch hanging loop when Whipstitching.

3. Using photo as a guide through step 6, cut four 4-inch lengths of bright purple. Thread one length from back to front through each top corner hole of sign, running yarn under several stitches on backside. Secure with glue.

4. Thread free end of lengths from front to back through holes indicated with blue dot on bunny's paws. Knot on backside, making lengths equal. Secure with glue.

5. Tie each of the remaining two lengths in a bow, then glue one bow to each paw at blue dot.

6. Glue white pompoms to bunny's face for muzzle. For nose, center and glue pink pompom above muzzle. ✀

FLORAL Mirrors

Designs by Ronda Bryce

Bring a touch of elegance, grace and beauty into your home with this pair of decorative ornaments accented with pearls, ribbon roses and antique-style buttons.

Skill Level: Beginner

Finished Sizes

Rose mirror: 3½ inches W x 3½ inches H

Heart mirror: 3⅞ inches W x 3⅞ inches H

Materials

- ⅔ sheet 7-count plastic canvas
- Uniek Needloft plastic canvas yarn as listed in color key
- #16 tapestry needle
- 2-inch octagonal mirror
- 2-inch square mirror
- 4 (½-inch) peach ribbon roses with leaves
- 4 (⅜-inch) Heart Throb Heirloom beige pearl heart buttons #214 from James Button and Trim
- 16 (5mm) round ivory pearl beads
- ½ yard ⅛-inch-wide ivory satin ribbon
- Sewing needle and beige sewing thread
- Tacky craft glue

Instructions

1. Cut and stitch plastic canvas according to graphs.

2. Overcast inside edges on front pieces following graphs.

3. Using sewing needle and beige sewing thread through step 4, stitch one pearl to each corner on rose mirror front and three pearls in a cluster to each corner on heart mirror front where indicated on graphs.

4. Sew peach ribbon roses to rose mirror front where indicated on graph. Sew heart buttons to heart mirror front where indicated on graph.

5. Center and glue wrong side of square mirror to wrong side of rose mirror back. Center and glue wrong side of octagonal mirror to wrong side of heart mirror back. Allow to dry.

6. Whipstitch wrong sides of corresponding fronts and backs together following graphs.

7. For hangers, cut ivory ribbon in half. For each mirror, thread one length through top center holes. Tie ends together in a knot to form a loop for hanging; trim excess. ✄

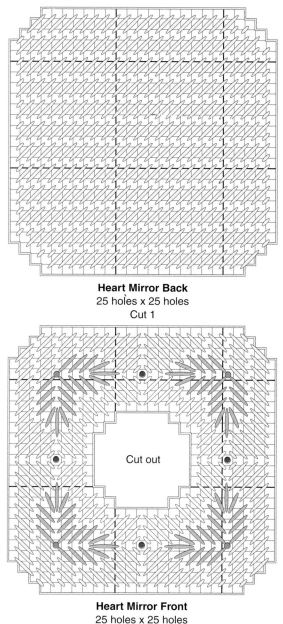

Heart Mirror Back
25 holes x 25 holes
Cut 1

Heart Mirror Front
25 holes x 25 holes
Cut 1

COLOR KEY
HEART

Plastic Canvas Yarn	Yards
▨ Fern #23	3
☐ White #41	3
☐ Flesh tone #56	4
● Attach pearl beads	
● Attach heart button	

Color numbers given are for Uniek Needloft plastic canvas yarn.

COLOR KEY
ROSE

Plastic Canvas Yarn	Yards
▨ Fern #23	3
▨ Beige #40	12
☐ Flesh tone #56	4
● Attach pearl bead	
● Attach ribbon rose	

Color numbers given are for Uniek Needloft plastic canvas yarn.

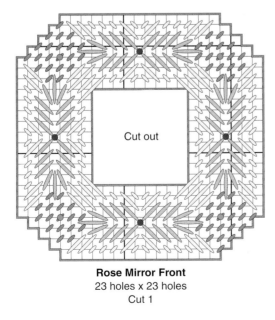

Rose Mirror Front
23 holes x 23 holes
Cut 1

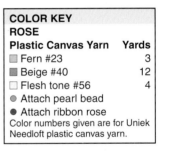

Rose Mirror Back
23 holes x 23 holes
Cut 1

MAY FLOWERS
Bouquet

Designs by Janna Britton

Stitch a bouquet of pretty spring flowers to dress up a little nook in your home sweet home!

Skill Level: Intermediate

Finished Size

2½ inches W x 4½ inches H

Materials

- ¼ sheet Uniek QuickCount 7-count plastic canvas
- Small amounts 7-count plastic canvas: bright pink, pastel yellow, pastel pink and bright purple
- Uniek Needloft plastic canvas yarn as listed in color key
- ⅜-inch-wide satin ribbon as listed in color key
- ⅛-inch-wide satin ribbon as listed in color key
- #16 tapestry needle
- 3-inch square green felt
- 8 inches 15-pound clear nylon line
- Low-temperature glue gun

Cutting & Stitching

1. Cut purple flowers from bright purple plastic canvas, large pink flowers from bright pink plastic canvas, small pink flowers and bow from pastel pink plastic canvas and pale yellow flowers from pastel yellow plastic canvas according to graphs.

2. Cut greenery from green plastic canvas according to graph, cutting away blue lines in stem area.

3. Cut green felt to fit back of bouquet area on greenery. Set aside.

4. Using Christmas green throughout, work uncoded background on bouquet area of greenery with Continental Stitches. At each green dot, work one to two long tails to mix with plastic canvas stems. Overcast bouquet area only following graph.

5. For leaves on greenery, work loose Straight Stitches with ⅛-inch-wide green ribbon, leaving ¼-inch-long loops.

6. Stitch bow following graph.

COLOR KEY	
Plastic Canvas Yarn	**Yards**
▢ Pink #07	2
▨ Watermelon #55	2
▧ Bright purple #64	1
Uncoded area is Christmas green #28 Continental Stitches	7
╱ Christmas green #28 Overcasting	
○ Eggshell #39 French Knot	4
⅜-Inch Satin Ribbon	
▨ Pink	2
⅛-Inch Satin Ribbon	
╱ Green Straight Stitch (loose)	1
Color numbers given are for Uniek Needloft plastic canvas yarn.	

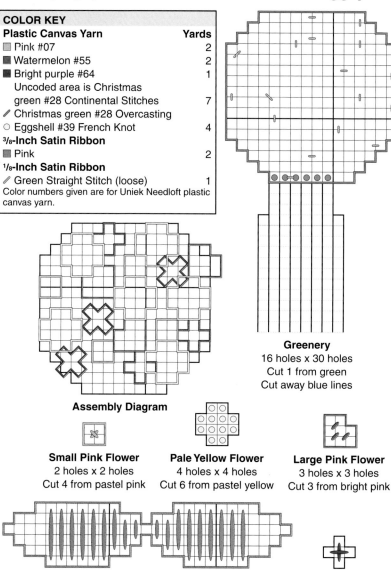

Greenery
16 holes x 30 holes
Cut 1 from green
Cut away blue lines

Assembly Diagram

Small Pink Flower
2 holes x 2 holes
Cut 4 from pastel pink

Pale Yellow Flower
4 holes x 4 holes
Cut 6 from pastel yellow

Large Pink Flower
3 holes x 3 holes
Cut 3 from bright pink

Bouquet Bow
27 holes x 6 holes
Cut 1 from pastel pink

Purple Flower
3 holes x 3 holes
Cut 6 from bright purple

May   May   May   May   May   May   May

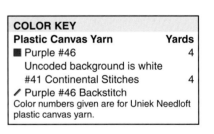

LATTICE
Heart

Design by Nancy Marshall

Dainty eyelet lace and ribbon roses add the perfect finishing touches to this sweet latticed heart!

Finished Size
4 inches W x 4 inches H

Materials
- Small amount 7-count plastic canvas
- Uniek Needloft plastic canvas yarn as listed in color key
- #16 tapestry needle
- 3 (½-inch) shocking pink ribbon roses with leaves
- 11 inches ¼-inch-wide white pre-gathered eyelet lace
- 7 inches ¼-inch-wide white satin ribbon
- 3½-inch x 4-inch piece white self-adhesive Presto felt from Kunin Felt
- Tacky craft glue

Skill Level: Beginner

Instructions
1. Cut plastic canvas according to graph.

2. Stitch heart following graph, working uncoded background with white Continental Stitches. Overcast with purple.

3. When background stitching and Overcasting are completed, work purple Backstitches.

4. Cut felt to fit heart. Set aside.

5. Using photo as a guide through step 6, glue eyelet lace to back of heart around edge.

6. Glue ends of ribbon to back of heart for hanger. Glue roses in a cluster to center top of heart front.

7. Apply felt to back of heart. ✂

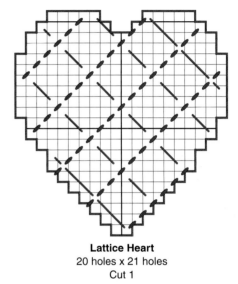

Lattice Heart
20 holes x 21 holes
Cut 1

COLOR KEY	
Plastic Canvas Yarn	**Yards**
■ Purple #46	4
Uncoded background is white #41 Continental Stitches	4
╱ Purple #46 Backstitch	
Color numbers given are for Uniek Needloft plastic canvas yarn.	

MAY FLOWERS
Bouquet

Fold edges back and tack ends to center; wrap ribbon around center. Overcast edges, leaving 2-inch to 3-inch tails; trim as desired.

Assembly
1. Use assembly diagram through step 4, following colors and shapes for flower placement and making sure ribbon leaves stay visible.

2. Cross Stitch purple flowers to greenery with bright purple. *Note: Purple flowers will not be Overcast.*

3. Overcast small pink flowers, then Cross Stitch to greenery. Work two outside stitches and Overcast large pink flowers, then attach to greenery with center stitch.

4. Work all but two eggshell French Knots for each pale yellow flower, then place on greenery and work final two French Knots. *Note: Pale yellow flowers will not be Overcast.*

5. Thread nylon line through center top hole. Knot ends together to form a loop for hanging; trim excess and place knot on backside.

6. Glue felt to backside of greenery, covering hanger knot. Glue bow to bouquet front at top of stems. ✂

May   May   May   May   May   May   May

BABY RATTLE
Frame

Design by Mary T. Cosgrove

This adorable project makes a terrific add-on for Baby's first birthday! Mother will surely want to tuck it away as a special keepsake.

Skill Level: Beginner

Finished Size
4½ inches W x 4½ inches H

Materials
- ⅓ sheet Uniek QuickCount 7-count plastic canvas
- Uniek Needloft plastic canvas yarn as listed in color key
- Bucilla pure silk 4mm ribbon as listed in color key
- #16 tapestry needle
- Nylon thread
- Fabric glue

Instructions
1. Cut and stitch plastic canvas according to graph.

2. When background stitching is completed, work turquoise Straight Stitches.

3. Overcast letters with white. Overcast inside edges of rattle with hot pink and outside edges with turquoise.

4. Use fabric glue to glue photo behind opening on rattle.

5. For hanger, cut desired length of nylon thread. Secure ends to yarn or silk ribbon on backside where indicated on graph. ✂

COLOR KEY	
Plastic Canvas Yarn	**Yards**
☐ White #41	3
4mm Pure Silk Ribbon	
■ Hot pink #24-552	3
☐ Turquoise #24-607	4
○ Attach hanger	

Color numbers given are for Uniek Needloft plastic canvas yarn and Bucilla 4mm pure silk ribbon.

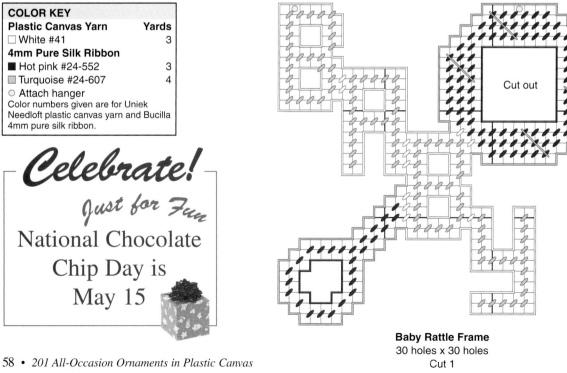

Baby Rattle Frame
30 holes x 30 holes
Cut 1

Celebrate!

Just for Fun

National Chocolate Chip Day is May 15

May   May   May   May   May   May   May

Skill Level: Beginner

Finished Sizes

Purple frame: 2¾ inches W x 3¼ inches H

Blue frame: 2⅔ inches W x 2¾ inches H

Green frame: 2¾ inches W x 3⅛ inches H

Materials

- ½ sheet Uniek QuickCount 7-count plastic canvas
- Uniek Needloft plastic canvas yarn as listed in color key
- #16 tapestry needle
- Fishing line
- Hot-glue gun

Instructions

1. Cut plastic canvas according to graphs, cutting out openings on frame fronts only. Frame backs will remain unstitched.

2. Stitch and Overcast hearts and flowers following graphs. Work French Knots when background stitching and Overcasting are completed.

3. Stitch frame fronts following graphs. Using adjacent colors, Overcast inside edges; Whipstitch wrong sides of corresponding fronts and backs

together, inserting photo before closing.

4. Using photo as a guide, glue yellow flowers to purple frame front, hearts to blue frame front and red flowers to green frame front.

5. For each hanger, thread desired length of fishing line from front to back through top center holes. Tie ends together in a knot to form a loop for hanging. ✂

HEARTS & Flowers Frames

Designs by Christina Laws

Display your homegrown treasures in this trio of colorful frames! They make a great gift for Grandma and Grandpa, too!

Green Frame Front & Back
18 holes x 20 holes
Cut 2
Stitch front only

Yellow Flower
5 holes x 5 holes
Cut 4

Flower Frame Heart
3 holes x 3 holes
Cut 6

Red Flower
3 holes x 3 holes
Cut 6

Blue Frame Front & Back
15 holes x 18 holes
Cut 2
Stitch front only

Purple Frame Front & Back
17 holes x 20 holes
Cut 2
Stitch front only

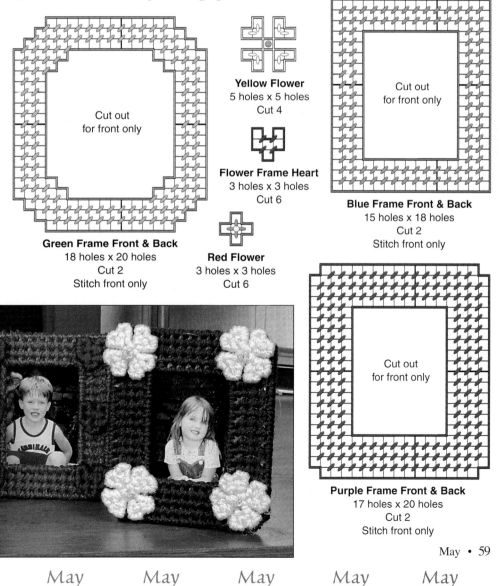

LULLABY BABY
Swings

Designs by Angie Arickx

*Celebrate the birth of your little boy or girl with
one of these sweet baby bear-in-a-swing ornaments!*

Skill Level: Intermediate

Finished Size

1⅞ inches W x 3⅝ inches H x
1 inch D

Materials

- ¼ sheet Uniek QuickCount 7-count plastic canvas
- Uniek Needloft plastic canvas yarn as listed in color key
- Uniek Needloft iridescent craft cord as listed in color key
- #16 tapestry needle
- 2 (1-inch) white flocked bears

Instructions

1. Cut plastic canvas according to graphs.

2. Stitch braces, seat bottoms and seat backs following graphs, working uncoded background on braces with white Continental Stitches.

3. Overcast inside and outside edges of braces with white. Backstitch letters when background stitching and Overcasting are completed.

4. With wrong sides facing, Whipstitch seat bottoms from purple dot to purple dot around side and back edges to bottom edge of corresponding seat backs, easing around curves as neces-

sary. Overcast remaining edges.

5. Overcast seat belts. Match green dots on seat belts to green dots on corresponding backs; tack in place. Match red dots on seat belts to red dots on seat bottoms; tack in place.

6. Place flocked bears in seats. Insert swing arms into bottom holes of brace.

7. Cut one 9-inch length of turquoise yarn. Attach length to top cut-out hole of boy's swing with a Lark's Head Knot. Tie ends together in a knot to form a loop for hanging. Repeat for girl's swing using watermelon yarn. ✄

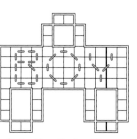

Baby Boy Swing Brace
12 holes x 11 holes
Cut 1

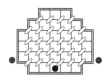

Swing Seat Bottom
7 holes x 6 holes
Cut 1 for each swing

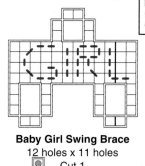

Baby Girl Swing Brace
12 holes x 11 holes
Cut 1

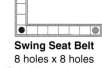

Swing Seat Belt
8 holes x 8 holes
Cut 1 for each swing

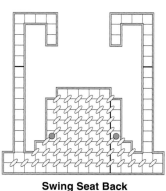

Swing Seat Back
15 holes x 15 holes
Cut 1 for each swing

COLOR KEY

BOY

Plastic Canvas Yarn	Yards
Uncoded areas are white #41 Continental Stitches	2
✎ Baby blue #36 Overcasting	1
✎ White #41 Overcasting	
✎ Turquoise #54 Backstitch and Overcasting	4
Iridescent Craft Cord	
☐ Blue #55049	2

Color numbers given are for Uniek Needloft plastic canvas yarn and iridescent craft cord.

COLOR KEY

GIRL

Plastic Canvas Yarn	Yards
Uncoded areas are white #41 Continental Stitches	2
✎ Pink #07 Overcasting	1
✎ White #41 Overcasting	
✎ Watermelon #55 Backstitch and Overcasting	4
Iridescent Craft Cord	
☐ Pink #55050	2

Color numbers given are for Uniek Needloft plastic canvas yarn and iridescent craft cord.

May   May   May   May   May

SUNNY
Days Kite

Design by Janna Britton

Make the most of those breezy spring days by stitching this friendly ornament featuring a smiling kite flying in a cloud-filled sky!

Skill Level: Beginner

Finished Size

$2\frac{7}{8}$ inches W x $4\frac{1}{8}$ inches H, including kite tail

Materials

- ¼ sheet Uniek QuickCount stiff 7-count plastic canvas
- Uniek Needloft plastic canvas yarn as listed in color key
- Kreinik Medium (#16) Braid as listed in color key
- #16 tapestry needle
- 13mm yellow Expression bead with sunglasses #1591-157N from The Beadery
- White felt
- 9 inches 40-pound clear monofilament
- Low-temperature glue gun

Instructions

1. Cut plastic canvas according to graph, carefully cutting away blue lines in tail area.

2. Cut felt to fit cloud and kite area of piece. Set aside.

3. Stitch and Overcast piece following graph, working uncoded area with white Continental Stitches.

4. When background stitching and Overcasting are completed, work periwinkle medium (#16) braid Backstitches and Straight Stitches.

5. Work royal Backstitches and Straight Stitches on red kite and cloud, threading yellow bead on royal Straight Stitch where indicated on graph.

6. Work Backstitches on tail as indicated, tying yarn in a knot at bottom of kite; trim yarn approximately ½ inch from knot.

7. For bows on tail, cut short lengths of Christmas red and royal yarn and tie in a knot around tail where indicated on graph. Trim ends as desired.

8. Secure ends of monofilament on backside below arrows. Glue felt to backside. ✄

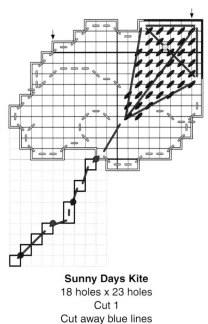

Sunny Days Kite
18 holes x 23 holes
Cut 1
Cut away blue lines

COLOR KEY

Plastic Canvas Yarn	Yards
■ Christmas red #02	2
Uncoded areas are white #41 Continental Stitches	5
╱ White #41 Overcasting	
╱ Royal #31 Backstitch and Straight Stitch	2
● Attach Christmas red #02 bow	
● Attach royal #32 bow	
Medium (#16) Braid	
╱ Periwinkle #9294 Backstitch and Straight Stitch	2
○ Attach yellow bead	

Color numbers given are for Uniek Needloft plastic canvas yarn and Kreinik Medium (#16) Braid.

Celebrate!
Just for Fun
National Hamburger Day is May 31

BABES IN
Blankets

Designs by Nancy Marshall

Add an extra-special touch to a baby shower gift by attaching one of these darling ornaments to the gift bow. It makes for two gifts in one!

Materials

Each Ornament

- ½ sheet Uniek QuickCount 7-count plastic canvas

- Uniek Needloft plastic canvas yarn as listed in color key

- #16 tapestry needle

- 1⅛-inch Happy Face from Annie's Attic

- ¼ yard ⅜-inch-wide flat white lace

- 6 inches ⅞-inch wide white grosgrain ribbon

- Small amount polyester fiberfill

- Small amount of doll hair in desired color

- Tacky craft glue

Girl

- 2-inch x 4¾-inch piece baby pink felt

Boy

- 2-inch x 4¾-inch piece baby blue felt

Skill Level: Beginner

Finished Size

2¼ inches W x 5⅛ inches H

Instructions

1. Cut plastic canvas according to graphs. Cut felt to fit back pieces.

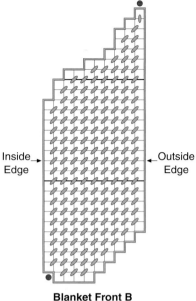

Inside Edge → ← Outside Edge

Blanket Front B
10 holes x 27 holes
Cut 1 for boy
Stitch as graphed
Cut 1 for girl
Reverse and stitch with pink

Blanket Back
14 holes x 32 holes
Cut 1 for boy
Stitch as graphed
Cut 1 for girl
Stitch with pink

COLOR KEY	
Plastic Canvas Yarn	**Yards**
Baby pink #07	8½
Bright blue #60	8½
Color numbers given are for Uniek Needloft plastic canvas yarn.	

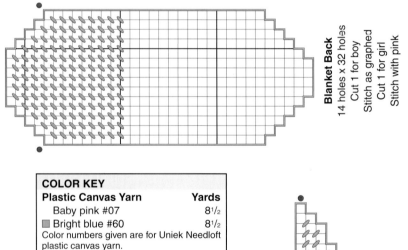

Outside Edge → ← Inside Edge

Blanket Front A
7 holes x 27 holes
Cut 1 for boy
Stitch as graphed
Cut 1 for girl
Reverse and stitch with pink

May   May   May

YELLOW ROSE
of Texas

Design by Ronda Bryce

The best part of this flower is that its beauty will never fade! Stitch it in your favorite color, and add a few drops of scented oil to the center.

Skill Level: Intermediate

Materials

- ½ sheet 7-count plastic canvas
- 3-inch Uniek QuickShape plastic canvas radial circle
- Uniek Needloft plastic canvas yarn as listed in color key
- #16 tapestry needle
- 8mm round white pearl bead
- ½ yard ⅝-inch-wide pre-gathered yellow eyelet trim
- ¼ yard ⅛-inch-wide ecru satin ribbon
- Sewing needle and pale yellow sewing thread

Finished Size

4 inches in diameter x 1¼ inches D

Instructions

1. Cut and stitch plastic canvas according to graphs.

2. Overcast rose base with lemon. Overcast small petals with yellow. Overcast bottom edges of medium and large petals with lemon; Overcast around side and top edges with yellow.

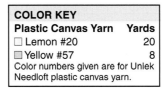

COLOR KEY

Plastic Canvas Yarn	Yards
☐ Lemon #20	20
☐ Yellow #57	8

Color numbers given are for Uniek Needloft plastic canvas yarn.

3. Using photo as a guide through step 7 and lemon yarn through step 4, overlap and tack bottom edges of small petals to base in or near the area shaded with blue.

4. Overlap and tack medium petals around small petals, then overlap and tack large petals around medium petals.

5. Using sewing needle and pale yellow sewing thread through step 6, stitch pearl to center of base.

6. Stitch yellow eyelet trim around backside of base around edge.

7. For hanger, thread ecru satin ribbon through hole along outer edge of base. Tie ends together in a knot at desired length; trim excess. ✂

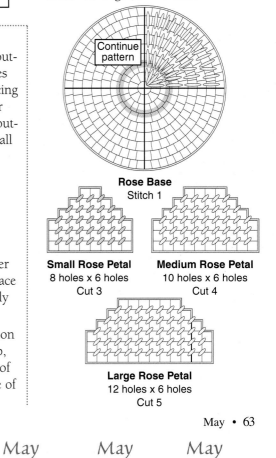

Continue pattern

Rose Base
Stitch 1

Small Rose Petal
8 holes x 6 holes
Cut 3

Medium Rose Petal
10 holes x 6 holes
Cut 4

Large Rose Petal
12 holes x 6 holes
Cut 5

BABES IN
Blankets

2. Stitch boy pieces with bright blue following graphs. Stitch girl pieces reversing fronts A and B and replacing bright blue with pink.

3. Using adjacent colors, Overcast front pieces along top and inside edges from red dot to red dot; Overcast top edges of back from red dot to red dot.

4. Using photo as a guide through step 8, for each blanket, glue lace along the following edges: top edge of back from red dot to red dot, top edge of side A from red dot to green dot, top and inside edges of Side B from red dot to red dot.

5. To assemble blankets, with right sides facing up, match outside and bottom edges of sides A and B to blanket back, placing B over A; Whipstitch together with adjacent colors around outside edges, stitching through all three thicknesses at bottom.

6. Lightly stuff blanket with fiberfill, then glue A and B together along front edge.

7. For each face, cut small lengths of hair, fraying if desired, and glue to top center back of face. Glue head in place on back piece, tucking slightly inside blanket front.

8. For each hanger, glue ribbon ends together, forming a loop, then glue to top center back of blanket. Glue felt to backside of blanket back. ✂

WEDDING &
Anniversary Globes

Designs by Angie Arickx

Whether the special occasion is a wedding, silver or golden anniversary, you'll want to make it extra special by stitching one of these beautiful, keepsake globes!

Skill Level: Intermediate

Finished Size
3 inches H x 2½ inches in diameter

Materials
Each globe
- ¼ sheet Uniek QuickCount 7-count plastic canvas
- 3 Uniek QuickShape plastic canvas hexagons
- Uniek Needloft plastic canvas yarn as listed in color key
- Uniek Needloft metallic craft cord as listed in color key
- #16 tapestry needle

Instructions
1. Cut plastic canvas according to graphs, cutting one each of globe cap, top half and bottom half for each globe.

2. Stitch inserts following graphs, working uncoded areas with white Continental Stitches.

3. Work Straight Stitches and Backstitches when background stitching is completed. Whipstitch wrong sides together with white.

4. Work globe top, bottom and cap following graphs. Before stitching, overlap spokes on top with spokes on bottom where shaded with blue. Overcast with white.

5. For hanger, matching metallic cord used on cap, cut an 8-inch length and thread ends from back to front through holes indicated on cap graph. Tie ends together in a knot to form a loop for hanging.

6. Using photo as a guide, place insert inside globe between spokes.

7. Place cap on globe putting points on cap between spokes. Using white, tack globe cap to top of globe with a running stitch, catching insert where indicated on graphs with green dots and making sure to run yarn under points of cap and under spokes. ✂

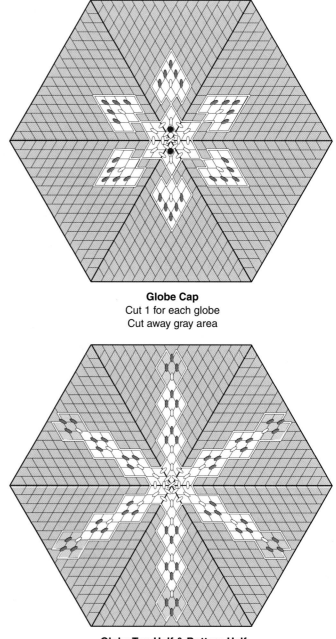

Globe Cap
Cut 1 for each globe
Cut away gray area

Globe Top Half & Bottom Half
Cut 2 for each globe
Cut away gray areas

June   June   June   June   June   June   June

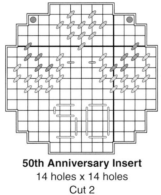

50th Anniversary Insert
14 holes x 14 holes
Cut 2

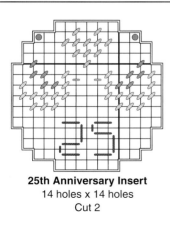

25th Anniversary Insert
14 holes x 14 holes
Cut 2

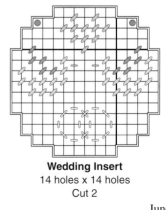

Wedding Insert
14 holes x 14 holes
Cut 2

June   June   June   June   June   June   June

CHOCOLATE
Layer Cake

Design by Ronda Bryce

This pretty ornament looks good enough to eat! Stitch it to make any special occasion memorable!

Skill Level: Beginner

Finished Size

2¼ inches H x 3 inches in diameter

Materials

- Small amount 7-count plastic canvas
- 3 (3-inch) Uniek QuickShape plastic canvas radial circles
- Uniek Needloft plastic canvas yarn as listed in color key
- 2 yards solid gold #55020 Uniek Needloft metallic craft cord
- 6 yards white #55033 Uniek Needloft iridescent craft cord
- #16 tapestry needle
- 4 (½ inch) red ribbon roses with leaves
- ¼ yard ⅜-inch-wide beige braid trim
- Sewing needle and beige sewing thread
- Tacky craft glue (optional)

Instructions

1. Cut cake sides and back from regular plastic canvas according to graphs.

2. Cut cake top from one radial circle and cake bottom from second radial circle following graph, cutting away gray area. Do not cut remaining radial circle, which is the plate.

3. Keeping craft cord smooth and flat, Continental Stitch cake plate with white iridescent; Overcast with solid gold.

4. Stitch cake top, back and sides following graphs. Cake bottom will remain unstitched.

5. Whipstitch top edges of cake sides to straight edges of cake top. Whipstitch joining sides of cake sides together with adjacent colors.

6. Using beige, Whipstitch cake back to cake sides and top, then Whipstitch sides and back to cake bottom.

7. Cut one length beige braid trim to fit bottom edge of cake back and one length to fit curved edge of cake top.

8. Using photo as a guide and sewing needle and beige sewing thread throughout, stitch trim to cake. Stitch cake to center top of plate. Sew three roses in a cluster to cake top. Sew remaining rose to plate at cake side.

9. For hanger, cut desired length of solid gold cord. Thread through center holes at back of cake slice; tie ends together in a knot to form a loop for hanging and trim as desired. Optional: Add a dab of glue to ends to prevent fraying. ✂

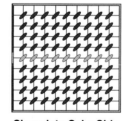

Chocolate Cake Back
16 holes x 10 holes
Cut 1

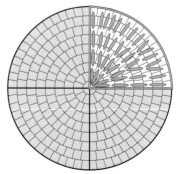

Chocolate Cake Side
10 holes x 10 holes
Cut 2

Chocolate Cake Top & Bottom
Cut 2, stitch 1
Cut away gray area

COLOR KEY

Plastic Canvas Yarn	Yards
■ Brown #15	3
▨ Beige #40	6

Color numbers given are for Uniek Needloft plastic canvas yarn.

Skill Level: Beginner

Finished Size

3⅜ inches W x 5¼ inches H, including flag pole

Materials

- ¼ sheet 7-count plastic canvas
- Coats & Clark Red Heart Classic worsted weight yarn Art. E267 as listed in color key
- #16 tapestry needle
- Fine gold yarn
- 3 (4-inch) lengths gold glitter stem
- Fabric glue

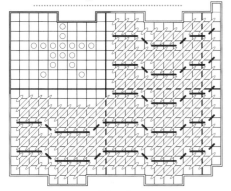

Flag A
22 holes x 19 holes
Cut 1

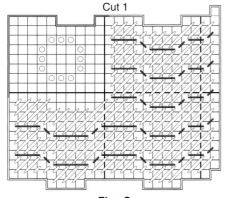

Flag B
22 holes x 19 holes
Cut 1

Flag C
22 holes x 19 holes
Cut 1

RIPPLING
Flags

Designs by Joan Green

One of June's lesser-known holidays is Flag Day. Show your respect for America's flag with this set of three commemorative ornaments.

Instructions

1. Cut plastic canvas according to graphs.

2. Stitch and Overcast pieces following graphs, working uncoded areas with Olympic blue Continental Stitches.

3. When background stitching and Overcasting are completed, work jockey red Backstitches with 2 full strands yarn. Using 2 plies of 4-ply strand white yarn, work French Knots.

4. For flag poles, glue one glitter stem to backside of each flag

along left edge, allowing 2½ inches to 3 inches of stem below bottom edge.

5. For each hanger, cut desired length of fine gold yarn. Glue ends together to center top backside of flag. ✄

COLOR KEY	
Worsted Weight Yarn	**Yards**
☐ White #1	14
Uncoded areas are Olympic blue #849 Continental Stitches	6
╱ Olympic blue #849 Overcasting	
╱ Jockey red #902 Backstitch	8
○ White #1 French Knot	
Color numbers given are for Coats & Clark Red Heart Classic worsted weight yarn Art. E267.	

June   June   June   June   June   June   June

CONGRATULATIONS
Graduate!

Design by Janna Britton & Joan Green

***Top off a graduate's gift with either one of these
congratulatory ornaments!***

Graduate

Skill Level: Intermediate

Finished Size

2⅝ inches W x 3 inches H x 2⅝ inches D

Materials

- ¼ sheet Uniek QuickCount clear 7-count plastic canvas
- Small amount Uniek QuickCount black 7-count plastic canvas
- Uniek Needloft plastic canvas yarn as listed in color key
- Uniek Needloft metallic craft cord as listed in color key
- ³⁄₁₆-inch-wide curling ribbon as listed in color key
- Kreinik Medium (#16) Braid as listed in color key
- DMC #3 pearl cotton as listed in color key
- #16 tapestry needle
- 1 yard DMC 6-strand rayon embroidery floss in school color
- 7 (5mm) round gold sequins

- 1-inch x 3-inch piece black felt
- 1½-inch square cardboard
- 24 inches 15-pound clear monofilament line
- Low-temperature glue gun

Cutting & Stitching

1. Cut head front, head back and year plaque from clear plastic canvas; cut cap band and cap from black plastic canvas according to graphs.

2. Cut felt to fit year plaque. Set aside.

3. Following graphs through step 7, stitch cap band, overlapping six holes before stitching. Overcast "point" on bottom edge.

4. Placing one corner of unstitched cap top in front, center cap top on top edge of hat band; tack in place with black yarn. Stitch cap top with black curling ribbon, running stitches through top holes of band as needed. Overcast top with black yarn.

5. Stitch and Overcast year plaque, working uncoded areas

with black Continental Stitches. Work Backstitches with medium (#16) braid.

6. Stitch head front and back, working uncoded area on head front with flesh tone Continental Stitches.

7. When background stitching is completed, work pearl cotton Backstitches on front. Whipstitch wrong sides of head front and back together.

8. For hair, cut 12 (3-inch) lengths of camel yarn. Thread two lengths through each hole indicated on graph to midpoint of yarn, leaving 1½ inches on both sides. Untwist hair and lightly glue to sides, leaving some fullness. Trim as desired.

Final Assembly

1. For tassel, wrap rayon embroidery floss around cardboard nine times. Tie a 6-inch length of floss around loops at top, knotting securely. Cut loops at bottom and remove cardboard. Tie another 6-inch length floss around tassel ¼ inch from top; knot securely. Trim as necessary.

2. Insert tassel tie from top to bottom through hole indicated on cap top, securing on inside. *Note: Tassel may be dampened to straighten floss as needed.*

3. Using photo as a guide through step 5, center year plaque under head and loosely tack together with flesh tone yarn.

4. Glue felt to back of plaque. Glue sequins to front of plaque where indicated on graph.

5. Tack cap to head with black yarn.

6. Cut monofilament into two 12-inch lengths. Thread one length through each side corner hole on cap top. Bring all four ends together and tie together in a knot above cap, checking for hanging balance.

Mortar Board

Skill Level: Beginner

Finished Size

$4\frac{1}{4}$ inches W x $4\frac{5}{8}$ inches H, including tassel

Materials

- Small amount 7-count plastic canvas
- Coats & Clark Red Heart worsted weight yarn Art. E267 as listed in color key
- $\frac{1}{8}$ inch-wide Plastic Canvas 7 Metallic Needlepoint Yarn

by Rainbow Gallery as listed in color key

- #16 tapestry needle
- $2\frac{1}{4}$-inch long silver tassel
- Fabric glue

Instructions

1. Cut plastic canvas according to graphs.

2. Cross Stitch silver button on mortar board and black Continental Stitches on both pieces following graphs. Overcast following graphs.

3. When background stitching and overcasting are completed,

embroider desired year on mortar board following numbers given.

4. Place hanger on tassel over stitched silver button. Using silver yarn, tack hanger in place where indicated on graph at silver button and at lower left side.

5. Place top over cap, covering unstitched area and stitch together, working over several stitches to secure.

6. Using fabric glue, glue ends of a 7-inch length of silver yarn to center top backside of top for hanger. ✂

COLOR KEY
GRADUATE

Plastic Canvas Yarn	Yards
■ Black #00	4
▨ Pink #07	1
▨ Cinnamon #41	1
□ White #41	1
■ Camel #43	3
Uncoded areas on plaque are black #00 Continental Stitches	
Uncoded areas on head front are flesh tone #56 Continental Stitches	2
⁄ Flesh tone #56 Whipstitching	
Metallic Craft Cord	
□ Gold #55001	2
³⁄₁₆-Inch Curling Ribbon	
■ Black	2
Medium #16 Braid	
▨ Gold #002J	2
#3 Pearl Cotton	
⁄ Medium brown #433 Backstitch	1
● Attach hair	
● Attach tassel	
● Attach sequin	

Color numbers given are for Uniek Needloft plastic canvas yarn and metallic craft cord, Kreinik Medium (#16) Braid and DMC #3 pearl cotton.

COLOR KEY
MORTAR BOARD

Worsted Weight Yarn	Yards
■ Black #12	9
1/8-Inch Metallic Needlepoint Yarn	
□ Silver #PM52	1
⁄ Silver #PM52 Backstitch and Straight Stitch	
⁄ Attach tassel	

Color numbers given are for Coats & Clark Red Heart Classic worsted weight yarn Art. E267 and Rainbow Gallery Plastic Canvas 7 Metallic Needlepoint Yarn.

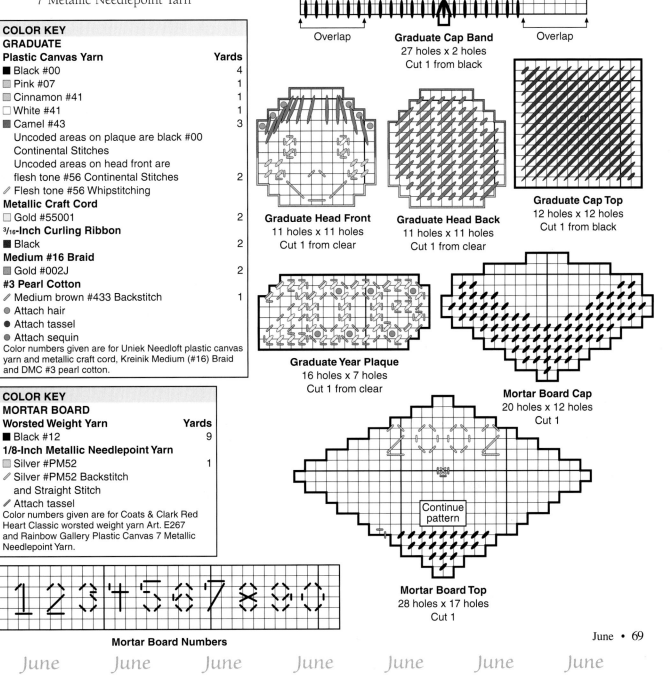

Graduate Cap Band
27 holes x 2 holes
Cut 1 from black

Graduate Head Front
11 holes x 11 holes
Cut 1 from clear

Graduate Head Back
11 holes x 11 holes
Cut 1 from clear

Graduate Cap Top
12 holes x 12 holes
Cut 1 from black

Graduate Year Plaque
16 holes x 7 holes
Cut 1 from clear

Mortar Board Cap
20 holes x 12 holes
Cut 1

Mortar Board Top
28 holes x 17 holes
Cut 1

Continue pattern

Mortar Board Numbers

LUCKY
Dice

Design by Alida Macor

Wish your graduate lots of luck with this pair of dice to hang on his or her car's rearview mirror!

Skill Level: Beginner

Finished Size

1½-inch cube

Materials

- ½ sheet 7-count plastic canvas
- Darice Bright Pearls pearlized metallic cord as listed in color key
- #16 tapestry needle
- 42 black sequins
- 2 yards ⅛-inch-wide white satin ribbon
- Sewing needle and transparent sewing thread

Instructions

1. Cut plastic canvas according to graphs.

2. Using white pearlized metallic cord, Continental Stitch all 12 sides.

3. With sewing needle and transparent sewing thread, sew sequins on one set of six sides; set aside. Repeat for second set.

4. Whipstitch one set together with white, forming a cube and making sure all opposite sides add up to seven: six and one, three and four, five and two. Repeat with second set.

5. Cut ribbon in half. Attach one length to one die through center holes of one edge with a Lark's Head Knot. Repeat with second die. Tie ribbon ends together in a knot, making one die higher than the other. ✄

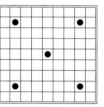
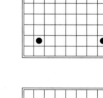
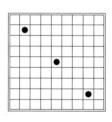
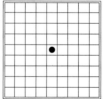

Dice Sides
9 holes x 9 holes
Cut 2 each

COLOR KEY

Pearlized Metallic Cord	Yards
Uncoded areas are white #3410-01 Continental Stitches	22
⁄ White #3410-01 Whipstitching	
● Attach black sequin	

Color number given is for Darice Bright Pearls Pearlized Metallic Cord.

GOLFING
Buddies

Designs by Judy Collishaw

Add humor and whimsy to your game of golf with this pair of golf-bag tags!

- 54 (½-inch) buttons
- 2 (6mm) gold jump rings
- 2 gold ball key chains
- Low-temperature glue gun

Cutting & Stitching

1. Cut plastic canvas according to graphs 71. Cut two shoes for each buddy, cutting away blue lines at bottom, leaving two cleats.

2. Following graphs through step 5, stitch and Overcast flag and golf club, working Backstitches on pole of flag and handle of club.

3. Stitch remaining pieces, working uncoded areas with peach Continental Stitches and leaving blue Whipstitch line on golf club holder unworked at this time.

4. When background stitching is completed, Straight Stitch eyes with 2 plies black yarn. Using pearl cotton for remainder of embroidery, work eyebrows with black, cheeks with very light carnation and mouths with red.

Continued on page 73

Skill Level: Intermediate

Finished Sizes

Flag holder: 4 inches W x 7½ inches H

Golf club holder: 4¾ inches W x 6 inches H

Materials

- 1 sheet 7-count plastic canvas
- Worsted weight yarn as listed in color key
- DMC #3 pearl cotton as listed in color key
- DMC #5 pearl cotton as listed in color key
- #16 tapestry needle
- 10mm red pompom

COLOR KEY

Plastic Canvas Yarn	Yards
Light brown	3
Medium blue	2
Burgundy	2
Gray	2
Eggshell	2
Mustard	1
Light blue	1
Kelly green	1
Grass green	1
Mint green	1
Uncoded areas are peach Continental Stitches	10
Dark brown Backstitch and Overcasting	2
White Overcasting	1
Peach Overcasting	
Black Straight Stitch	1
Gray Backstitch	
#3 Pearl Cotton	
Very light carnation #894 Straight Stitch	2
#5 Pearl Cotton	
Black #310 Straight Stitch	1
Red #321 Backstitch and Straight Stitch	
Attach button leg	
Attach jump ring	
Attach pompom	

Color numbers given are for DMC pearl cotton.

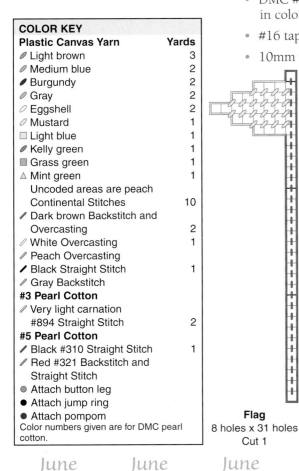

Flag
8 holes x 31 holes
Cut 1

Golf Club
7 holes x 28 holes
Cut 1

Sun Visor
11 holes x 4 holes
Cut 1

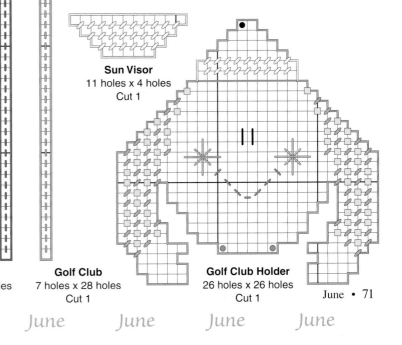

Golf Club Holder
26 holes x 26 holes
Cut 1

BUTTERFLY
Trio

Designs by Christina Laws

Fluttering butterflies add delicate beauty outdoors, while these sparkling ornaments bring it indoors!

Skill Level: Beginner

Finished Size
4⅛ inches W x 4¼ inches H

Materials

- ½ sheet Uniek QuickCount clear 7-count plastic canvas
- Small amount black 7-count plastic canvas
- Worsted weight yarn as listed in color key
- Uniek Needloft metallic craft cord as listed in color key
- Uniek Needloft metallic iridescent craft cord as listed in color key
- Uniek Needloft metallic holographic craft cord as listed in color key
- #16 tapestry needle
- 6 (5mm) movable eyes
- Fishing line
- Hot-glue gun

Instructions

1. Cut butterflies from clear plastic canvas; cut antennae from black plastic canvas according to graphs, cutting away blue lines on antennae.

2. Stitch and Overcast pieces following graphs, working uncoded areas on red butterfly with red Continental Stitches, on blue butterfly with light blue Continental Stitches and on purple butterfly with lavender Continental Stitches. Antennae will remain unstitched.

3. When background stitching is completed, work Backstitches to form mouths and to separate upper and lower wings.

4. Using photo as guide, glue eyes to fronts of heads and antennae to backs of heads.

5. Thread desired length of fishing line through top center hole of head. Tie ends together in a knot to form a loop for hanging. ✄

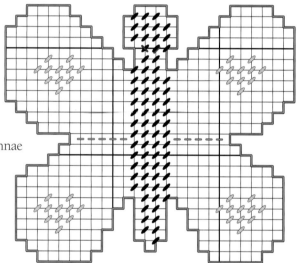

Blue Butterfly
27 holes x 24 holes
Cut 1

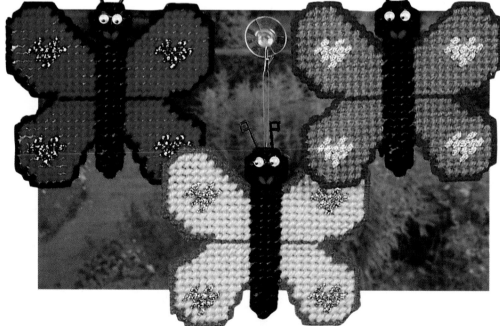

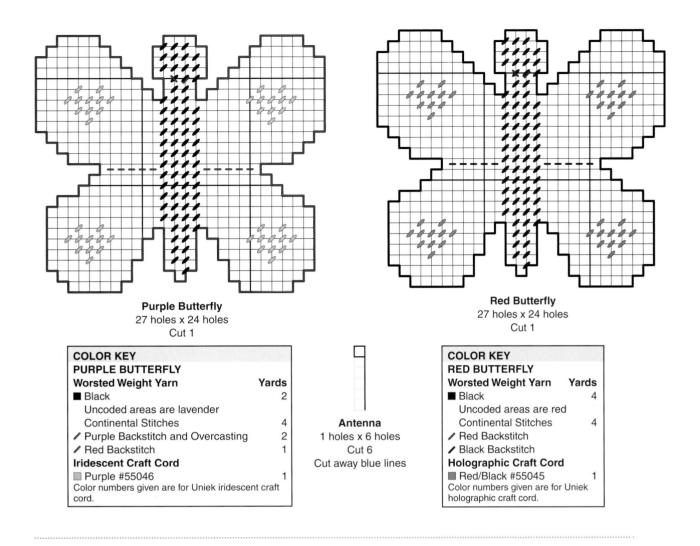

Purple Butterfly
27 holes x 24 holes
Cut 1

COLOR KEY
PURPLE BUTTERFLY

Worsted Weight Yarn	Yards
■ Black	2
Uncoded areas are lavender Continental Stitches	4
✎ Purple Backstitch and Overcasting	2
✎ Red Backstitch	1
Iridescent Craft Cord	
▨ Purple #55046	1

Color numbers given are for Uniek iridescent craft cord.

Antenna
1 holes x 6 holes
Cut 6
Cut away blue lines

Red Butterfly
27 holes x 24 holes
Cut 1

COLOR KEY
RED BUTTERFLY

Worsted Weight Yarn	Yards
■ Black	4
Uncoded areas are red Continental Stitches	4
✎ Red Backstitch	
✎ Black Backstitch	
Holographic Craft Cord	
▨ Red/Black #55045	1

Color numbers given are for Uniek holographic craft cord.

GOLFING Buddies
Continued from page 71

5. Overcast holders. Overcast all but cleats on shoes. Overcast around side and bottom edges of sun visor, then Whipstitch top edge of visor to blue Whipstitch line on golf club holder. *Note: Visor will be a little off center.*

Assembly

1. Use photo as a guide throughout assembly. Glue golf club and flag to corresponding holders. Glue pompom to flag holder where indicated on graph.

2. Cut a 1-yard length of peach yarn, then secure approximately 1 inch under stitches on back of flag holder above hole indicated for attaching button leg, coming out behind hole.

3. Thread on 14 buttons, going down through one hole of each button. Thread yarn through hole indicated on one shoe, back up through second hole of each button, from front to back of hole indicated and up through yarn on back of holder. Trim yarn as necessary and glue ends to secure.

4. Repeat steps 2 and 3 for second leg of flag holder, then for both legs of golf club holder, using 13 buttons for each of his two legs.

5. Attach jump rings to holes indicated on holders, then insert key chains through

jump rings. ✂

Golf Shoe
7 holes x 4 holes
Cut 2, reverse 1,
for each tag
Cut away blue lines

Flag Holder
26 holes x 26 holes
Cut 1

ALL-AMERICAN
Bears

Designs by Angie Arickx

Add a patriotic touch to your home with this set of three friendly bears!

Skill Level: Intermediate

Finished Sizes

Heart bear: 4⅛ inches W x 4⅛ inches H

Window bear: 4⅛ inches W x 4⅛ inches H

Flag-holding bear: 4⅜ inches W x 6 inches H

Materials

- 1 sheet Uniek QuickCount 7-count plastic canvas
- Uniek Needloft plastic canvas yarn as listed in color key
- #16 tapestry needle
- 2 (20mm) suction cups with hooks
- 3½ inches magnetic strip (optional)
- Hot-glue gun

Instructions

1. Cut plastic canvas according to graphs.

2. Stitch and Overcast pieces following graphs, working uncoded areas on heart and flag-holding bears with maple Continental Stitches and uncoded areas on window bear front and back with royal Continental Stitches.

3. Cut an 8-inch length of maple yarn and thread through top center hole of heart bear. Tie ends together in a knot to form a loop for hanging.

4. Glue wrong sides of window bears together, leaving hands unglued. Insert hooks of suction cups through holes indicated with green dots on front or back.

5. Hang remaining bear from flag or if desired, cut a 2-inch length of magnetic strip and glue to back of bear, glue remaining strip to back of flag. ✂

Heart Bear
27 holes x 27 holes
Cut 1

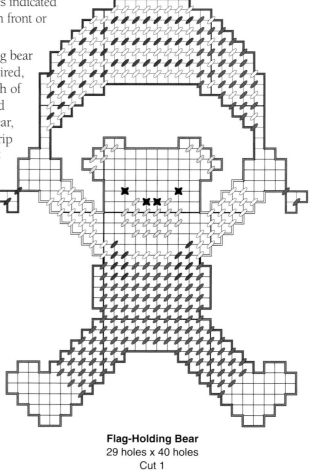

Flag-Holding Bear
29 holes x 40 holes
Cut 1

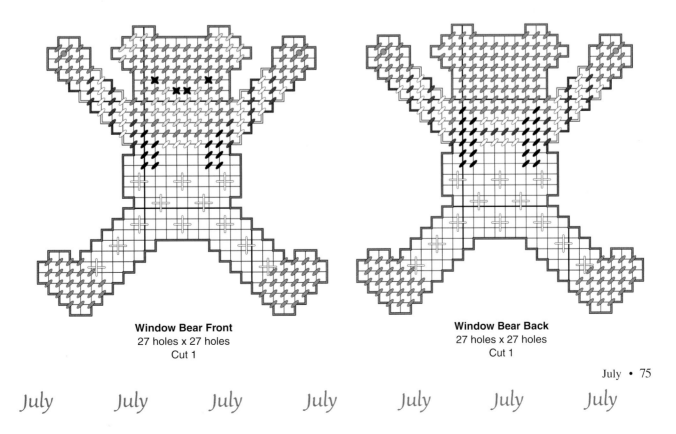

Window Bear Front
27 holes x 27 holes
Cut 1

Window Bear Back
27 holes x 27 holes
Cut 1

July   *July*   *July*   *July*   *July*   *July*   *July*

FISH
Family

Design by Michele Wilcox

This family of brightly colored, tropical fish makes an eye-catching accent for your bathroom!

Skill Level: Beginner

Finished Size

5½ inches W x 5¼ inches H

Materials

• ⅓ sheet Uniek QuickCount 7-count plastic canvas

• Uniek Needloft plastic canvas yarn as listed in color key

• #3 pearl cotton: 6 inches cream and as listed in color key

• #16 tapestry needle

• Hot-glue gun

Instructions

1. Cut plastic canvas according to graphs.

2. Stitch pieces following graphs, working two small fish with watermelon as graphed, one with turquoise and one with yellow.

3. Overcast fish with adjacent colors. Work French Knot eyes with black pearl cotton.

4. For hanger, thread cream pearl cotton from front to back through holes indicated on large fish, knotting ends in back.

5. Glue fish together using photo as a guide. ✂

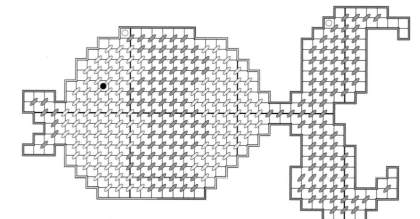

Large Fish
36 holes x 20 holes
Cut 1

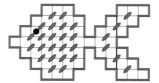

Small Fish
13 holes x 7 holes
Stitch 2 as graphed,
1 with turquoise and
1 with yellow

COLOR KEY	
Plastic Canvas Yarn	**Yards**
▨ Turquoise #54	8
▪ Watermelon #55	4
☐ Yellow #58	7
#3 Pearl Cotton	
● Black French Knot	1
○ Attach hanger	
Color numbers given are for Uniek Needloft plastic canvas yarn.	

FIRST
Mate Frame

Design by Susan Leinberger

Display a favorite photo in this handsome, nautical project. Use it as a frame or ornament!

Skill Level: Intermediate

Finished Size

5½ inches W x 5¼ inches H

Materials

- Uniek QuickShape plastic canvas star
- 4½-inch plastic canvas radial circle from Darice
- Small amount 7-count plastic canvas (optional)
- Coats & Clark Red Heart Super Saver worsted weight yarn Art. E301: 2 yards cherry red #319 and as listed in color key
- Darice Bright Jewels metallic cord as listed in color key
- #16 tapestry needle
- Seam sealant (optional)
- Tacky craft gun

Instructions

1. Cut plastic canvas according to graphs, cutting away gray areas on star frame back and on life preserver frame front.

2. If desired, cut one 12-hole x 24-hole piece from regular plastic canvas for frame support; it will remain unstitched.

3. Continental Stitch uncoded background on frame front with white. Following graph, embroider letters and anchors with soft navy when background stitching is completed.

4. Overcast inner and outer edges of frame front with alternating stitches of white yarn and gold metallic craft cord.

5. Cut four 16-inch lengths cherry red yarn. Using photo as a guide, wrap one length around life preserver frame front at each point indicated by arrow.

6. Using soft navy, Backstitch star frame back following graph, leaving center area unstitched. Overcast inner and outer edges where indicated with gold metallic craft cord.

7. If using frame support, Whipstitch top edge of frame support to star frame back with white where indicated.

8. Glue frame front to frame back where indicated at green lines on frame back graph, leaving top open. Cut photo to size and insert through top opening.

9. If using hanger, cut desired length of gold metallic craft cord and thread through top hole of star frame back; tie ends together in a knot or bow to from a loop for hanging. Apply seam sealant to ends to prevent fraying. ✄

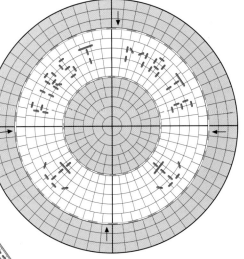

Life Preserver Frame Front
Cut 1
Cut away gray areas

Star Frame Back
Cut 1
Cut away gray areas

COLOR KEY	
Worsted Weight Yarn	**Yards**
Uncoded areas on front are white #311 Continental Stitches	5
⁄ White #311 Overcasting and Whipstitching	
⁄ Soft navy #387 Backstitch and Straight Stitch	2
Metallic Craft Cord	
⁄ Gold #3411-01 Overcasting	4
Color numbers given are for Coats & Clark Red Heart Super Saver worsted weight yarn Art. E301 and Darice Bright Jewels metallic craft cord.	

PATRIOTIC
Trio

Designs by Janelle Giese

Uncle Sam, Betsy Ross and a striped heart make for a festive and patriotic set!

Skill Level: Beginner

Finished Size

Sam: 2⅞ inches W x 5 inches H

Betsy: 2½ inches W x 4⅝ inches H

Heart: 3⅝ inches W x 3⅜ inches H

Materials

- ½ sheet 7-count plastic canvas
- Coats & Clark Red Heart Classic worsted weight yarn Art. E267 as listed in color key
- Kreinik Medium (#16) Braid as listed in color key
- DMC #5 pearl cotton as listed in color key
- DMC 6-strand embroidery floss as listed in color key
- #16 tapestry needle
- Thick white glue

Instructions

1. Cut plastic canvas according to graphs.

2. Stitch and Overcast pieces following graphs, working uncoded areas on Betsy with white Continental Stitches and uncoded areas on Sam and heart with Olympic blue Continental Stitches. Work Cross Stitches for Sam's vest with 2 strands gold braid.

3. When background stitching and Overcasting are completed, use 1 ply medium salmon to embroider cheeks. Use 1 strand gold for embroidery on heart, Sam's hat and bib of Betsy's apron.

4. Work highlights on Sam's shoes with a full strand white yarn. Work remaining embroidery with black pearl cotton, passing over each eye four times.

5. Tie a 6-inch length gold braid in a small bow; trim ends. Glue to Betsy's cap where indicated on graph.

6. For each ornament, thread ends of a length of black pearl cotton from front to back through holes indicated on graph. Tie ends together in a knot to form a loop for hanging, allowing loop to extend 3 inches above top of ornament. ✄

COLOR KEY

Worsted Weight Yarn

		Yards
☐	White #1	7
▧	Sea coral #246	3
■	Coffee #365	2
▨	True blue #822	1
■	Olympic blue #849	5
■	Cherry red #912	4

Uncoded areas on Betsy are white #1 Continental Stitches

Uncoded areas on Sam and flag are Olympic blue #849 Continental Stitches

⁄ White #1 Straight Stitch

Medium (#16) Braid

☐	Gold #002	6

⁄ Gold #002 Backstitch, Straight Stitch and Cross Stitch

#5 Pearl Cotton

✔ Black #310 Backstitch and Straight Stitch

6-Strand Embroidery Floss

✕	Medium salmon #3712 Cross Stitch	1

● Attach hanger

Color numbers given are for Coats & Clark Red Heart Classic worsted weight yarn Art. E267, Kreinik Medium (#16) Braid, and DMC #3 pearl cotton and 6-strand embroidery floss.

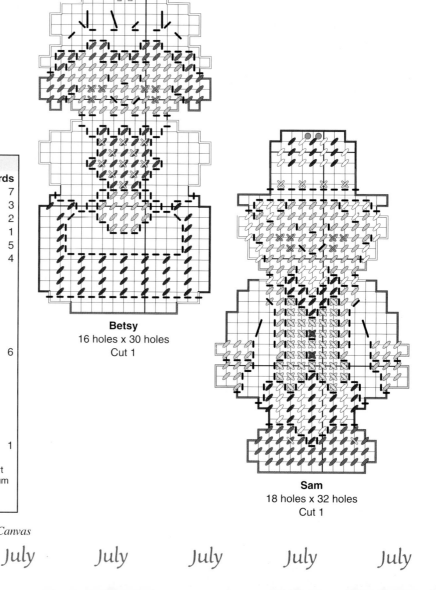

Betsy
16 holes x 30 holes
Cut 1

Sam
18 holes x 32 holes
Cut 1

July   July   July   July   July   July   July

Heart
23 holes x 22 holes
Cut 1

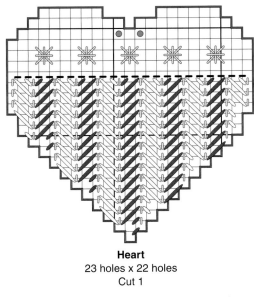

Celebrate

Just for Fun!

National Country
Music Day
is July 4

July   July   July   July   July   July   July

STAR
Ornaments

Design by Ruby Thacker

Hang this trio of ornaments in a sunny window to reflect a rainbow of patriotic charm!

Skill Level: Beginner

Finished Size

5½ inches W x 5½ inches H

Materials

- 6 (3¼ inch) plastic canvas star shapes from Darice
- Uniek Needloft plastic canvas yarn as listed in color key
- #16 tapestry needle
- 2 (19mm x 22mm) ruby acrylic drop beads
- 19mm x 22mm crystal acrylic drop bead
- 1 yard silver lamé cord
- Tacky craft glue

Instructions

1. Cut plastic canvas according to graph, cutting away gray area in center of each star.

2. Stitch four stars with red as graphed; stitch remaining two replacing red with dark royal.

3. Place wrong sides of two stars with matching colors together, then Whipstitch together along outside edges with adjacent color and along inside edges with white.

4. Use ruby beads with red stars and crystal bead with dark royal star. For each ornament, cut a 4-inch length of silver lamé cord. Thread cord through bead and through hole indicated on graph, allowing bead to hang freely. Tie a small knot next to canvas; glue to secure.

5. For each hanger, thread an 8-inch length of silver lamé cord through top hole of star. Tie ends together in a knot to form a loop for hanging. ✂

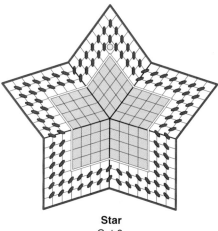

Star
Cut 6,
cutting away gray area
Stitch 4 as graphed
Stitch 2 replacing red
with dark royal

COLOR KEY	
Plastic Canvas Yarn	**Yards**
■ Red #01	12
Dark royal #48	6
✎ White #41 Whipstiching	1
○ Attach drop bead	
Color numbers given are for Uniek Needloft plastic canvas yarn.	

FOURTH OF JULY
Rockets

Design by Nancy Marshall

Set off your own fireworks with this eye-catching ornament! Curled wire adds a touch of zip!

5. Glue rockets together, placing center rocket on top of two outside rockets.

6. Thread desired length of monofilament through top center hole of center rocket. Tie ends together in a knot to form a loop for hanging. ✂

Skill Level: Beginner

Finished Size

5½ inches W x 5½ inches H

Materials

- ⅓ sheet Uniek QuickCount 7-count plastic canvas
- Uniek Needloft plastic canvas yarn as listed in color key
- #16 tapestry needle
- 3 (7-inch) lengths each red, white and blue Wire Art plastic-coated wire from Duncan Enterprises
- ¼-inch metal or wooden rod
- Wire cutters
- Needle-nose pliers
- Monofilament
- Tacky craft glue

Instructions

1. Cut plastic canvas according to graphs.

2. Stitch and Overcast pieces following graphs.

3. Wrap each length of wire around metal or wooden rod, leaving 1 inch straight at one end of each wire.

4. Using photo as a guide through step 5, insert straight end of coils through holes indicated at bottom of each rocket, wrapping end around itself, then squeezing with pliers.

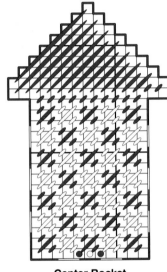

Center Rocket
15 holes x 24 holes
Cut 1

Right Rocket
15 holes x 24 holes
Cut 1

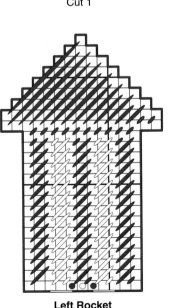

Left Rocket
15 holes x 24 holes
Cut 1

COLOR KEY	
Plastic Canvas Yarn	**Yards**
■ Christmas red #02	6
■ Royal #31	5
☐ White #41	5
● Attach red wire	
○ Attach white wire	
● Attach blue wire	
Color numbers given are for Uniek Needloft plastic canvas yarn.	

Celebrate
Just for Fun!

National Pecan Pie Day is July 12

SUMMERTIME
Sue & Bill

Designs by Janelle Giese

Stitch old-time favorite characters—Sunbonnet Sue and Overall Bill—as they enjoy a harvest of summer watermelon!

Skill Level: Beginner

Finished Size

Both Sue and Bill: 3⅛ inches W x 4½ inches H

Materials

- ¼ sheet 7-count plastic canvas
- Uniek Needloft plastic canvas yarn as listed in color key
- DMC #5 pearl cotton as listed in color key
- #16 tapestry needle

Instructions

1. Cut plastic canvas according to graphs.

2. Stitch and Overcast pieces following graphs, working uncoded areas with red Continental Stitches. Use two strands watermelon yarn for stitching on watermelon slices and 2 strands sail blue to stitch Bill's overall cuff.

3. When background stitching and Overcasting are completed, Backstitch watermelon rind with moss and Straight Stitch watermelon seeds with black, passing over each seed two times.

4. Work all remaining embroidery with black pearl cotton.

5. For each ornament, thread ends of a length of black pearl cotton from front to back through holes indicated on graph. Tie ends together in a knot to form a loop for hanging, allowing loop to extend 3 inches above top of ornament. ✂

COLOR KEY

Plastic Canvas Yarn	Yards
■ Cinnamon #14	1
▨ Moss #25	3
▨ Sail blue #35	3
☐ Beige #40	5
▨ Watermelon #55	4
▨ Flesh tone #56	1
Uncoded areas are red #01 Continental Stitches	3
╱ Red #01 Overcasting	
╱ Holly #27 Overcasting	1
╱ Black #00 Straight Stitch	1
╱ Moss #25 Backstitch	
#5 Pearl Cotton	
╱ Black #310 Backstitch and Straight Stitch	1
● Attach hanger	

Color numbers given are for Uniek Needloft plastic canvas yarn and DMC #5 pearl cotton.

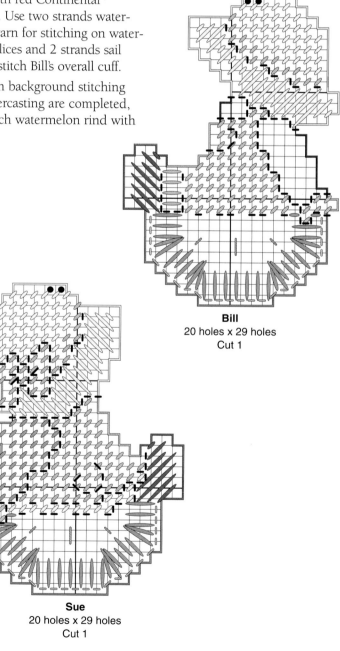

Bill
20 holes x 29 holes
Cut 1

Sue
20 holes x 29 holes
Cut 1

FIRECRACKER
& Flag

Designs by Kathleen J. Fischer

Overcast each of these festive ornaments
with metallic yarn to add a touch of sparkle!

Skill Level: Beginner

Finished Sizes

Firecracker: 3⅛ inches W x 3⅛
inches H

Flag: 3⅛ inches W x 2¾ inches H

Materials

Each Ornament

- ¼ sheet Uniek QuickCount 7-count plastic canvas
- Worsted weight yarn as listed in color key
- ⅛ inch-wide Plastic Canvas 7 Metallic Needlepoint Yarn by Rainbow Gallery as listed in color key
- #16 tapestry needle
- Nylon thread
- Tacky craft glue

Firecracker

- 2 (1-inch) lengths silver tinsel stems

Flag

- ⅞-inch Dress It Up gold star combo button #0553 from James Button and Trim

Instructions

1. Cut plastic canvas according to graphs.

2. For firecracker, following graphs, stitch front piece with white; stitch firecracker only on back piece.

3. Place front on top of back piece, matching star edges. Using silver metallic yarn, Whipstitch front to back around all edges of star, stitching through stripes on firecracker (see photo). Overcast remaining firecracker edges with red worsted weight yarn.

4. Stitch flag front following graph. Flag back will remain unstitched.

5. Whipstitch front and back together with red metallic yarn and blue worsted weight yarn.

6. For each ornament, cut desired length of nylon thread. Thread length through hole indicated on graph. Tie ends together in a knot to form a loop for hanging.

7. Using photo as a guide, glue silver tinsel stems to top backside of firecracker.

8. Center and glue star button to blue section of flag. ✂

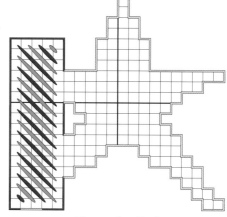

Firecracker Back
20 holes x 20 holes
Cut 1

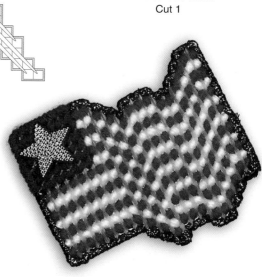

Firecracker Front
19 holes x 20 holes
Cut 1

JUICY
Strawberry

Design by Ronda Bryce

Strawberry lovers will enjoy displaying this pretty ornament! Beads and ribbon add the finishing touches!

Skill Level: Beginner

Finished Size

2 inches W x 2½ inches H

Materials

- Small amount 7-count plastic canvas
- Uniek Needloft plastic canvas yarn as listed in color key
- #16 tapestry needle
- ½ yard ¼-inch-wide green satin ribbon
- 12mm x 10mm black heart pony bead
- 21 (⅜-inch) black bugle beads
- Sewing needle and red sewing thread

Instructions

1. Cut plastic canvas according to graph.

2. Stitch and Overcast strawberry, working uncoded area with burgundy Continental Stitches.

3. Using sewing needle and red sewing thread through step 5, stitch bugle beads to strawberry where indicated on graph.

4. Cut a 12-inch length of green ribbon. Make a multi-looped bow and tack to center top front of strawberry. Attach heart to center of bow.

5. For hanger, fold remainder of ribbon in half and tack to center top back. ✂

COLOR KEY	
Plastic Canvas Yarn	**Yards**
■ Red #01	3
■ Christmas red #02	1
Uncoded area is burgundy #03 Continental Stitches	1
I Attach bugle bead	
Color numbers given are for Uniek Needloft plastic canvas yarn.	

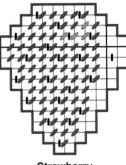

Strawberry
12 holes x 14 holes
Cut 1

FIRECRACKER
& Flag

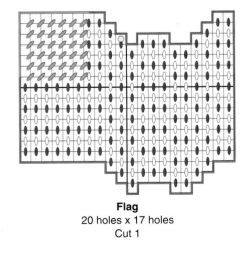

Flag
20 holes x 17 holes
Cut 1

COLOR KEY	
FLAG	
Worsted Weight Yarn	**Yards**
■ Red	2
■ Blue	1
□ White	1
⅛-Inch Metallic Needlepoint Yarn	
■ Red #PC5	1
○ Attach hanger	
Color numbers given are for Rainbow Gallery Plastic Canvas 7 Metallic Needlepoint Yarn.	

NAUTICAL
Trio

Designs by Joan Green

Dress up a window with this set of three nautical ornaments including a lighthouse, sailboat and anchor.

Skill Level: Beginner

Finished Sizes

Lighthouse: 1¾ inches W x 4½ inches H

Sailboat: 3⅜ inches W x 4 inches H

Anchor: 2¾ inches W x 3⅜ inches H

Materials

- ⅓ sheet 7-count plastic canvas
- Coats & Clark Red Heart Classic worsted weight yarn Art. E267 as listed in color key
- Coats & Clark Red Heart Super Saver worsted weight yarn Art. E300 as listed in color key
- Coats & Clark Red Heart kids worsted weight yarn Art. E711 as listed in color key
- #16 tapestry needle
- 3 (7-inch) lengths fine gold yarn
- Fabric glue

Instructions

1. Cut plastic canvas according to graphs.

2. Stitch and Overcast pieces following graphs, working uncoded areas with white Continental Stitches.

3. When background stitching and Overcasting are completed, work embroidery on lighthouse and sailboat following graphs, using 4 plies yellow and 2 plies black.

4. For each ornament, glue ends of one length fine gold yarn to top backside, allowing loop to extend 3 inches above top of ornament. ✂

COLOR KEY	
Worsted Weight Yarn	**Yards**
■ Black #12	2
■ Tangerine #253	2
■ Gold #321	2
■ Skipper blue #848	3
■ Jockey red #902	6
☐ Yellow #2230	4
Uncoded areas are white #1 Continental Stitches	2
⁄ White #1 Overcasting	
⁄ Black #12 Straight Stitch	
⁄ Yellow #2230 Straight Stitch	
Color numbers given are for Coats & Clark Red Heart Classic worsted weight yarn Art. E267, Super Saver worsted weight yarn Art. E300 and kids worsted weight yarn Art. E711.	

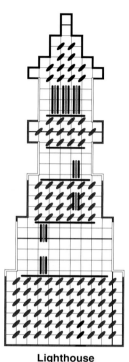

Lighthouse
11 holes x 31 holes
Cut 1

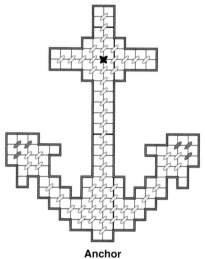

Anchor
18 holes x 22 holes
Cut 1

Sailboat
22 holes x 26 holes
Cut 1

August   August   August   August   August   August   August

SPOT &
Ginger

Designs by Ruby Thacker

Dog and cat owners will be tickled pink when you present them with one or both of these cute ornaments to display at home!

Skill Level: Beginner

Finished Size

Spot: 3¼ inches W x 3⅞ inches H

Ginger: 3⅝ inches W x 4 inches H

Materials

- ½ sheet 7-count plastic canvas
- Uniek Needloft plastic canvas yarn as listed in color key
- DMC 6-strand embroidery floss as listed in color key
- #16 tapestry needle
- 2 (8-inch) lengths gold lamé thread
- Hot-glue gun

Instructions

1. Cut plastic canvas according to graphs.

2. Stitch and Overcast pieces following graphs, leaving Long Stitches at top of front legs unworked at this time. Do not Overcast neck areas on bodies and Long Stitch areas at top of front legs where indicated with arrows.

3. When background stitching and Overcasting are completed, work ultra dark beaver gray embroidery.

4. Using photo as a guide, glue areas with Continental Stitches on tails to backs of corresponding bodies.

5. Lay front legs over corresponding bodies, placing top row of holes on front legs over neck areas of bodies, then work Long Stitches through both layers; Whipstitch edges together.

6. Cut one 6-inch length each of red and royal yarn. Tie each in a bow; trim ends as desired. Using photo as a guide, glue red bow to left side of dog collar and royal bow to left side of cat collar.

7. For hangers, thread one length gold lamé thread through top center hole of each ornament. Tie ends together in a knot to form a loop for hanging. ✂

Spot Tail
8 holes x 13 holes
Cut 1

COLOR KEY

SPOT

Plastic Canvas Yarn	Yards
■ Cinnamon #14	4
▨ Sandstone #16	3
☐ White #41	4
✎ Red #01 Straight Stitch and Whipstitching	1
6-Strand Embroidery Floss	
✎ Ultra dark beaver gray #844 Backstitch	4

Color numbers given are for Uniek Needloft plastic canvas yarn and DMC 6-strand embroidery floss.

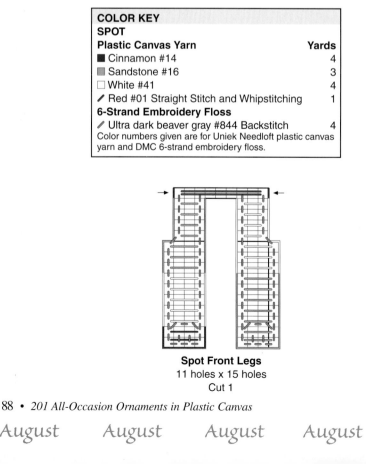

Spot Front Legs
11 holes x 15 holes
Cut 1

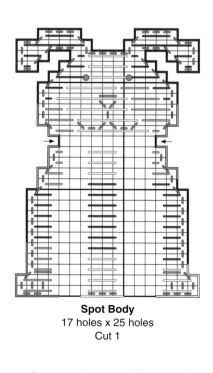

Spot Body
17 holes x 25 holes
Cut 1

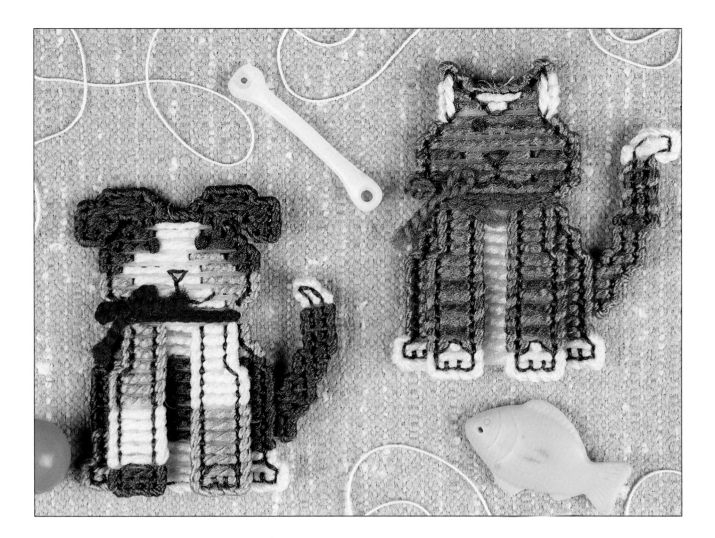

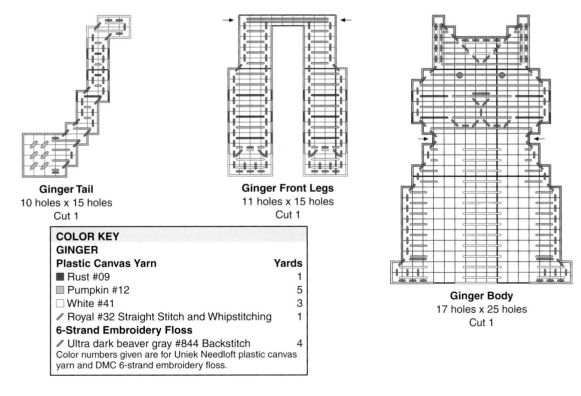

Ginger Tail
10 holes x 15 holes
Cut 1

Ginger Front Legs
11 holes x 15 holes
Cut 1

Ginger Body
17 holes x 25 holes
Cut 1

COLOR KEY	
GINGER	
Plastic Canvas Yarn	**Yards**
■ Rust #09	1
▨ Pumpkin #12	5
☐ White #41	3
✎ Royal #32 Straight Stitch and Whipstitching	1
6-Strand Embroidery Floss	
✎ Ultra dark beaver gray #844 Backstitch	4
Color numbers given are for Uniek Needloft plastic canvas yarn and DMC 6-strand embroidery floss.	

FRIENDSHIP
Blooms

Design by Janelle Giese

Celebrate a friendship that has grown over time with this pretty, floral ornament!

Skill Level: Intermediate

Finished Size
5 inches W x 5½ inches H

Materials
- ¼ sheet Uniek QuickCount 7-count plastic canvas
- Uniek Needloft plastic canvas yarn as listed in color key
- DMC #3 pearl cotton as listed in color key
- DMC #5 pearl cotton as listed in color key
- DMC 6-strand embroidery floss as listed in color key
- #16 tapestry needle

Instructions
1. Cut plastic canvas according to graph.

2. Stitch piece following graph, working uncoded areas with rust Continental Stitches.

3. Overcast flowers with adjacent colors, leaves with Christmas green and flowerpot with maple.

4. Work black #5 pearl cotton embroidery, passing over each eye three times. Cross Stitch cheeks with two plies very dark salmon embroidery floss.

5. Using #3 pearl cotton, work light topaz Smyrna Cross Stitches

on flowerpot and Straight Stitches on flowers; work ultra dark coffee brown letters on flowerpot.

6. Thread ends of a length of black #5 pearl cotton from front to back through holes indicated on graph. Tie ends together in a knot to form a loop for hanging, allowing loop to extend 3 inches above top of ornament. ✄

COLOR KEY

Plastic Canvas Yarn — Yards

		Yards
■	Christmas red #02	3
■	Maple #13	1
■	Fern #23	3
■	Christmas green #28	2
□	Yellow #57	2
■	Bright orange #58	3
	Uncoded areas are rust #09 Continental Stitches	5

#3 Pearl Cotton

╱	Light topaz #726 Straight Stitch	3
╱	Ultra dark coffee brown #938 Backstitch and Straight Stitch	3

#5 Pearl Cotton

╱	Black #310 Backstitch and Straight Stitch	5

6-Strand Embroidery Floss

✕	Very dark salmon #347 Cross Stitch	1
○	Attach hanger	

Color numbers given are for Uniek Needloft plastic canvas yarn and DMC pearl cotton and 6-strand embroidery floss.

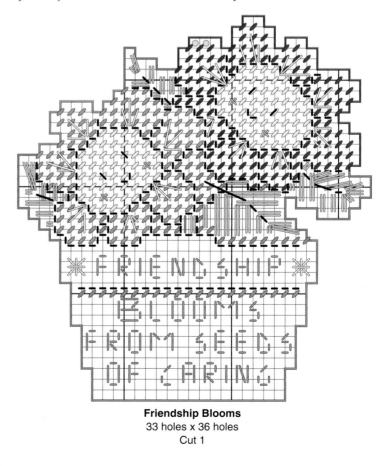

Friendship Blooms
33 holes x 36 holes
Cut 1

Skill Level: Beginner

Finished Size

4⅞ inches W x 4⅝ inches H

Materials

- ¼ sheet 7-count plastic canvas
- Coats & Clark Red Heart Classic worsted weight yarn Art. E267 as listed in color key
- DMC #5 pearl cotton as listed in color key
- DMC 6-strand embroidery floss as listed in color key
- #16 tapestry needle
- 18 inches ⅛-inch-wide white satin ribbon
- Thick tacky glue

Instructions

1. Cut plastic canvas according to graph.

2. Stitch and Overcast piece following graph, working uncoded areas with sea coral Continental Stitches.

3. When background stitching and Overcasting are completed, work Backstitches for cheeks with medium salmon embroidery floss. Work shoe highlights with two plies white yarn.

4. Work all remaining embroidery with black pearl cotton, passing over each eye three times and wrapping pearl cotton

FRIENDS Forever

Design by Janelle Giese

Delight a friend with this sweet ornament that will show your affection!

around needle two times for French Knot buttons.

5. For hanger, thread ends of a length of black pearl cotton from front to back through holes indicated on graph. Tie ends together

in a knot to form a loop for hanging, allowing loop to extend 3 inches above top of ornament.

6. Cut white satin ribbon into four 4½-inch lengths. Tie each in a tiny bow. Using photo as a guide, glue bows to hair. ✂

COLOR KEY

Worsted Weight Yarn	Yards
☐ White #1	2
■ Black #12	2
☐ Maize #261	2
■ Medium clay #280	1
▨ Warm brown #336	1
▨ Light seafoam #683	2
☐ Pale rose #755	2
Uncoded areas are sea coral #246 Continental Stitches	3
╱ Sea coral Overcasting	
╱ White #1 Straight Stitch	
#5 Pearl Cotton	
╱ Black #310 Backstitch and Straight Stitch	6
● Black #310 French Knot	
6-Strand Embroidery Floss	
╱ Medium salmon #3712 Backstitch	1
● Attach hanger	

Color numbers given are for Coats & Clark Red Heart Classic worsted weight yarn Art. E267 and DMC pearl cotton and 6-strand embroidery floss.

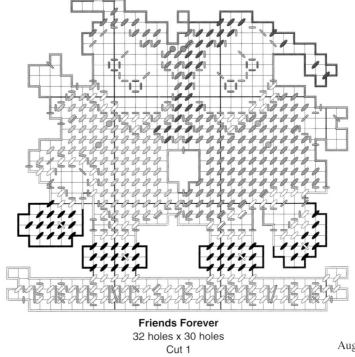

Friends Forever
32 holes x 30 holes
Cut 1

SUNFLOWER
Doorknob Ornament

Design by Sue Penrod

Dress up your bedroom or bathroom
door with this quick-to-stitch doorknob cover!

Skill Level: Intermediate

Finished Size

Sunflower: 1⅜ inches square

Doorknob cover: 2¾ inches
from front to back x 2¼ inches in
diameter

Butterflies: 1⅜ inches W x ⅞
inches H, including antennae

Materials

- ½ sheet light blue 10-count
  plastic canvas
- ½ sheet clear 10-count plastic
  canvas
- #3 pearl cotton as listed in
  color key
- #22 tapestry needle
- 24 inches (¼-inch-wide) light
  blue satin ribbon
- 4 (1-inch) pieces black craft
  whiskers
- Hot-glue gun

Project Note

Refer to photo throughout.

Instructions

1. Cut doorknob cover from light
blue plastic canvas according to
graph, carefully trimming out
bars indicated in blue from ribbon slots in bottom right corner
of each strip.

2. Cut sunflower pieces, leaves and
butterflies from clear plastic canvas
according to graphs.

3. Following graphs through step
6, stitch doorknob cover, then
Whipstitch tab on right side to
corresponding bar on left side.
Carefully Whipstitch tips together
at top, overlapping them; tie off
securely.

4. Stitch butterflies following
graph. Overcast bodies with
black; Overcast wings with adjacent colors.

5. Stitch leaves, leaving center
unstitched; Overcast with green.

6. For sunflowers, stitch one as
graphed for top; stitch only topaz
portions on remaining one for
bottom. Overcast top with adjacent colors; Overcast entire bottom, including unstitched center,
with topaz.

Assembly

1. Following graph and Fig. 1
and keeping ribbon smooth and
flat, weave blue ribbon through
slots in bottom of strips, threading ribbon down through slot, up
over next strip and down
through its slot, etc. Ends of
strips will overlap slightly. Pull
ribbon gently to leave ends of
even length.

2. Glue stitched leaves to closed
end of doorknob cover. Lay sunflower top on sunflower bottom,
alternating positions of petals.
Lock pieces together by gently
pulling bottom petals up through
adjacent pairs of top petals. Glue
assembled sunflower on top of
leaves.

3. Glue two whiskers to each
butterfly's head for antennae; trim
antennae to about ⅝ inch.

4. Glue one butterfly to each

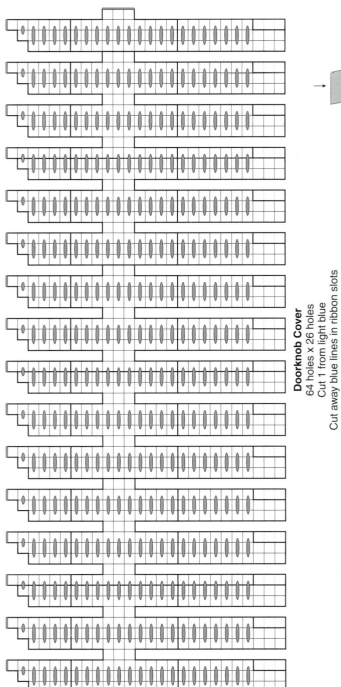

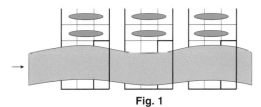

Fig. 1

Doorknob Cover
64 holes x 26 holes
Cut 1 from light blue
Cut away blue lines in ribbon slots

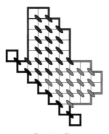

Butterfly
9 holes x 11 holes
Cut 2 from clear

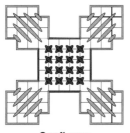

Sunflower
11 holes x 11 holes
Cut 2 from clear
Stitch 1 as graphed for top
Stitch 1, omitting brown
for bottom

ribbon streamer on doorknob cover, positioning butterflies 1–2 inches from ribbon ends.

5. Place cover on doorknob. Gently draw ribbon ends to gather cover close to shaft of doorknob. It is not necessary to tie ribbon to keep cover in place; if you do so, tie it loosely so cover can be removed as desired and to avoid breaking plastic canvas. ✄

COLOR KEY	
#3 Pearl Cotton	**Yards**
Blue	4
Topaz	4
Green	3
Lavender	2
Purple	2
Brown	1
Black	1

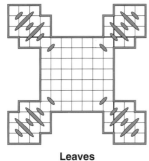

Leaves
13 holes x 13 holes
Cut 1 from clear

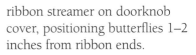

DREAM Catchers

Designs by Ruby Thacker

Native American folklore says a dream catcher hanging over you will bring peaceful dreams and sweet sleep. Stitch this pair for yourself or to share with a friend.

Skill Level: Advanced

Finished Size
3¼ inches in diameter

Materials

Each Ornament
- 2 (3-inch) plastic canvas radial circles
- Uniek Needloft plastic canvas yarn as listed in color key
- #16 tapestry needle
- 2 yards gold lamé thread
- 2¼ yards silver lamé thread
- 110 seed beads in assorted colors
- 2 (¾-inch) gold feather charms
- Seam sealant
- Hot-glue gun

Cutting & Stitching

1. For each ornament, cut one inner circle for concho and two outer circles from plastic canvas radial circles according to graphs, cutting away gray area.

2. Following graphs through step 3, stitch two outer circles with sandstone for one ornament and two replacing sandstone with brown for remaining ornament. Whipstitch wrong sides together with adjacent colors.

3. Stitch and Overcast conchos with gray.

Dream Catcher Web

1. Cut 1½ yards gold lamé thread for sandstone dream catcher and 1½ yards silver lamé thread for brown dream catcher.

2. For each ornament, begin first round of web by threading lamé thread through one hole indicated with red dot; tie in a knot, leaving a 2- to 3-inch tail. Bring needle up at next red dot, then down through loop created, pulling till snug but not overly tight. Continue around circle.

3. For next round, bring needle up through loop on first round, then down through new loop created. Continue around until desired number of rounds is reached. *Note: Brown and silver sample has four rounds; sandstone and gold sample has six rounds.*

4. When final loop is made, tie thread around loop and trim excess. Bring tail made at beginning over to first-round loop beside it and tie to top of loop; trim excess. Apply a drop of seam sealant to knots to secure.

Assembly

1. For hangers, cut one 10-inch

length each of gold and silver lamé thread. Thread hangers through one outside hole of corresponding dream catcher. Tie ends together in a knot to form a loop for hanging.

2. For sandstone and gold dream catcher, tie one gold feather charm to one end of remaining gold lamé thread. String on 35 seed beads, then tie on remaining gold feather charm next to last bead. Trim excess.

3. Using photo as a guide, hot glue beads and one stitched concho to one side of dream catcher.

4. For brown and silver dream catcher, cut silver lamé thread in half. Tie one seed bead to one end of one length. String on 38 seed beads, then tie on last bead. Trim excess. Repeat with remaining beads and silver lamé thread.

5. Using photo as a guide, hot glue beads and remaining stitched concho to one side of dream catcher.

6. Add a drop of seam sealant to each knot on lamé threads to secure. ✄

CAPE HATTERAS
Lighthouse

Design by Nancy Dorman

Distinctive diagonal stripes set the lighthouse at Cape Hatteras apart from all others. Stitch the ornament version in minutes!

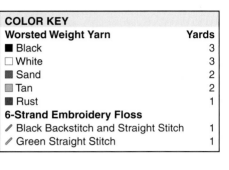

COLOR KEY

Worsted Weight Yarn	Yards
■ Black	3
□ White	3
■ Sand	2
■ Tan	2
■ Rust	1
6-Strand Embroidery Floss	
✎ Black Backstitch and Straight Stitch	1
✎ Green Straight Stitch	1

Skill Level: Beginner

Finished Size

$3\frac{1}{2}$ inches W x $5\frac{1}{2}$ inches H

Materials

- $\frac{1}{4}$ sheet 7-count plastic canvas
- Worsted weight yarn as listed in color key
- 6-strand embroidery floss as listed in color key
- #16 tapestry needle

Instructions

1. Cut plastic canvas according to graph.

2. Stitch and Overcast piece following graph. When background stitching and Overcasting are completed, work embroidery with 6-strand embroidery floss.

3. Attach hanger as desired. ✂

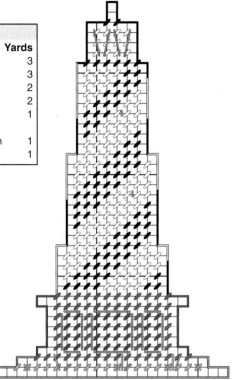

Cape Hatteras
23 holes x 37 holes
Cut 1

DREAM
Catchers

COLOR KEY

Plastic Canvas Yarn	Yards
Brown #15	4
■ Sandstone #16	4
□ Gray #38	1
Color numbers given are for Uniek Needloft plastic canvas yarn.	

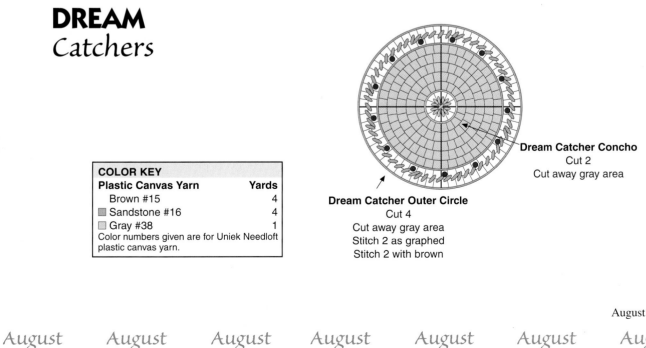

Dream Catcher Concho
Cut 2
Cut away gray area

Dream Catcher Outer Circle
Cut 4
Cut away gray area
Stitch 2 as graphed
Stitch 2 with brown

CUDDLY
Koalas

Designs by Susan D. Fisher

Give Baby something to look at in his crib with this set of cute koala ornaments hung up as a mobile!

Skill Level: Beginner

Finished Size

Koala with balloons: 3¾ inches W x 7¼ inches H

Koala with blocks: 4⅜ inches W x 5½ inches H

Mama and baby: 5⅛ inches W x 5⅜ inches H

Materials

- 2 sheets 7-count plastic canvas
- Coats & Clark Red Heart Super Saver worsted weight yarn Art. E301 as listed in color key
- #16 tapestry needle
- 6 (1-inch) lengths magnetic strip (optional)

Instructions

1. Cut plastic canvas according to graphs (page 98).

2. Stitch and Overcast pieces following graphs, working uncoded areas with warm brown Continental Stitches.

3. When background stitching and Overcasting are completed, work embroidery with 2 plies black and a full strand of soft white.

4. Using photo as a guide through step 5 for koala with blocks, tack upper right corner of green block to hand on koala with grass green yarn.

5. Using warm brown, tack shoulder of arm to body where indicated on graph, placing hand over grass green block; tack hand in place.

6. Attach hangers as desired on koalas or glue two magnetic strips to back of each piece. ✂

Koala With Balloons
25 holes x 48 holes
Cut 1

COLOR KEY
KOALA WITH BALLOONS

Worsted Weight Yarn	Yards
■ Black #312	5
□ Soft white #316	3
■ Cherry red #319	2
▨ Buff #334	3
■ Amethyst #356	2
▨ Raspberry #375	1
▨ Grass green #687	2
Uncoded areas are warm brown #336 Continental Stitches	11
╱ Warm brown #336 Overcasting	
╱ Black #312 Backstitch and Straight Stitch	
● Black #312 French Knot	
╱ Soft white #312 Straight Sttich	

Color numbers given are for Coats & Clark Red Heart Super Saver worsted weight yarn Art. E301.

Graphs Continued on page 98

August   August   August   August   August   August   August

CUDDLY
Koalas
Continued from page 96

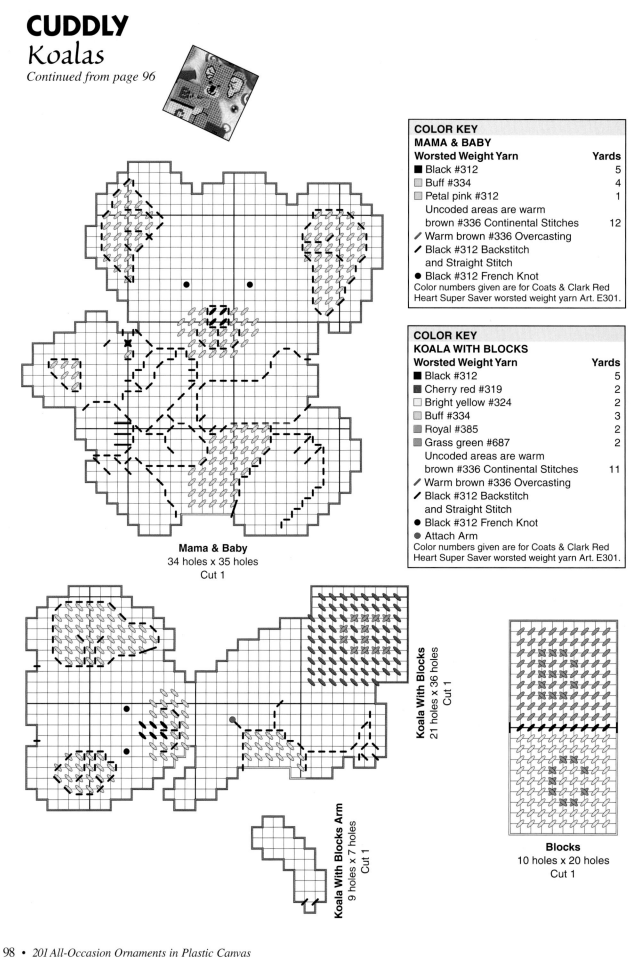

Continued from page 96

COLOR KEY
MAMA & BABY

Worsted Weight Yarn	Yards
■ Black #312	5
☐ Buff #334	4
☐ Petal pink #312	1
Uncoded areas are warm brown #336 Continental Stitches	12
╱ Warm brown #336 Overcasting	
╱ Black #312 Backstitch and Straight Stitch	
● Black #312 French Knot	

Color numbers given are for Coats & Clark Red Heart Super Saver worsted weight yarn Art. E301.

COLOR KEY
KOALA WITH BLOCKS

Worsted Weight Yarn	Yards
■ Black #312	5
■ Cherry red #319	2
☐ Bright yellow #324	2
☐ Buff #334	3
▨ Royal #385	2
▨ Grass green #687	2
Uncoded areas are warm brown #336 Continental Stitches	11
╱ Warm brown #336 Overcasting	
╱ Black #312 Backstitch and Straight Stitch	
● Black #312 French Knot	
● Attach Arm	

Color numbers given are for Coats & Clark Red Heart Super Saver worsted weight yarn Art. E301.

Mama & Baby
34 holes x 35 holes
Cut 1

Koala With Blocks
21 holes x 36 holes
Cut 1

Koala With Blocks Arm
9 holes x 7 holes
Cut 1

Blocks
10 holes x 20 holes
Cut 1

August   *August*   *August*   *August*   *August*   *August*   *August*

Skill Level: Beginner

Finished Size

3¼ inches W x 3¼ inches H

Materials

- Small amount 7-count plastic canvas
- Worsted weight yarn as listed in project note and color key
- #16 tapestry needle

Project Note

Instructions and yardage given are for one shell. Light and medium shades of the same color should be used for each shell stitched. Samples were stitched in shades of lavender, seafoam and peach.

Instructions

1. Cut plastic canvas according to graph.

2. Continental Stitch shell with light shade of desired color following graph. Using medium shade, Overcast shell, then work Straight Stitches.

3. Attach hanger as desired. ✂

SCALLOP
Seashells

Design by Nancy Dorman

Collecting shells is a fun seaside activity for people of all ages. Stitch a collection of perfect shells with this simple pattern!

COLOR KEY	
Worsted Weight Yarn	**Yards**
▨ Light Shade	6
■ Medium shade Straight Stitch and Overcasting	4

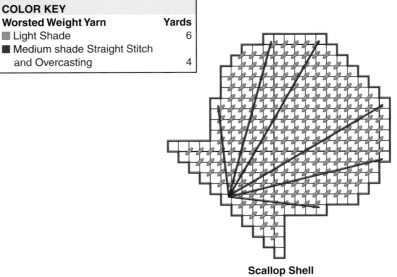

Scallop Shell
21 holes x 21 holes
Cut 1

SCHOOL
Bus

Design by Ronda Bryce

Get your child's school year off to a great start by giving this charming ornament to his or her school bus driver!

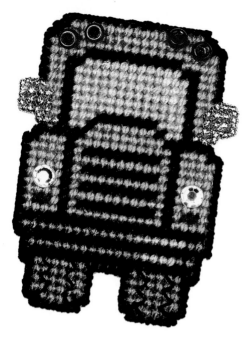

Skill Level: Beginner

Finished Size

3¾ inches W x 5 inches H

Materials

- ¼ sheet 7-count plastic canvas
- Uniek Needloft plastic canvas yarn as listed in color key
- Uniek Needloft metallic craft cord as listed in color key
- DMC 6-strand embroidery floss as listed in color key
- #16 tapestry needle
- 4 (6mm x 9mm) red pony beads #2931 from Westrim Crafts
- 2 (10mm) round acrylic crystal faceted jewels #7413 from Westrim Crafts
- Craft glue

Instructions

1. Cut plastic canvas according to graph.

2. Stitch and Overcast piece following graph working uncoded areas with tangerine Continental Stitches. When background stitching and Overcasting are completed, work black floss Backstitches and red yarn French Knots, working French Knots loosely.

3. Glue red pony beads over French Knots. Glue round crystal jewels for headlights where indicated on graph.

4. For hanger, thread ends of desired length of black yarn

from front to back through top two center holes of bus, knotting ends on backside. ✂

COLOR KEY	
Plastic Canvas Yarn	**Yards**
■ Black #00	6
■ Red #01	2
□ Silver #37	4
▨ Gray #38	3
□ White #41	1
Uncoded areas are tangerine #11 Continental Stitches	6
● Red #01 French Knot	
Metallic Craft Cord	
■ Solid silver #55021	1
6-Strand Embroidery Floss	
⁄ Black #310 Backstitch	1
○ Attach round crystal jewel	
Color numbers given are for Uniek Needloft plastic canvas yarn and metallic craft cord and DMC 6-strand embroidery floss.	

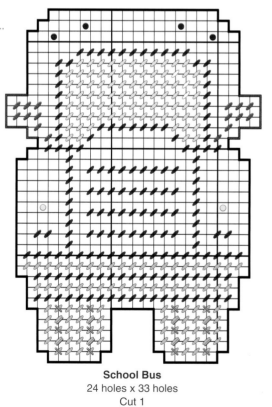

School Bus
24 holes x 33 holes
Cut 1

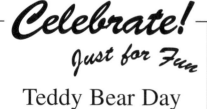

Celebrate!
Just for Fun
Teddy Bear Day
is Sept. 9

Skill Level: Beginner

Finished Size

5 inches W x 3¾ inches H

Materials

- ¼ sheet Uniek QuickCount 7-count plastic canvas
- Coats & Clark Red Heart kids worsted weight yarn Art. E711 as listed in color key
- Anchor #3 pearl cotton from Coats & Clark as listed in color key
- #16 tapestry needle
- ½ yard ⅝-inch-wide rainbow strip ribbon by Offray
- 5 assorted school theme buttons
- Black felt
- Tacky craft glue

Instructions

1. Cut plastic canvas according to graph.

2. Stitch and Overcast piece following graph, working uncoded area in center with black Continental Stitches.

3. When background stitching is completed, work white pearl cotton Backstitches and Straight Stitches.

4. Glue buttons to ornament, snipping off shanks as needed before gluing.

5. Tie a bow in center of rainbow stripe ribbon, then glue tail ends to wrong side of ornament, adjusting lengths as needed for hanging balance.

6. Cut felt ¼ inch smaller all around than ornament; glue to backside. ✂

COLOR KEY

Plastic Canvas Yarn	Yards
☐ Yellow #2230	1
■ Crayon #2930	5
Uncoded area is black #2012 Continental Stitches	5
✎ Blue #2845 Overcasting	2
#3 Pearl Cotton	
✎ White #1 Backstitch and Straight Stitch	

Color numbers given are for Coats & Clark Red Heart kids worsted weight yarn Art. E711 and Anchor #3 pearl cotton.

September   September

#1
Teacher

Design by Susan Leinberger

Show appreciation for your child's teacher with this bright and colorful ornament decorated with miniature school supplies!

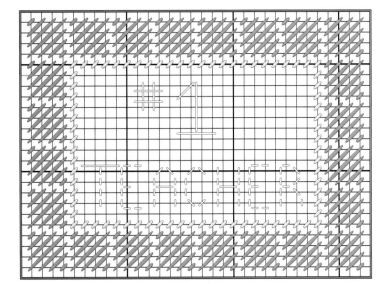

#1 Teacher
33 holes x 25 holes
Cut 1

KITTY IN
the Window

Designs by Michele Wilcox

Every cat lover knows how her kitty loves to sit in a window watching the birds and squirrels play in the yard! Stitch this pretty ornament to capture that moment!

Skill Level: Beginner

Finished Size

5⅜ inches W x 4⅝ inches H

Materials

- ⅓ sheet Uniek QuickCount 7-count plastic canvas
- Uniek Needloft plastic canvas yarn as listed in color key
- DMC #3 pearl cotton: 6 inches white and as listed in color key
- #16 tapestry needle
- Hot glue gun or tacky craft glue

Instructions

1. Cut plastic canvas according to graphs.

2. Stitch and Overcast pieces fol-lowing graphs. When background stitching is completed, work pearl cotton French Knots on kitty and flowers.

3. Using photo as a guide, glue flower box below window, then glue on kitty, flowers and leaves as desired.

4. For hanger, thread ends of white pearl cotton from front to back through holes indicated on graph; tie ends in a knot on backside. ✁

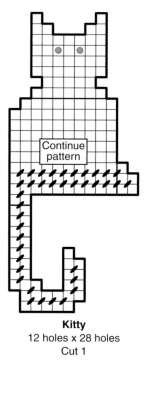

Kitty
12 holes x 28 holes
Cut 1

Window Box Flower
6 holes x 6 holes
Cut 4

Window Box Leaf
5 holes x 5 holes
Cut 3

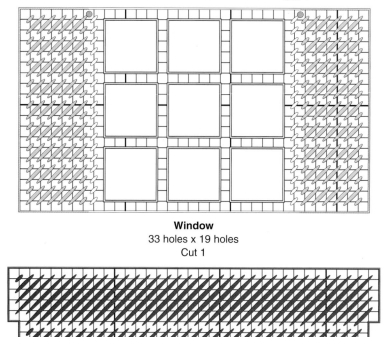

Window
33 holes x 19 holes
Cut 1

Window Box
35 holes x 9 holes
Cut 1

COLOR KEY	
Plastic Canvas Yarn	**Yards**
■ Black #00	5
■ Red #01	8
▨ Christmas green #28	4
▨ Sail blue #35	6
☐ White #41	6
☐ Yellow #57	5
#3 Pearl Cotton	
● Red #321 French Knot	2
● Very dark emerald green #909 French Knot	1
● Attach hanger	
Color numbers given are for Uniek Needloft plastic canvas yarn and DMC #3 pearl cotton.	

BOOKWORM
Buddy

Design by Janna Britton

As your child discovers the joy of reading, stitch her this cute-as-a-bug ornament for hanging by her desk!

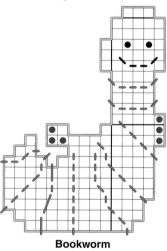

Skill Level
Beginner

Finished Size
2⅜ inches W x 3¼ inches H

Materials
- ¼ sheet 7-count plastic canvas
- Uniek Needloft plastic canvas yarn as listed in color key
- DMC #3 pearl cotton as listed in color key
- #16 tapestry needle
- 2 inches 24-gauge silver wire
- ¼-inch wooden dowel
- Wire cutters
- Small amount apple green felt from Kunin
- 2 (¾-inch x 1½-inch) pieces unlined white paper
- Stapler
- 9 inches 40-pound clear monofilament
- Low-temperature glue gun

Instructions
1. Cut plastic canvas according to graphs. Cut felt to fit bookworm; set aside.

2. Stitch plastic canvas following graphs, working uncoded background on bookworm with fern Continental Stitches.

3. Whipstitch two long edges of book cover together with yellow, then Overcast remaining edges.

4. Overcast bookworm with fern, then work pearl cotton Backstitches and French Knots.

5. For pages of book, place one piece of paper on top of the other,

fold in half, then staple together in fold. Glue pages to wrong side of book with staple at center. Trim pages as necessary to fit.

6. Using photo as a guide, tack book to bookworm with fern where indicated on graphs with red dots.

7. Using Fig. 1 as a guide, wrap 24-gauge wire around dowel to form eyeglasses. Fit over eyes, inserting ear pieces through holes to backside, then bend ends to secure, or wrap ear pieces around edges to backside.

8. Thread monofilament through yarn at center top back of bookworm; knot ends. Glue felt to wrong side of bookworm. ✂

Fig. 1

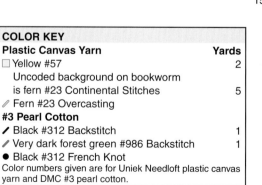

Bookworm
15 holes x 21 holes
Cut 1

COLOR KEY	
Plastic Canvas Yarn	**Yards**
☐ Yellow #57	2
Uncoded background on bookworm is fern #23 Continental Stitches	5
⁄ Fern #23 Overcasting	
#3 Pearl Cotton	
⁄ Black #312 Backstitch	1
⁄ Very dark forest green #986 Backstitch	1
● Black #312 French Knot	
Color numbers given are for Uniek Needloft plastic canvas yarn and DMC #3 pearl cotton.	

Book Cover
5 holes x 7 holes
Cut 2

Skill Level: Beginner

Finished Size

3½ inches W x 3¾ inches H

Materials

- Small amount 7-count plastic canvas
- Coats & Clark Red Heart Super Saver worsted weight yarn Art. E301 as listed in color key
- ⅛-inch-wide Plastic Canvas 7 Metallic Needlepoint Yarn by Rainbow Gallery as listed in color key
- 7 inches ¹⁄₁₆-inch-wide gold #PM51 Plastic Canvas 10 Metallic Needlepoint Yarn by Rainbow Gallery
- #16 tapestry needle
- 7mm and 9mm round acrylic faceted stones by The Beadery from Designs by Joan Green:

  January and July: ruby #017

  February: dark amethyst #002

  March and December: turquoise #026

  April: crystal #006

  May: emerald #007

  August: mint #013

  September: dark sapphire #020

  October: pink #015

  November: topaz #023

- 7mm and 9mm round acrylic cabochons by The Beadery from Designs by Joan Green:

  June: antique white pearl #427

- Jewel glue
- Fabric glue

Project Note

For the stones and cabochons, use 9mm for children and 7mm for grandchildren, selecting the correct one for the month in which they were born.

Instructions

1. Cut plastic canvas according to graph.

GRANDMA'S
Tree of Life

Design by Joan Green

Delight a grandmother with this beautiful keepsake ornament adorned with birthstones for each of her children and grandchildren!

2. Stitch and Overcast piece following graph.

3. Using jewel glue, attach stones and cabochons to leaf area of tree, placing randomly or in family groupings (parent with children) as in photo.

4. Fasten ends of gold ¹⁄₁₆-inch-wide metallic yarn to top center backside of tree with fabric glue, forming a loop for hanging. ✂

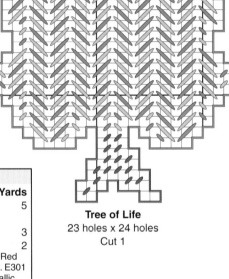

Tree of Life
23 holes x 24 holes
Cut 1

COLOR KEY	
Plastic Canvas Yarn	**Yards**
▨ Paddy green #368	5
⅛-Inch Metallic Needlepoint Yarn	
▨ Emerald #PC4	3
▨ Bronze #PC21	2
Color numbers given are for Coats & Clark Red Heart Super Saver worsted weight yarn Art. E301 and Rainbow Gallery Plastic Canvas 7 Metallic Neddlepoint Yarn.	

THREE IN
The Family

Designs by Lee Lindeman

Add an artistic touch to your home decor with this set of three unique family ornaments! They're sure to be an interesting conversation starter!

Skill Level

Beginner

Finished Size

Mother: $3\frac{1}{4}$ inches W x 6 inches H

Daughter: $2\frac{3}{8}$ inches W x $4\frac{1}{2}$ inches H

Son: $3\frac{1}{8}$ inches W x $5\frac{3}{8}$ inches H

Materials

- $\frac{1}{2}$ sheet 7-count plastic canvas
- Coats & Clark Red Heart Super Saver worsted weight yarn Art. E300 as listed in color key
- #16 tapestry needle
- Fine gold cord or braid
- $57\frac{1}{2}$ inches 19-gauge black wire
- Small round-nose pliers
- Small wire cutters
- Hot-glue gun or tacky craft glue

Instructions

1. Cut plastic canvas according to graphs.

2. Stitch and Overcast pieces following graphs, working uncoded areas with light clay Continental Stitches. Work black French Knots when background stitching

is completed.

3. From 19-gauge wire cut the following: for the mother, 11($1\frac{1}{2}$-inch) lengths for hair and four 3-inch lengths for arms and legs; for the daughter, six 1-inch lengths for hair, two 2-inch lengths for arms and two $2\frac{1}{2}$-inch lengths for legs; for the son, four 1-inch lengths for hair, two 2-inch lengths for arms and two 3-inch lengths for legs.

4. Using photo as a guide through step 5, curl one end of each length of wire with round-nose pliers.

5. For each ornament, place straight ends of wire on wrong

side of one stitched piece at head for hair, at shoulders for arms and at bottom edge for legs, cutting excess on straight ends of wire as needed. Glue in place, making sure to keep glue away from edges to allow for Whipstitching.

6. Whipstitch wrong sides of corresponding pieces together with black.

7. For each ornament, thread desired length of gold cord or braid through top center hole. Tie ends together in a knot to form a loop for hanging. ✂

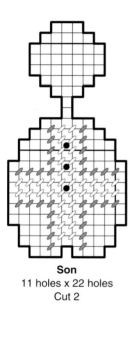

Son
11 holes x 22 holes
Cut 2

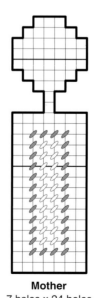

Mother
7 holes x 24 holes
Cut 2

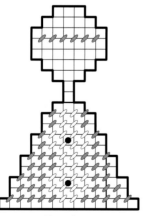

Daughter
13 holes x 19 holes
Cut 2

COLOR KEY	
Worsted Weight Yarn	**Yards**
■ Medium clay #280	6
□ White #311	6
Uncoded areas are light clay #275	
Continental Stitches	5
✏ Black #312 Whipstitching	8
● Black #312 French Knot	
Color numbers given are for Coats & Clark Red Heart Super Saver worsted weight yarn Art. E300.	

VINTAGE
Car

Design by Ronda Bryce

Delight an old-time car collector with this classic car ornament stitched in black, just like the very first Model-T cars!

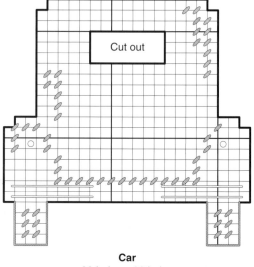

Car
23 holes x 23 holes
Cut 1

Skill Level: Beginner

Finished Size

3½ inches W x 3½ inches H

Materials

- Small amount clear 7-count plastic canvas
- ¼ sheet black 7-count plastic canvas
- 3-inch Uniek QuickShape plastic canvas radial circle
- Uniek Needloft plastic canvas yarn as listed in color key
- Uniek Needloft metallic craft cord as listed in color key
- #16 tapestry needle
- 2 (6mm x 9mm) red pony beads #2931 from Westrim Crafts
- Craft glue

Instructions

1. Cut car from black plastic canvas according to graph. Cut one 2-hole x 29-hole piece from clear plastic canvas for wheel cover rim. Cut five outermost rows of holes from plastic canvas radial circle for wheel cover.

2. Stitch and Overcast car following graph. When background stitching and Overcasting are completed, work white/silver Straight Stitches and French Knots, working French Knots loosely.

3. Using black through step 4, Continental Stitch wheel cover rim and wheel cover, working a Cross Stitch at center of cover.

4. Whipstitch short edges of cover rim together, forming a cir-cle, then Whipstitch rim to cover. Using photo as a guide, center assembled wheel cover under window on car, then Whipstitch rim to car.

5. Glue red pony beads over French Knots for taillights.

6. For hanger, thread ends of a desired length of black yarn from front to back through top center hole of car, knotting ends on backside. ✄

COLOR KEY	
Plastic Canvas Yarn	**Yards**
☐ Silver #37	1
☐ Gray #38	2
Uncoded areas are black #00	
Continental Stitches	10
⁄ Black #00 Overcasting	
Metallic Craft Cord	
⁄ White/silver #55008 Straight Stitch	1
○ White/silver #55008 French Knot	
Color numbers given are for Uniek Needloft plastic canvas yarn and metallic craft cord.	

Skill Level: Beginner

Finished Size

5¼ inches W x 4 inches H, including hanger

Materials

- Small amount 7-count plastic canvas
- Uniek Needloft plastic canvas yarn as listed in color key
- Uniek Needloft metallic craft cord as listed in color key
- #16 tapestry needle
- 24 inches 26-gauge wire
- Small amount white felt
- Low-temperature glue gun

Instructions

1. Cut plastic canvas according to graph. Cut felt to fit canvas.

2. Stitch and Overcast piece following graph, working uncoded area with white Continental Stitches.

3. Work gold metallic craft cord embroidery when background stitching and Overcasting are completed.

COLOR KEY

Plastic Canvas Yarn	Yards
Uncoded area is white #41 Continental Stitches	6
✐ White #41 Overcasting	
Metallic Craft Cord	
■ Black #55000	3
▢ Gold #55001	3
✐ Gold #55001 Backstitch and Straight Stitch	
● Gold #55001 French Knot	

Color numbers given are for Uniek Needloft plastic canvas yarn and metallic craft cord.

GOLDEN Notes

Design by Janna Britton

Reward your child for learning that difficult piece of music by stitching this golden-accented ornament for her!

4. For hanger, cut a 24-inch length of gold metallic craft cord. Slide 26-gauge wire into cord. Leaving a 3-inch tail on one end, form a triple bow with 1- to 1¼-inch loops. Wrap cord around center, then leave another 3-inch tail.

5. Using photo as a guide, glue ends of tails to back of stitched piece, centering for hanging balance. Glue felt to back of piece over tail ends. ✄

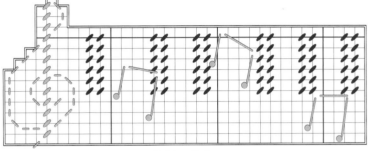

Golden Notes
34 holes x 14 holes
Cut 1

QUILT
Blocks

Designs by Janna Britton

Share this set of pretty quilt blocks with a needlecrafting friend! Tiny charms and coat hangers make each dainty quilt simply delightful!

Skill Level: Beginner

Finished Sizes

Quilts A and B: 3⅛ inches W x 3 inches H, excluding hanger

Quilt C: 3¼ inches W x 3⅛ inches H, excluding hanger

Materials

- 1 sheet Uniek QuickCount soft 7-count plastic canvas
- Coats & Clark Red Heart Classic worsted weight yarn Art. E267 as listed in color key
- Coats & Clark Red Heart Super Saver worsted weight yarn Art. E301 as listed in color key
- DMC 6-strand embroidery floss as listed in color key
- #16 tapestry needle
- 10 inches ⅛-inch-wide baby pink satin ribbon
- Sewing Treasures by La Mode scissors and spool button #1359 from Blumenthal Lansing Co.
- Funtastics by Streamline gold scissors button #Q148 by Blumenthal Lansing Co.
- Spool, sewing machine and scissors brass charms
- 3 (18-inch) lengths 18-gauge bare stem wire
- Needle-nose pliers
- Clear acrylic spray sealer
- Low-temperature glue gun

Instructions

1. Cut plastic canvas according to graphs.

2. Stitch and Overcast pieces following graphs, working uncoded areas on quilt A with lavender Continental Stitches and on quilts B and C with raspberry Continental Stitches.

3. Work Backstitches on quilt B with 6-strands ultra dark dusty rose embroidery floss.

4. For each of the three hangers, fold wire in half using needle-nose pliers. Following Fig. 1 throughout, twist ¾ inches of the folded end together and bend into hook. Shape remaining wire into hanger, overlapping ends. Cut excess with wire cutters.

5. Fold each quilt in half over overlapping ends of a hanger and glue together, keeping glue from edges so it does not come out along sides and end.

6. Spray brass charms with acrylic sealer and allow to dry. Snip shank off scissors and spool button with pliers.

7. Using photo as a guide through step 9, tie pink satin ribbon in a bow around hanger of quilt A, then glue brass charms to quilt where indicated on graph.

8. Tie desired length of ultra dusty rose floss in a bow around hanger of quilt B, then glue scissors and spool button to quilt where indicated on graph.

9. For quilt C, tie a 10-inch length of lavender yarn in a bow around hanger at bottom of twisted hook, then wrap tails around hanger, gluing ends

inside fold of quilt. Glue gold scissors button to quilt where indicated on graph. ✄

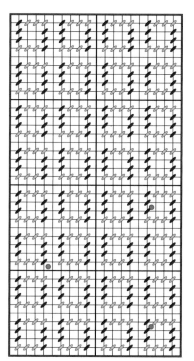

Quilt A
20 holes x 40 holes
Cut 1

Quilt B
20 holes x 40 holes
Cut 1

September   September   September   September   September   September

COLOR KEY
QUILT A

Worsted Weight Yarn	Yards
■ Raspberry #375	4
▨ Lily pink #719	4
Uncoded areas are lavender #358 Continental Stitches	8
╱ Lavender Overcasting	
● Attach charm	

Color numbers given are for Coats & Clark Red Heart Classic worsted weight yarn Art. E267 and Super Saver worsted weight yarn Art. E301.

COLOR KEY
QUILT B

Worsted Weight Yarn	Yards
■ Lavender #358	4
▨ Lily pink #719	5
Uncoded areas are raspberry #375 Continental Stitches	6
╱ Raspberry #375 Overcasting	
6-Strand Embroidery Floss	
╱ Ultra dark dusty rose #3350 Backstitch	3
● Attach button	

Color numbers given are for Coats & Clark Red Heart Classic worsted weight yarn Art. E267 and Super Saver worsted weight yarn Art. E301 and DMC 6-strand embroidery floss.

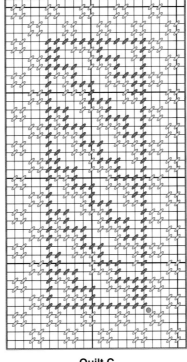

Quilt C
21 holes x 41 holes
Cut 1

COLOR KEY
QUILT C

Worsted Weight Yarn	Yards
■ Lavender #358	5
▨ Lily pink #719	5
Uncoded areas are raspberry #375 Continental Stitches	7
● Attach button	

Color numbers given are for Coats & Clark Red Heart Classic worsted weight yarn Art. E267 and Super Saver worsted weight yarn Art. E301.

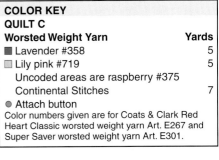
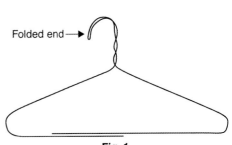

Folded end →

Fig. 1

SPOOKY
Window Ornaments

Designs by Angie Arickx

This pair of Halloween window ornaments is just right for adding a fun and spooky touch to your home or car windows!

Skill Level: Intermediate

Finished Sizes

Jack-o'-lantern: 5 inches W x 5 inches H

Spiderweb with spider: 5 inches W x 5 inches H

Materials

- 1 sheet Uniek QuickCount 7-count plastic canvas
- Uniek Needloft plastic canvas yarn as listed in color key
- #16 tapestry needle
- 2 (30mm) suction cups with hooks
- Hot-glue gun

Continued on page 115

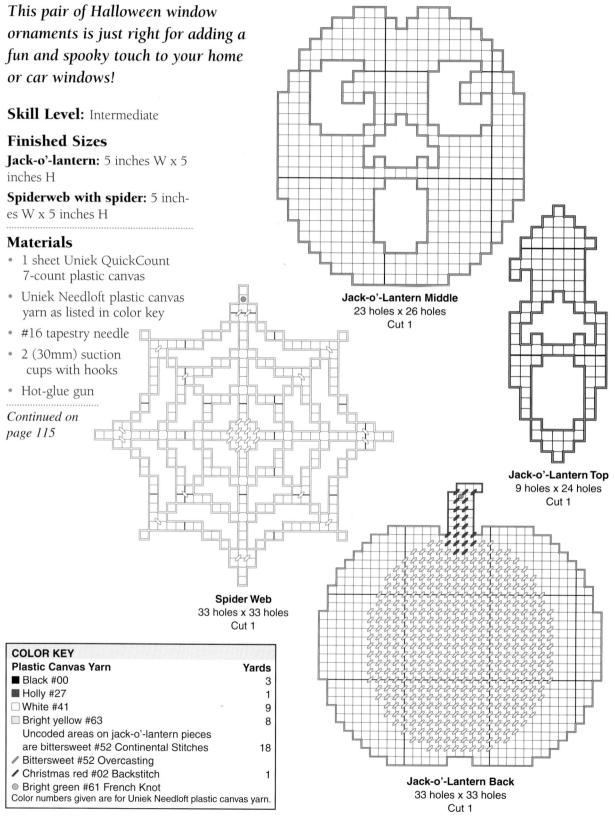

Jack-o'-Lantern Middle
23 holes x 26 holes
Cut 1

Jack-o'-Lantern Top
9 holes x 24 holes
Cut 1

Spider Web
33 holes x 33 holes
Cut 1

Jack-o'-Lantern Back
33 holes x 33 holes
Cut 1

COLOR KEY

Plastic Canvas Yarn	Yards
■ Black #00	3
■ Holly #27	1
□ White #41	9
▢ Bright yellow #63	8
Uncoded areas on jack-o'-lantern pieces are bittersweet #52 Continental Stitches	18
⁄ Bittersweet #52 Overcasting	
⁄ Christmas red #02 Backstitch	1
● Bright green #61 French Knot	
Color numbers given are for Uniek Needloft plastic canvas yarn.	

October   October   October   October   October   October   October

GHOST &
Pumpkin

Design by Michele Wilcox

Hang this scary ghost and jack-o'-lantern ornament on your front doorknob to welcome trick-or-treaters into your home—if they dare!

Skill Level: Beginner

Finished Size

5 inches W x 8⅝ inches H

Materials

- ½ sheet Uniek QuickCount 7-count plastic canvas
- Uniek Needloft plastic canvas yarn as listed in color key
- #3 pearl cotton: 3½ inches white and as listed in color key
- #16 tapestry needle
- Hot-glue gun

Instructions

1. Cut plastic canvas according to graphs.

2. Stitch and Overcast pumpkin and ghost following graphs, working uncoded area on pumpkin with pumpkin Continental Stitches.

3. When background stitching is completed, work eyes and mouth on ghost with black pearl cotton, passing over each four times.

4. Using photo as a guide, place pumpkin in curve of tail at bottom of ghost; glue in place.

5. For hanger, thread white pearl cotton from front to back through holes indicated on head. Knot ends on backside. ✂

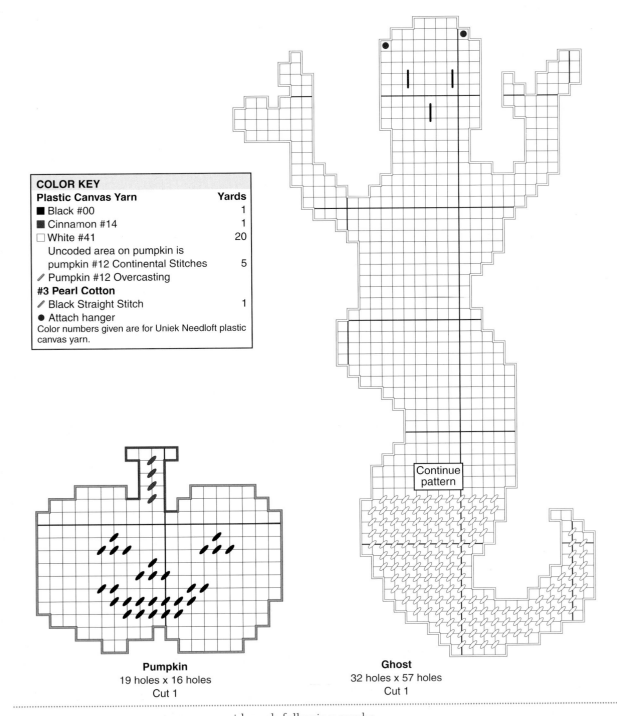

COLOR KEY

Plastic Canvas Yarn	Yards
■ Black #00	1
■ Cinnamon #14	1
□ White #41	20
Uncoded area on pumpkin is pumpkin #12 Continental Stitches	5
╱ Pumpkin #12 Overcasting	
#3 Pearl Cotton	
╱ Black Straight Stitch	1
● Attach hanger	

Color numbers given are for Uniek Needloft plastic canvas yarn.

Pumpkin
19 holes x 16 holes
Cut 1

Ghost
32 holes x 57 holes
Cut 1

Continue pattern

SPOOKY
Window Ornaments

Continued from page 112

Instructions

1. Cut plastic canvas according to graphs (this page and page 112).

2. Stitch and Overcast jack-o'-lantern pieces following graphs, working uncoded areas with bittersweet Continental Stitches.

3. Stitch and Overcast spider and spiderweb following graphs. When background stitching and Overcasting are completed, work Backstitches and French Knots on spider.

4. Use photo as a guide through step 5. For jack-o'-lantern, with right sides facing up, center and glue middle piece over back piece, then glue top piece over middle piece, aligning mouth and nose holes. Glue spider to web.

5. Insert hooks of suction cups through holes indicated on graphs with blue dots. ✂

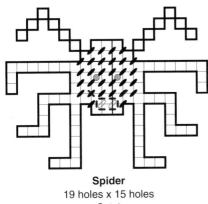

Spider
19 holes x 15 holes
Cut 1

HALLOWEEN
Friends

Design by Janelle Giese

Who can resist this trio of trick-or-treaters? Stitch this ornament as a delightful decoration for your Halloween party!

Skill Level: Beginner

Finished Size

4½ inches W x 5¼ inches H

Materials

- ¼ sheet 7-count plastic canvas
- Coats & Clark Red Heart Classic worsted weight yarn Art. E267 as listed in color key
- DMC #5 pearl cotton as listed in color key
- DMC 6-strand embroidery floss as listed in color key
- #16 tapestry needle

Instructions

1. Cut plastic canvas according to graph.

2. Stitch and Overcast piece following graph, working uncoded areas on pumpkin with orange Continental Stitches and uncoded areas on witch hat and dress with soft navy Continental Stitches.

3. When background stitching and Overcasting are completed, Cross Stitch cheeks with two plies medium shell pink. Use a full strand yellow to Backstitch buckle on hat and work French Knot nose on pumpkin, wrapping yarn two times around needle.

4. Work black #5 pearl cotton embroidery, passing over eyes on ghost and pumpkin four times, placing eyes on pumpkin between two yellow Continental Stitches (see photo). Work French Knot eyes on witch, wrapping pearl cotton two times around needle.

5. Work Straight Stitch under pumpkin's nose by bringing needle up in same hole as French Knot, drape stitch around base of nose, then draw needle back down through same hole.

6. For hanger, thread ends of a length of black #5 pearl cotton from front to back through holes indicated on graph. Tie ends together in a knot to form a loop for hanging, allowing loop to extend 3 inches above top of ornament. ✂

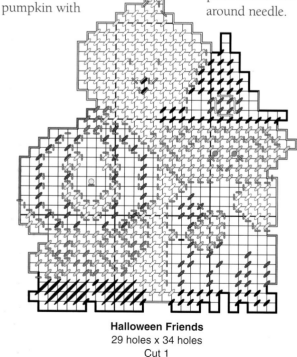

Halloween Friends
29 holes x 34 holes
Cut 1

COLOR KEY	
Worsted Weight Yarn	**Yards**
☐ White #1	3
■ Black #12	3
☐ Yellow #230	3
☐ Sea coral #246	2
■ Tangerine #253	1
■ Warm brown #336	1
■ Purple #596	1
■ Medium sage #632	1
☐ Kiwi #651	2
Uncoded areas on pumpkin are orange #245 Continental Stitches	2
Uncoded areas on witch hat and dress are soft navy #853 Continental Stitches	2
╱ Orange #245 Overcasting	
╱ Soft navy #853 Overcasting	
╱ Yellow #230 Backstitch	
○ Yellow #230 French Knot	
#5 Pearl Cotton	
╱ Black #310 Backstitch	1
● Black #310 French Knot	
6-Strand Embroidery Floss	
✕ Medium shell pink #3722 Cross Stitch	1
○ Attach hanger	
Color numbers given are for Coats & Clark Red Heart Classic worsted weight yarn Art. E267 and DMC #5 pearl cotton and 6-strand embroidery floss.	

Skill Level: Beginner

Finished Size

3¾ inches W x 4⅝ inches H

Materials

- ¼ sheet Uniek QuickCount clear 7-count plastic canvas
- ¼ sheet Uniek QuickCount white 7-count plastic canvas
- Uniek Needloft plastic canvas yarn as listed in color key
- #16 tapestry needle
- 10 inches 15-pound clear monofilament
- Low-temperature glue gun

Instructions

1. Cut ghost from white plastic canvas; cut BOO and jack-o'-lantern from clear plastic canvas according to graphs.

2. Stitch and Overcast pieces following graphs, working uncoded areas on jack-o'-lantern with bittersweet Continental Stitches and uncoded background on BOO with black Continental Stitches.

3. When background stitching and Overcasting are completed, work Backstitches and Straight Stitches.

4. Using photo as a guide, glue pieces together.

5. For hanger, attach monofilament to ghost with a Lark's Head Knot where indicated on graph with blue dots. Tie ends together in a knot to form a loop for hanging. ✂

BOO to You!

Design by Janna Britton

It is doubtful this friendly ghost and jack-o'-lantern will scare anybody, so stitch up several to share with your friends!

COLOR KEY	
Plastic Canvas Yarn	**Yards**
■ Black #00	2
▨ Pumpkin #12	1
■ Cinnamon #14	1
▨ Holly #27	1
☐ White #41	6
Uncoded background on BOO is black #00 Continental Stitches	
Uncoded areas on jack-o'-lantern pieces are bittersweet #52 Continental Stitches	6
╱ Black #00 Backstitch	
╱ Bittersweet #52 Backstitch and Overcasting	
╱ Cinnamon #14 Backstitch	
Color numbers given are for Uniek Needloft plastic canvas yarn.	

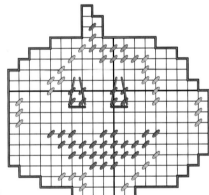

Boo
9 holes x 6 holes
Cut 1 from clear

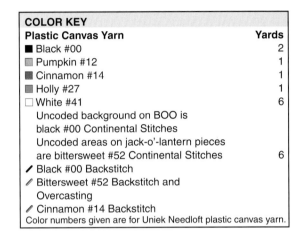

Boo to You! Jack-o'-Lantern
19 holes x 18 holes
Cut 1 from clear

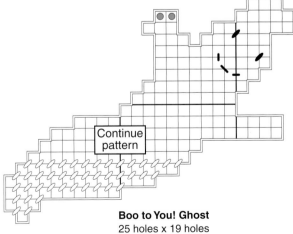

Boo to You! Ghost
25 holes x 19 holes
Cut 1 from white

PUMPKIN
Pals

Designs by Nancy Marshall

Easy-to-coil green wire adds a festive accent to this pair of fun and friendly Halloween characters!

Skill Level: Beginner

Finished Sizes
Cat: 3⅛ inches W x 5⅛ inches H

Ghost: 4¾ inches W x 7 inches H, including wire hanger

Materials
Each ornament

- ½ sheet Uniek QuickCount 7-count plastic canvas
- Uniek Needloft plastic canvas yarn as listed in color key
- #16 tapestry needle
- ⅛-inch dowel rod
- Tacky craft glue

Cat

- DMC 6-strand embroidery floss as listed in color key
- 2 (7mm) round movable eyes
- ½ yard each Wire Art white and green plastic-coated wire from Duncan Enterprises
- Paper crimper from Fiskars
- Wire cutters
- Monofilament

Ghost

- 3 (½-inch) lengths green chenille stem
- ¾ yard plastic-coated green wire from Wire Art Inc.

Cutting & Stitching
1. Cut plastic canvas according to graphs.

2. Stitch and Overcast pieces following graphs, working uncoded areas on cat pieces with black Continental Stitches.

3. When background stitching and Overcasting are completed,
work Backstitches on cat pieces, ghost and pumpkins.

Cat Assembly
1. For whiskers, run white plastic-coated wire through paper crimper, then cut in six 2-inch lengths. Insert three whiskers into each hole indicated on each side of nose, pushing ½ inch to backside of head. Bend ½-inch ends back to secure. Arrange whiskers as desired.

2. Using photo as a guide throughout assembly, glue movable eyes to head above nose. Glue head to body.

3. For pumpkin vine, wrap 2 inches on one end of green wire around dowel rod to form coil; remove from rod. Insert other end of wire through hole indicated at base of pumpkin stem. Pull wire through until coiled section meets stitched piece.

4. Wrap wire once around stem, then wrap around tail, securing on backside of cat.

5. Insert monofilament through a top center hole of tail. Tie ends together in a knot to form a loop for hanging.

Ghost Assembly
1. Using photo as a guide throughout assembly, for stems, glue one green chenille stem to center backside of each pumpkin.

2. Glue pumpkins to ghost, making sure they are positioned under wire insertion holes.

3. Insert one end of wire from front to back through one of
ghost's hands where indicated on graph, bending back 1 inch to temporarily hold wire in place.

4. Wrap wire close to insertion point on front around dowel rod two or three times to form coil; remove rod. Push coil close to adjacent pumpkin's stem. Slip wire behind stem, then bring wire over to next pumpkin and repeat for remaining two pumpkins.

5. Insert wire from front to back through remaining hand. Bend wire to form a loop over ghost's head, adding coils at even intervals. Twist ends of wire together behind first insertion point. ✂

COLOR KEY
GHOST

Plastic Canvas Yarn	Yards
■ Black #00	1
□ White #41	9
▨ Bright orange #58	2
╱ Black #00 Backstitch	
╱ Bittersweet #52 Backstitch and Overcasting	3
● Insert green plastic-coated wire	

Color numbers given are for Uniek Needloft plastic canvas yarn.

COLOR KEY
CAT

Plastic Canvas Yarn	Yards
▨ Pink #07	1
▨ Holly #27	1
□ White #41	1
▨ Bright orange #58	1
Uncoded areas are black #00 Continental Stitches	7
╱ Black #00 Overcasting	
╱ Bittersweet #52 Backstitch and Overcasting	1
╱ White #41 Straight Stitch	
6-Strand Embroidery Floss	
╱ Light steel gray #318 Backstitch	1
○ Insert whiskers	
● Insert green plastic-coated wire	

Color numbers given are for Uniek Needloft plastic canvas yarn and DMC 6-strand embroidery floss.

Pumpkin Pals Cat Pumpkin
11 holes x 9 holes
Cut 1

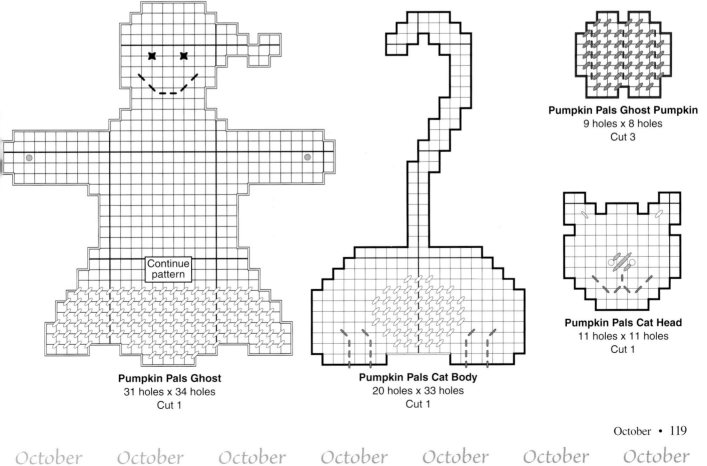

Pumpkin Pals Ghost
31 holes x 34 holes
Cut 1

Pumpkin Pals Cat Body
20 holes x 33 holes
Cut 1

Pumpkin Pals Ghost Pumpkin
9 holes x 8 holes
Cut 3

Pumpkin Pals Cat Head
11 holes x 11 holes
Cut 1

Continue pattern

SWINGING
Witch

Design by Lee Lindeman

This colorful witch is taking a rest from flying on her broomstick and is enjoying an autumn swing!

Skill Level: Intermediate

Finished Size

4 inches W x 8 inches H x 4 inches D, including ropes on swing, excluding tree branch

Materials

- 1 sheet 7-count plastic canvas
- Coats & Clark Red Heart Classic worsted weight yarn Art. E267 as listed in color key
- Coats & Clark Red Heart Super Saver worsted weight yarn Art. E300 as listed in color key
- #16 tapestry needle
- 2 black seed beads
- Sewing needle and black sewing thread
- Small amount fiberfill
- Orange polymer clay
- Small amounts gold and black felt
- 30 inches 48-pound hemp cord
- 8-inch x ½-inch in diameter tree branch with several shoots
- Designer tacky glue
- Hot-glue gun

Cutting & Stitching

1. Cut head pieces, body pieces, sleeves, hands and legs from plastic canvas according to graphs (page 122). Also cut four 2-hole x 5-hole pieces for feet and two 14-hole x 8-hole pieces for swing seat.

2. Continental Stitch feet with black and swing seats with hot red. Stitch remaining pieces fol-lowing graphs, reversing two sleeves before stitching. Work body front as graphed; work body back entirely with black Continental Stitches.

3. When background stitching is completed, work Turkey Loop Stitches on head front over bar indicated, making loops approxi-mately ½-inch long. Work Turkey Loop Stitches on head back, cov-ering lavender area.

4. Using sewing needle and black sewing thread, attach black seed beads to head front for eyes where indicated on graph.

5. Whipstitching wrong sides of pieces together and following graphs through step 8, Overcast top and bottom edges of body front and back. Whipstitch together along side edges.

6. Whipstitch head pieces togeth-er, working Turkey Loop Stitches for hair along lavender edges and stuffing with a tiny amount of fiberfill before closing.

7. Overcast wrist edges of sleeve pieces. For each sleeve, Whipstitch two pieces together along remaining edges. Whipstitch two hand pieces together for each hand.

8. For each leg, Whipstitch two pieces together. Whipstitch two foot pieces together with black for each foot. Whipstitch swing seats together with hot red.

Assembly

1. Use photo as a guide through-out assembly. For swing ropes, cut two 12½-inch lengths of hemp cord.

2. Following Fig. 1, thread one length from top to bottom through one corner hole of swing seat, across short length of seat and from bottom to top at corner hole. Tie end in a knot to cord ¾ inch above seat.

3. Repeat with remaining 12½-inch length on other side of swing, keeping knots same dis-tance from seat. Tie remaining end of both lengths around main part of branch, making sure lengths are even; hot glue to secure. Add a bit of glue to cord knots to secure.

4. Using glue gun through step 5, center and glue neck of head inside top opening of body. Stuff body with small amount of fiber-fill, then glue to swing seat, mak-ing sure back edges of body and seat are even.

5. Glue one foot to bottom of each leg at right angles. Glue legs to bottom edge of body front and to swing seat.

6. Glue one hand in each sleeve at top of wrist opening. Glue shoul-ders of sleeves to shoulder areas of body back. Glue rope to hands.

7. For nose, roll orange polymer clay into a ½-inch-long x ¼-inch in diameter cone shape and bake according to manufacturer's directions. Using tacky glue, attach to face.

8. Using patterns given (page 122), cut bat and hat brim from black felt; cut cape from gold felt. Slip hat brim over tip of hat to hairline; hot glue in place. Using tacky glue, center and glue bat to cape, then glue cape around neck.

9. For hanger, wrap and glue remaining cord around branch, tying ends together in a knot to form a loop; add a dab of glue to knot. ✄

SWINGING
Witch
Continued from page 120

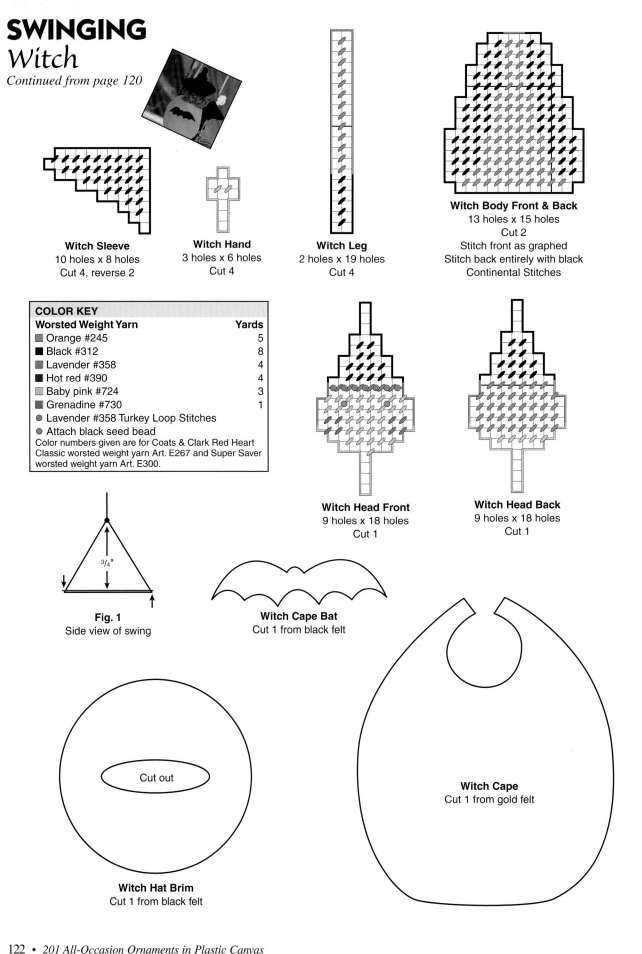

Witch Sleeve
10 holes x 8 holes
Cut 4, reverse 2

Witch Hand
3 holes x 6 holes
Cut 4

Witch Leg
2 holes x 19 holes
Cut 4

Witch Body Front & Back
13 holes x 15 holes
Cut 2
Stitch front as graphed
Stitch back entirely with black
Continental Stitches

COLOR KEY

Worsted Weight Yarn	Yards
Orange #245	5
Black #312	8
Lavender #358	4
Hot red #390	4
Baby pink #724	3
Grenadine #730	1
● Lavender #358 Turkey Loop Stitches	
● Attach black seed bead	

Color numbers given are for Coats & Clark Red Heart Classic worsted weight yarn Art. E267 and Super Saver worsted weight yarn Art. E300.

Witch Head Front
9 holes x 18 holes
Cut 1

Witch Head Back
9 holes x 18 holes
Cut 1

3/4"

Fig. 1
Side view of swing

Witch Cape Bat
Cut 1 from black felt

Cut out

Witch Hat Brim
Cut 1 from black felt

Witch Cape
Cut 1 from gold felt

October   October   October   October   October   October   October

Skill Level: Beginner

Finished Sizes

Jack-o'-lantern A: 2⅝ inches W x 3¼ inches H

Jack-o'-lantern B: 3¼ inches W x 3⅛ inches H

Materials

- ¼ sheet 7-count plastic canvas
- Uniek Needloft plastic canvas yarn as listed in color key
- #16 tapestry needle
- 2 (8-inch) lengths gold lamé thread

Instructions

1. Cut plastic canvas according to graphs.

2. Stitch and Overcast pumpkins following graph.

3. For each ornament, thread one length gold lamé thread through top hole of stem. Tie ends together in a knot to form a loop for hanging. ✂

JOLLY
Jack-O'-Lanterns

Designs by Ruby Thacker

Slanted Gobelin Stitches make this pair of creepy jack-o'-lanterns frightfully quick and easy to stitch.

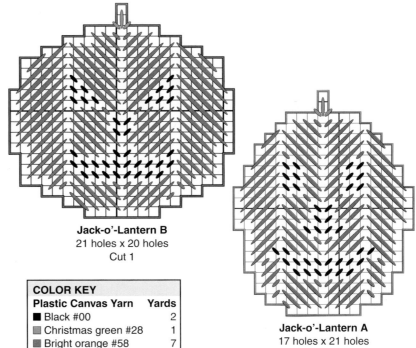

Jack-o'-Lantern B
21 holes x 20 holes
Cut 1

Jack-o'-Lantern A
17 holes x 21 holes
Cut 1

COLOR KEY	
Plastic Canvas Yarn	**Yards**
■ Black #00	2
▨ Christmas green #28	1
▨ Bright orange #58	7
Color numbers given are for Uniek Needloft plastic canvas yarn.	

GHOSTLY
Pumpkin

Design by Kathleen J. Fischer

This small ornament is also just the right size for making into a refrigerator magnet!

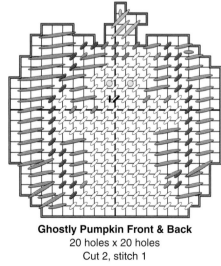

Skill Level: Beginner

Finished Size

3⅛ inches W x 3⅛ inches H

Materials

- ¼ sheet Uniek QuickCount 7-count plastic canvas
- Worsted weight yarn as listed in color key
- #5 pearl cotton as listed in color key
- #16 tapestry needle
- 2 (4mm) black beads
- Sewing needle and black sewing thread
- Nylon thread

Instructions

1. Cut front and back according to graph. Back will remain unstitched.

2. Stitch front following graph. When background stitching is completed, work pearl cotton Backstitches for mouth.

3. With sewing needle and black sewing thread, attach beads where indicated on graph.

4. Whipstitch front and back together following graph.

5. For hanger, thread desired amount of nylon thread through top hole on stem. Tie ends together in a knot to form a loop for hanging. ✂

Ghostly Pumpkin Front & Back
20 holes x 20 holes
Cut 2, stitch 1

COLOR KEY	
Worsted Weight Yarn	**Yards**
■ Orange	3
□ White	2
■ Rust	1
▨ Medium green	1
■ Dark green	1
#5 Pearl Cotton	
╱ Black Backstitch	1
○ Attach 4mm bead	

October   October   October   October   October   October   October

Skill Level: Beginner

Finished Size

5 inches W x 5 inches H

Materials:

- ⅓ sheet Uniek QuickCount 7-count plastic canvas
- Uniek Needloft plastic canvas yarn as listed in color key
- #16 tapestry needle
- 12 inches ½-inch-wide orange Halloween print ribbon
- 2 (10mm) oval movable eyes
- 15 gold star sequins
- Monofilament
- Tacky craft glue

Instructions

1. Cut plastic canvas according to graph.

2. Stitch and Overcast bat following graph. When stitching horizontal stitches in center of bat, work two stitches per hole as necessary to cover canvas.

3. Tie ribbon in a bow around neck, trimming ends to desired length. Glue ribbon tails to bat.

4. Using photo as a guide, glue movable eyes to head and star sequins to wings.

5. Thread monofilament through top center hole of head. Tie ends together in a knot to form a loop for hanging. ✂

Design by Nancy Marshall

Golden stars and a spooky orange bow add extra Halloween touches to this not-so-scary bat!

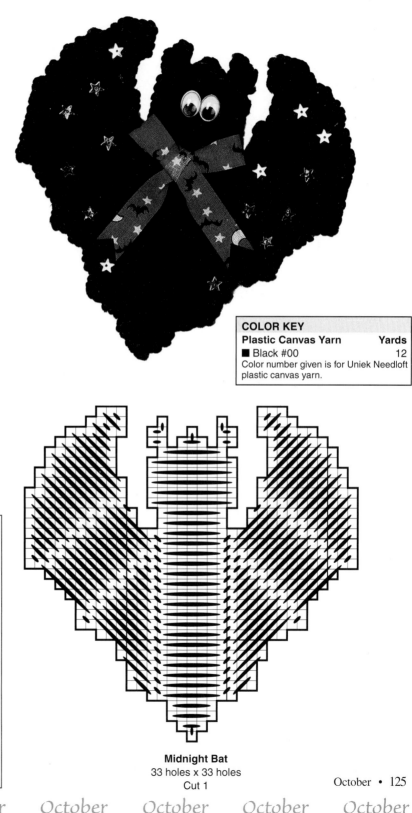

COLOR KEY

Plastic Canvas Yarn	Yards
■ Black #00	12

Color number given is for Uniek Needloft plastic canvas yarn.

Midnight Bat
33 holes x 33 holes
Cut 1

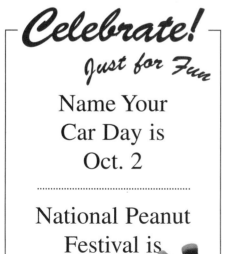

Celebrate!
Just for Fun

Name Your Car Day is Oct. 2

National Peanut Festival is Oct. 13

PUMPKIN
Mini-Mobile

Design by Lee Lindeman

Three smiling pumpkins hanging from a stick will swing and sway as they hang in your home!

Skill Level: Beginner

Finished Sizes

Pumpkin A: 2 inches W x 2¼ inches H

Pumpkin B: 2⅛ inches W x 2⅜ inches H

Pumpkin C: 1¾ inches W x 2½ inches H

Materials

• ¼ sheet 7-count plastic canvas
• Coats & Clark Red Heart Super Saver worsted weight yarn Art. E300 as listed in color key
• #16 tapestry needle
• 6 small black beans
• Thin gold cord
• 14 inches ¼-inch-wide yellow ribbon
• White acrylic craft paint
• Small paintbrush
• 6 inch x ¼-inch in diameter tree branch with several shoots
• Tacky craft glue

Instructions:

1. Cut plastic canvas according to graphs, making sure not to cut off "teeth" on pumpkins B and C.

2. Stitch pumpkins with orange following graphs, reversing one pumpkin A and one pumpkin B before stitching. Whipstitch corresponding pieces together with orange and medium celery.

3. Paint teeth on pumpkins B and C with white acrylic paint; allow to dry.

4. For hangers, cut three different lengths of thin gold cord as desired. For each pumpkin, thread one length through hole indicated on pumpkin stem. Tie ends together in a knot to form a loop for hanging, then glue knot inside hole; allow to dry.

5. Using photo as a guide through step 6, glue one black bean into each pumpkin eye; allow to dry. Slip gold cord hangers over branch and glue in place; allow to dry.

6. If desired, add a dab of white paint to center of each bean for eye highlight; allow to dry.

7. Cut a 6-inch length of yellow satin ribbon. Glue ends to a top center point of branch, forming a loop for hanging. Tie remaining ribbon in a bow and glue to ends of loop; allow to dry. ✂

COLOR KEY	
Worsted Weight Yarn	**Yards**
▨ Orange #245	24
✎ Medium celery #616 Whipstitching	2
✎ Orange #245 Backstitch and Straight Stitch	
○ Attach gold cord hanger	
Color numbers given are for Coats & Clark Red	

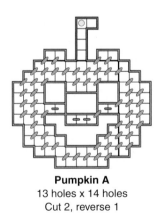

Pumpkin A
13 holes x 14 holes
Cut 2, reverse 1

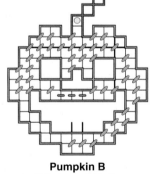

Pumpkin B
13 holes x 15 holes
Cut 2, reverse 1

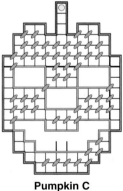

Pumpkin C
11 holes x 16 holes
Cut 2

October   October   October   October   October   October   October

COUNT YOUR
Blessings

Design by Janelle Giese

Remember to count your blessings on Thanksgiving as well as every day!

Skill Level: Beginner

Finished Size

4⅛ inches W x 3⅝ inches H

Materials

- ¼ sheet Uniek QuickCount 7-count plastic canvas
- Uniek Needloft plastic canvas yarn as listed in color key
- Kreinik Medium (#16) Braid as listed in color key
- Kreinik ⅛-inch-wide Ribbon as listed in color key
- DMC #5 pearl cotton as listed in color key
- #16 tapestry needle

Instructions

1. Cut plastic canvas according to graph.

2. Stitch piece following graph, working uncoded background with eggshell Continental

Stitches. Do not work vertical bar highlighted with blue at this time.

3. Following graph, Overcast edges around left side and bottom from arrow to arrow.

4. Using gold metallic ribbon, Overcast remaining sign edges, filling in bar highlighted with blue while Overcasting. Using curry braid, Overcast sign and stitch blue bar a second time, keeping curry stitches sparse to resemble the look of twisted cording.

5. Work embroidery with pearl cotton, medium (#16) braid and

yarn following graph, wrapping yarn around needle once for French Knots.

6. For hanger, secure curry braid on backside of stitched piece. Work a French Knot in one of the holes indicated on graph for hanger, wrapping needle twice. Allow braid to loop 2 inches above top edge, then work a second French Knot where indicated, securing braid on backside. ✂

Count Your Blessings
27 holes x 23 holes
Cut 1

COLOR KEY	
Plastic Canvas Yarn	**Yards**
■ Red #01	1
□ Rust #09	1
■ Pumpkin #12	1
■ Cinnamon #14	1
□ Moss #25	1
□ Beige #40	2
□ Camel #43	1
■ Purple #46	1
Uncoded areas are eggshell #39 Continental Stitches	4
● Bright purple #64 French Knot	1
Medium (#16) Braid	
╱ Curry #2122 Backstitch and Straight Stitch	5
● Curry #2122 French Knot	
⅛-Inch Ribbon	
□ Gold #002	2
#5 Pearl Cotton	
╱ Black #310 Backstitch and Straight Stitch	3
● Attach hanger	
Color numbers given are for Uniek Needloft plastic canvas yarn, Kreinik Meduim (#16) Braid and ⅛-inch Ribbon, and DMC #5 pearl cotton.	

November November November November November November

Skill Level: Beginner

Finished Size

3 inches W x 3⅛ inches H

Materials

- Uniek QuickShape plastic canvas hexagon
- Acrylic plastic canvas yarn: 1¼ inches red and as listed in color key
- Lamé thread as listed in color key
- 6-strand embroidery floss as listed in color key
- #16 tapestry needle
- 12 inches thin gold cord
- Hot-glue gun

Instructions

1. Cut body and legs, tail feathers and head from plastic canvas hexagon according to graph.

2. Stitch and Overcast pieces following graph, working two Long Stitches on each side of body where indicated.

3. When background stitching and Overcasting are completed, work brown yarn Backstitches at center and Straight Stitches over tail feather edges. Work gold lamé thread Backstitches on tail feathers and black floss French Knots on head for eyes.

4. Using photo as a guide throughout, glue red yarn behind beak for wattle. Glue head to top of body, then glue body to center front of tail feathers over cutout section.

5. If hanger is desired, thread an 8-inch length of gold lamé thread through top center hole of turkey. Tie ends together in a knot to form a loop for hanging. ✄

Design by Ruby Thacker

A precut hexagon shape makes stitching this pretty turkey a snap! When finished, it makes a great place marker at your Thanksgiving table!

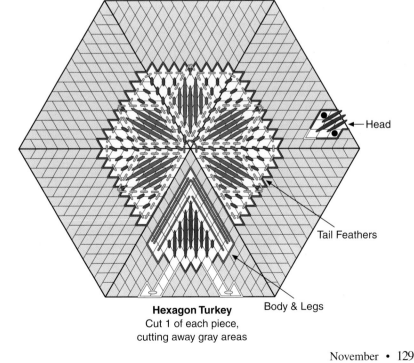

Hexagon Turkey
Cut 1 of each piece,
cutting away gray areas

COLOR KEY	
Plastic Canvas Yarn	**Yards**
■ Rust	3
■ Brown	2
☐ Medium yellow	1
✎ Brown Backstitch and Straight Stitch	
Lamé Thread	
✎ Gold Backstitch	6
6-Strand Embroidery Floss	
● Black French Knot	1

→ Head

Tail Feathers

Body & Legs

AUTUMN
Leaves

Designs by Joan Green

Stitch the multi-hued splendor of autumn with this set of three collectible fall leaves!

Materials

- ¼ sheet 7-count plastic canvas
- Coats & Clark Red Heart Classic worsted weight yarn Art. E267 as listed in color key
- Coats & Clark Red Heart Super Saver worsted weight yarn Art. E300 as listed in color key
- Coats & Clark Red Heart kids worsted weight yarn Art. E711 as listed in color key
- 21 inches ¹⁄₁₆-inch-wide gold #PM51 Plastic Canvas 10 Metallic Needlepoint Yarn by Rainbow Gallery
- #16 tapestry needle
- Fabric glue

Skill Level: Beginner

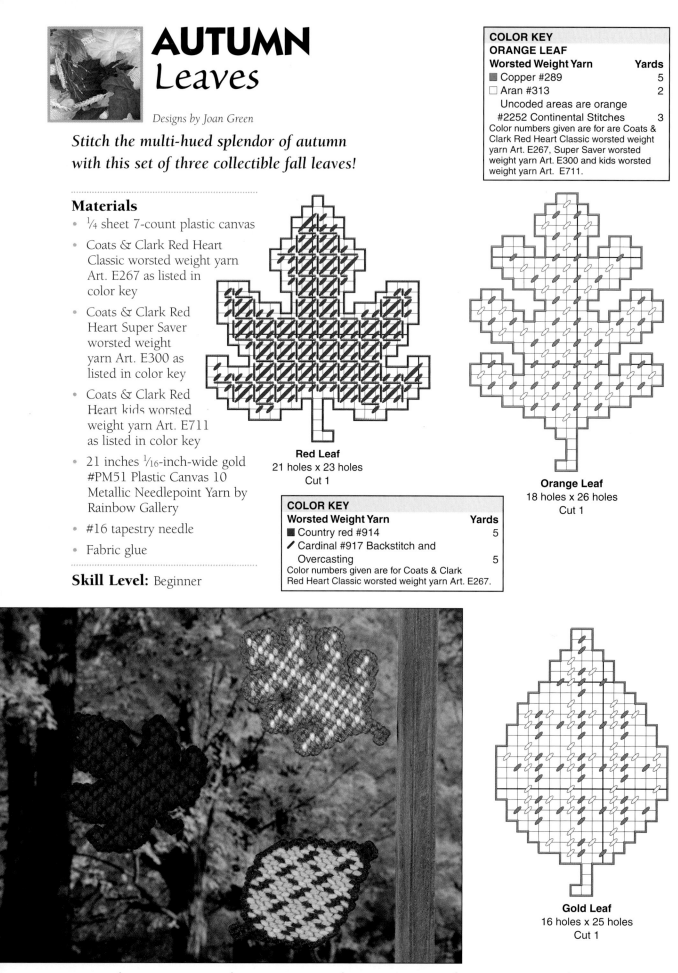

COLOR KEY	
ORANGE LEAF	
Worsted Weight Yarn	**Yards**
■ Copper #289	5
□ Aran #313	2
Uncoded areas are orange #2252 Continental Stitches	3
Color numbers given are for are Coats & Clark Red Heart Classic worsted weight yarn Art. E267, Super Saver worsted weight yarn Art. E300 and kids worsted weight yarn Art. E711.	

Red Leaf
21 holes x 23 holes
Cut 1

COLOR KEY	
Worsted Weight Yarn	**Yards**
■ Country red #914	5
✦ Cardinal #917 Backstitch and Overcasting	5
Color numbers given are for Coats & Clark Red Heart Classic worsted weight yarn Art. E267.	

Orange Leaf
18 holes x 26 holes
Cut 1

Gold Leaf
16 holes x 25 holes
Cut 1

Skill Level: Beginner

Finished Size

2⅛ inches W x 1⅞ inches H x ⅞ inches D

Materials

- ¼ sheet Uniek QuickCount 7-count plastic canvas
- Uniek Needloft plastic canvas yarn as listed in color key
- #16 tapestry needle
- 1-inch flocked bear (sample is gray)
- Hot-glue gun

Instructions

1. Cut plastic canvas according to graphs.

2. Stitch and Overcast headband, overlapping two holes of band while Overcasting. Stitch canoe sides and base following graphs.

3. With wrong sides facing and using gold, Whipstitch one long side of canoe base to canoe sides around side and bottom edges from dot to dot. Overcast remaining edges.

4. For hanger, cut a 10-inch length of gold yarn. Attach ends to canoe base where indicated on graph, wrapping around edges and weaving ends under yarn on inside of canoe.

5. Using photo as a guide, glue headband on bear. Glue bear in canoe. ✂

LITTLE INDIAN *Bear*

Design by Angie Arickx

This little Indian is looking for adventure as he floats down a river in his tiny canoe!

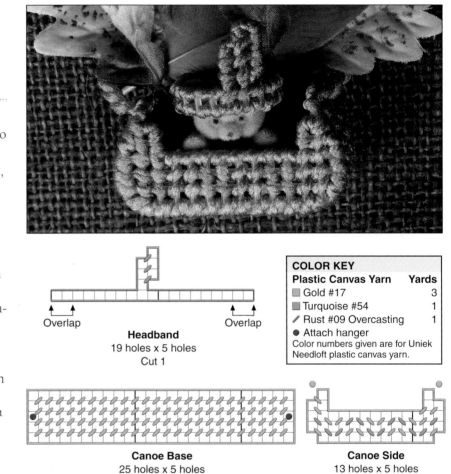

Headband
19 holes x 5 holes
Cut 1

Overlap — Overlap

Canoe Base
25 holes x 5 holes
Cut 1

Canoe Side
13 holes x 5 holes
Cut 2

COLOR KEY

Plastic Canvas Yarn	Yards
▦ Gold #17	3
▦ Turquoise #54	1
╱ Rust #09 Overcasting	1
● Attach hanger	

Color numbers given are for Uniek Needloft plastic canvas yarn.

AUTUMN *Leaves*

COLOR KEY
GOLD LEAF

Worsted Weight Yarn	Yards
▦ Mid brown #339	4
☐ Honey gold #645	3
Uncoded areas are gold #321 Continental Stitches	4

Color numbers given are for are for Coats & Clark Red Heart Classic worsted weight yarn Art. E267 and Super Saver worsted weight yarn Art. E300.

Finished Sizes

Gold leaf: 2½ inches W x 3¾ inches H

Red leaf: 3¼ inches W x 3½ inches H

Orange leaf: 2¾ inches W x 4 inches H

Instructions

1. Cut plastic canvas according to graphs.

2. Stitch pieces following graphs, working uncoded areas on gold leaf with gold Continental Stitches and uncoded areas on orange leaf with orange Continental Stitches.

3. Overcast leaves following graphs. Work Backstitches on red leaf with 2 plies cardinal.

4. Cut ¹⁄₁₆-inch-wide gold metallic yarn into three 7-inch lengths. For each ornament, glue ends of one length to top center backside with fabric glue, forming a loop for hanging. ✂

SQUIRREL'S
Harvest

Design by Lee Lindeman

Squirrel lovers will enjoy this cute autumn ornament! Stitch this dimensional squirrel collecting a harvest of acorns to tide him over the winter!

Skill Level: Beginner

Finished Sizes

Squirrel with acorn: 4½ inches W x 4½ inches H x 1¼ inches D

Leaf: 2 inches W x 3⅛ inches H

Assembled sample: 9½ W x 10 inches L x 5 inches H

Materials

- 2 sheets 7-count plastic canvas
- Coats & Clark Red Heart Super Saver worsted weight yarn Art. E300 as listed in color key
- Coats & Clark Red Heart kids worsted weight yarn Art. E711 as listed in color key
- Acrylic worsted weight yarn as listed in color key
- #16 tapestry needle
- 3mm round black bead
- 2 (6mm) round brown animal eyes
- 4 acorns
- Light taupe felt or synthetic suede
- Small amount fiberfill
- 7½-inch x ½-inch in diameter tree branch with several shoots
- Sewing needle and black sewing thread
- Clear thread (optional)
- 12 inches thin gold cord
- Hot-glue gun

Cutting & Stitching

1. Cut plastic canvas according to graphs. Cut two ears from light taupe felt or synthetic suede using pattern given.

2. Stitch squirrel pieces following graphs, working uncoded areas with light taupe Continental Stitches and reversing one body, two arms and two legs before stitching.

3. Following graph, stitch four leaves with orange, reversing two before stitching; stitch four leaves with burgundy, reversing two. Stitch two leaves each with gold, yellow and mid brown, reversing one of each color before stitching.

4. For each leaf, Whipstitch wrong sides of two leaves of the same color together with leaf color.

5. Using adjacent colors through step 6, Whipstitch wrong sides of body pieces together, stuffing with fiberfill before closing.

6. For each arm and each leg, Whipstitch wrong sides of two pieces together, stuffing with a small amount of fiberfill before closing.

Final Assembly

1. Use photo as a guide throughout assembly. Glue arms and legs to squirrel, making sure bottom edges of body and legs are even, or are in right position to glue to tree branch.

2. Following graph throughout, fold bottom edge of each ear together and glue into stitches on head. Glue eyes to head. Using sewing needle and black sewing thread, attach black bead for nose to front edge of head.

3. Glue acorn between front paws, then glue squirrel to branch. If desired, tack squirrel to branch with clear thread for more stability. Glue leaves to branch. Glue remaining acorns in a cluster to branch and leaves.

4. For hanger, thread gold cord through hole indicated. Tie ends together in a knot to form a loop for hanging. ✂

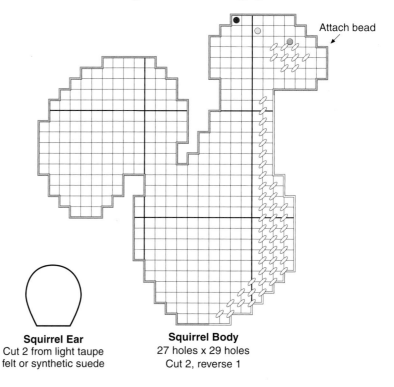

Squirrel Ear
Cut 2 from light taupe
felt or synthetic suede

Squirrel Body
27 holes x 29 holes
Cut 2, reverse 1

Attach bead

COLOR KEY

Worsted Weight Yarn	Yards
■ Orange #245	10
□ Aran #313	3
Gold #321	5
Mid brown #339	5
Burgundy #376	10
Yellow #2230	5
Uncoded areas are light	
taupe Continental Stitches	20

⊘ Light taupe Whipstitching
○ Attach ear
● Attach eye
● Attach hanger

Color numbers given are for Coats & Clark
Red Heart Super Saver worsted weight
yarn Art. E300 and kids worsted weight
yarn Art. E711.

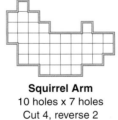

Squirrel Arm
10 holes x 7 holes
Cut 4, reverse 2

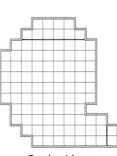

Squirrel Leg
11 holes x 12 holes
Cut 4, reverse 2

Squirrel's Harvest Leaf
12 holes x 20 holes
Cut 14
Stitch 4 as graphed, reversing 2
Stitch 4 with burgundy, reversing 2
Stitch 2 with gold, reversing 1
Stitch 2 with yellow, reversing 1
Stitch 2 with mid brown, reversing 1

Skill Level: Beginner

Finished Size

4⅛ inches W x 5⅜ inches H

Materials

- ¼ sheet Uniek QuickCount 7-count plastic canvas
- Uniek Needloft plastic canvas yarn as listed in color key
- Kreinik Heavy (#32) Braid as listed in color key
- Kreinik Medium (#16) Braid as listed in color key
- DMC #5 pearl cotton as listed in color key
- #16 tapestry needle

Instructions

1. Cut plastic canvas according to graph.

2. Stitch piece following graph, working uncoded background with beige Continental Stitches. Do not work beige Continental Stitches over four corners of sampler. Overcast with maple.

3. When background stitching and Overcasting are completed, embroider lettering with pearl cotton, wrapping pearl cotton around needle once for French Knots. Work gold braid Backstitches along edges.

4. Work large Cross Stitch and French Knots on each side of word "Thankful" with curry braid, wrapping braid one time around needle for French Knots.

5. For top band of decorative stitching, work tangerine Back-stitches first, using a full strand yarn. Using gold braid, work Herringbone Stitch (Fig. 1) next. Backstitch lines at top and bottom of band last with curry braid.

6. For decorative work in middle, work Backstitches and Cross Stitches in center area with curry braid; work Cross Stitches above

Fig. 1
Herringbone Stitch

and below curry stitching with gold braid.

7. For bottom band, work gold braid embroidery, including the three Cross Stitches above bottom band. Using curry braid, work Running Stitches over gold Cross Stitches. Work Chain Stitches at top and bottom of band.

8. For hanger, secure gold braid on backside of sampler and work a Straight Stitch across one of the bars indicated for attaching hanger. Allow braid to loop 2½ inches above sampler, then work Straight Stitch across second bar indicated for attaching hanger, securing yarn on backside. ✂

THANKFUL *Sampler*

Design by Janelle Giese

Friends and family add much to enrich our lives. Stitch this meaningful sampler to share with those you love!

COLOR KEY	
Plastic Canvas Yarn	**Yards**
☐ Tangerine #11	2
☐ Maple #13	3
Uncoded areas are beige #40 Continental Stitches	13
╱ Tangerine #11 Backstitch	
Heavy (#32) Braid	
╱ Gold #002 Straight Stitch, Cross Stitch and Herringbone Stitch	5
Medium (#16) Braid	
╱ Curry #2122 Backstitch, Cross Stitch and Running Stitch	4
⟿ Curry #2122 Chain Stitch	
● Curry #2122 French Knot	
#5 Pearl Cotton	
╱ Very dark garnet #902 Backstitch	1
╱ Ultra dark coffee brown #938 Backstitch	4
● Ultra dark coffee brown #938 French Knot	
● Attach hanger	
Color numbers given are for Uniek Needloft plastic canvas yarn, Kreinik Heavy (#32) Braid and Medium (#16) Braid, and DMC #5 pearl cotton.	

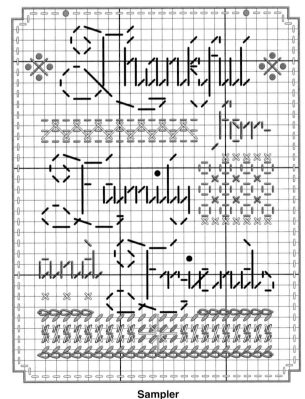

Sampler
27 holes x 35 holes
Cut 1

BUTTON
Turkey

Design by Kathleen J. Fischer

Invite your children to help you with this colorful turkey ornament! After you've finished the stitching, your kids can help sew on the button head!

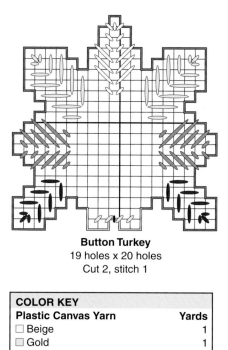

Button Turkey
19 holes x 20 holes
Cut 2, stitch 1

COLOR KEY	
Plastic Canvas Yarn	**Yards**
☐ Beige	1
☐ Gold	1
▨ Orange	1
■ Rust	1
Uncoded area is brown	
Continental Stitches	2
╱ Brown Straight Stitch	
⅛ Inch Metallic Needlepoint Yarn	
■ Bronze #PC21 Whipstitching	
Color number given is for Rainbow Gallery Plastic Canvas 7 Metallic Needlepoint Yarn.	

Skill Level: Beginner

Finished Size

3 inches W x 3⅛ inches H

Materials

- Small amount 7-count plastic canvas
- Worsted weight yarn: 8 inches red and as listed in color key
- ⅛-inch-wide Plastic Canvas 7 Metallic Needlepoint Yarn by Rainbow Gallery as listed in color key
- #16 tapestry needle
- 1-inch 2-hole white button
- 2 (4mm) round black beads
- Sewing needle and black sewing thread
- Nylon thread
- Tacky craft glue

Instructions

1. Cut plastic canvas according to graph. Back will remain unstitched.

2. Stitch front following graph, working uncoded area with brown Continental Stitches. Work brown Straight Stitch when background stitching is completed.

3. For wattle, thread red yarn from back to front through one hole of button, leaving a 1-inch tail. Bring yarn down front, around to back and through second hole.

4. Slip needle under yarn on front, wrapping second stitch around first stitch. Continue wrapping yarn around first stitch to back of button, tying off when tails meet.

5. Using photo as a guide, place button on turkey front. Using sewing needle and black sewing thread, attach beads to button front and button to turkey front through holes on button. Secure button with tacky glue.

6. Whipstitch front and back together following graph.

7. Thread desired amount of nylon thread through top hole of turkey. Tie ends together in knot to form a loop for hanging. ✄

Celebrate!
Just for Fun
Forget-Me-Not
Day is
Nov. 19

Skill Level: Beginner

Finished Size

4³⁄₈ inches W x 4³⁄₄ inches H

Materials

- ¼ sheet Uniek QuickCount 7-count plastic canvas
- Coats & Clark Red Heart Classic worsted weight yarn Art. #267 as listed in color key
- DMC #5 pearl cotton as listed in color key
- #16 tapestry needle

Instructions

1. Cut plastic canvas according to graph.

2. Stitch and Overcast piece following graph, working uncoded areas with warm brown Continental Stitches.

3. When background stitching and Overcasting are completed, use a full strand honey gold to Backstitch buckle on hat.

4. Work black #5 pearl cotton embroidery, passing over eyes on turkey four times. Work French Knot eyes on Indian and pilgrim, wrapping pearl cotton two times around needle.

THANKSGIVING
Friends

Design by Janelle Giese

Celebrate the season with family and friends, while also remembering the friendships formed at our nation's very first Thanksgiving Day!

5. Thread ends of a length of black #5 pearl cotton from front to back through holes indicated on graph. Tie ends together in a knot to form a loop for hanging, allowing loop to extend 3 inches above top of ornament. ✂

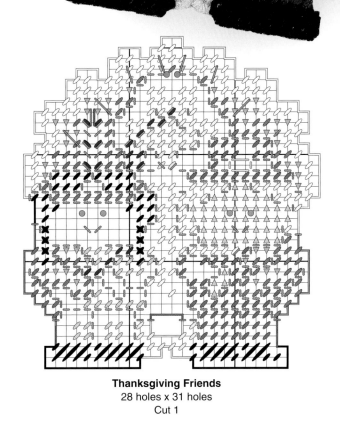

Thanksgiving Friends
28 holes x 31 holes
Cut 1

November   November   November   November   November   November

FALLING
Leaves

Design by Janna Britton

A twig adds the perfect authentic autumn touch to this festive fall project! Hang it just so and it spells out "FALL"!

Skill Level: Beginner

Finished Size

Approximately 9 inches W x 9½ inches H

Materials

- ¼ sheet Uniek QuickCount brown 7-count plastic canvas
- Uniek Needloft plastic canvas yarn as listed in color key
- #16 tapestry needle
- 9-inch twig with several shoots
- 2 yards 24-gauge gold craft wire from The Beadery
- Wire cutters
- ⅛-inch wooden dowel

Instructions

1. Cut plastic canvas according to graphs.

2. Stitch pieces following graphs, working uncoded areas with cinnamon Continental Stitches. Do not Overcast.

3. Use photo as a guide through step 6. For hanger, cut a 10-inch length of gold craft wire. Wrap ends around twig, spaced approximately 3 inches apart.

4. For letters, cut four 4-inch lengths of gold craft wire. Thread one length through top center hole of each letter; twist wire around itself to secure. Wrap remaining ends around twig between hanger ends, spelling the word FALL and twisting wires for different lengths and shaping.

5. Cut three 6-inch to 8-inch lengths of craft wire. Thread one length through bottom center hole of three leaves, twisting wire around itself to secure. Curl wire around dowel rod and hang from twig as desired.

6. Wire three remaining leaves to top of twig or hanger as desired. ✄

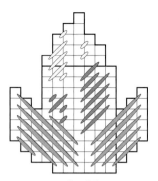

Leaf A
13 holes x 15 holes
Cut 2

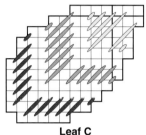

Leaf C
13 holes x 11 holes
Cut 2

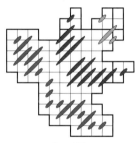

Leaf B
12 holes x 12 holes
Cut 2

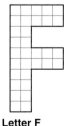

Letter F
5 holes x 10 holes
Cut 1

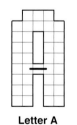

Letter A
5 holes x 9 holes
Cut 1

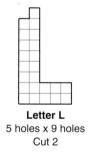

Letter L
5 holes x 9 holes
Cut 2

COLOR KEY

Plastic Canvas Yarn	Yards
■ Red #01	2
■ Burgundy #03	1
□ Tangerine #11	1
■ Maple #13	1
□ Beige #40	2
▨ Bittersweet #52	2
Uncoded areas are cinnamon #14 Continental Stitches	4
✔ Cinnamon #14 Straight Stitch	

Color numbers given are for Uniek Needloft plastic canvas yarn.

CHRISTMAS
Friends

Design by Janelle Giese

Enchant a special someone with this delightful ornament featuring Santa, an elf and a friendly snowman!

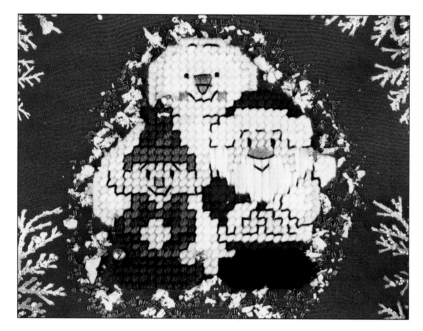

Skill Level: Beginner

Finished Size

4⅝ inches W x 4¾ inches H

COLOR KEY

Worsted Weight Yarn	Yards
☐ White #1	5
■ Black #12	1
☐ Sea coral #246	2
☐ Paddy green #686	1
■ Forest green #689	2
☐ Light coral rose #749	1
☐ Pale blue #815	2
■ Cherry red #912	1
☐ Cardinal #917	1
Uncoded areas are white # 1 Continental Stitches	
⁄ Light coral rose #749 Straight Stitch	
⁄ Medium coral #252 Straight Stitch	1
#5 Pearl cotton	
⁄ Black #310 Backstitch and Straight Stitch	6
● Black #310 French knot	
○ Attach gold jingle bell	
○ Attach hanger	

Color numbers given are for Coats & Clark Red Heart Classic worsted weight yarn Art. E267 and DMC #5 pearl cotton.

Materials

- ¼ sheet Uniek Needloft 7-count plastic canvas
- Coats & Clark Red Heart Classic worsted weight yarn Art. E267 as listed in color key
- DMC #5 pearl cotton as listed in color key
- #16 tapestry needle
- 4 (6mm) gold jingle bells

Instructions

1. Cut plastic canvas according to graph.

2. Continental Stitch and Overcast piece following graph, working uncoded areas with white Continental Stitches and working white Long Stitches for Santa's beard as indicated.

3. When background stitching and Overcasting are completed, work snowman's nose with full strand medium coral, passing over center stitch three times. Stitch Santa's nose with full strand light coral rose passing over area three times.

4. Work remaining embroidery with black pearl cotton, stitching eyes on elf and Santa four times and wrapping pearl cotton around needle two times for snowman's eyes.

5. Using black pearl cotton, attach gold jingle bells to elf and Santa where indicated on graph.

6. For hanger, cut a 7-inch length of black pearl cotton. Thread ends from front to back through holes indicated on graph. Knot ends together on backside so loop extends 3 inches above top of ornament; trim excess. ✂

Christmas Friends
30 holes x 31 holes
Cut 1

December   December   December   December   December   December

Skill Level: Beginner

Finished Size

5⅛ inches W x 5¼ inches H

Materials

- ¼ sheet 7-count plastic canvas
- Uniek Needloft plastic canvas yarn as listed in color key
- #16 tapestry needle
- 12 inches ⅜-inch-wide striped Christmas ribbon
- 2 (6mm) black cabochons
- 9 (½-inch to ⅝-inch) Christmas light bulbs in assorted colors
- 9 inches Wire Art black plastic-coated wire from Duncan Enterprises
- Wire cutters
- Needle-nose pliers
- White felt (optional)
- Plastic monofilament
- Hot-glue gun

Instructions

1. Cut plastic canvas according to graph.

SNOWMAN
With Lights

Design by Nancy Marshall

This cheery little snowman is ready to help you hang your Christmas lights! Won't he look adorable on your tree?

2. Stitch and Overcast snowman following graph, working uncoded area with white Continental Stitches.

3. Work black Backstitches for mouth. Glue cabochons to face for eyes where indicated on graph.

4. Using photo as a guide through step 6, tie Christmas ribbon around neck for scarf; trim ends to desired length and glue to body.

5. Insert 1 inch black wire under a few stitches on backside of one mitten; twist wire around itself to secure. Bring wire to front between thumb and fingers of mitten.

6. Thread Christmas light bulbs on wire, securing with a small

amount of glue. Fasten remaining end of wire to back of mitten on other side, trimming excess as needed; place wire between thumb and fingers of mitten.

7. For hanger, thread desired length of plastic monofilament through top center hole of head; tie ends together in a knot to form a loop for hanging. ✂

COLOR KEY	
Plastic Canvas Yarn	**Yards**
■ Christmas red #02	3
☐ Holly #27	2
Uncoded area is white	
#41 Continental Stitches	7
⁄ White #41 Overcasting	
✎ Black #00 Backstitch	1
● Attach black cabochon	
Color numbers given are for Uniek Needloft plastic canvas yarn.	

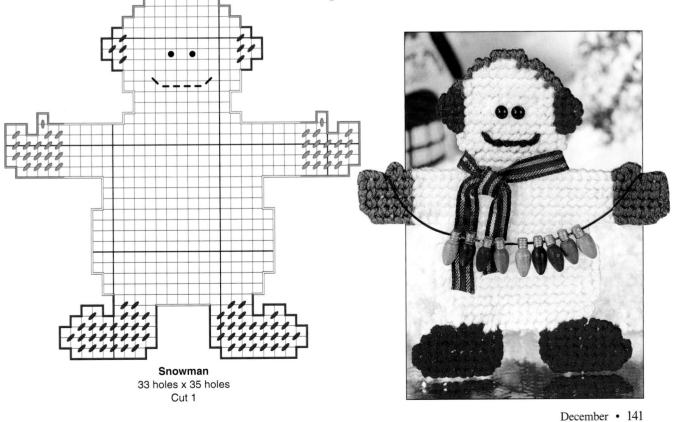

Snowman
33 holes x 35 holes
Cut 1

FESTIVE GIFT
Packages

Designs by Ruby Thacker

Discover a world of miniature dreams with this pair of enchanting ornaments! Tiny gift boxes, adorned with bows, pinecones and holly berries each have darling miniatures inside!

Skill Level: Beginner

Finished Size

2¼ inches W x 2¾ inches H x 2¼ inches D

Materials

- ½ sheet 7-count plastic canvas
- Uniek Needloft plastic canvas yarn as listed in color key
- Uniek Needloft solid metallic craft cord as listed in color key
- #16 tapestry needle
- 2 (24-inch) lengths ⅜-inch-wide coordinating ribbon
- Shredded gift packaging in coordinating colors
- Miniature pinecones and berries
- 4 miniature toy and candy ornaments
- 2 (8-inch) lengths gold lamé thread
- Hot-glue gun

Instructions

1. For each package, cut three box sides, one box bottom, three lid sides and one lid top from plastic canvas according to graphs.

2. Stitch pieces for one gift package with holly as graphed; stitch pieces for second gift package replacing holly with red.

3. Overcast bottom edges of lid sides with solid gold.

4. Following graphs through step 6, for each package, Whipstitch three box sides together along short edges making one long strip, then Whipstitch sides to three edges of box bottom.

5. Whipstitch lid sides together along short edges making one long strip, then Whipstitch lid sides to three edges of lid top.

6. Place lid on box. Overcast around front opening, Whipstitching lid sides to box sides while Overcasting.

7. Using photo as a guide through step 9, and using one 24-inch-length ribbon for each box, wrap and glue ribbon around stitched portions of package. Make a multi-loop bow and glue to top. Add cones and berries as desired to center of bow.

8. For hangers, thread an 8-inch length gold lamé thread down through center of lid. Tie ends together in a knot on wrong side to form a loop for hanging.

9. Stuff boxes with small amount shredded packaging, then glue two ornaments in each box. ✄

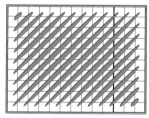

Lid Top
14 holes x 14 holes
Cut 2
Stitch 1 as graphed
Stitch 1 with red

Lid Side
14 holes x 3 holes
Cut 6
Stitch 3 as graphed
Stitch 3 replacing holly with red

Box Side
13 holes x 10 holes
Cut 6
Stitch 3 as graphed
Stitch 3 with red

Box Bottom
13 holes x 13 holes
Cut 2
Stitch 1 as graphed
Stitch 1 with red

COLOR KEY	
Plastic Canvas Yarn	**Yards**
Red #01	12
■ Holly #27	12
Solid Metallic Craft Cord	
╱ Solid gold #55020 Overcasting	2
Color numbers given are for Uniek Needloft plastic canvas yarn and solid metallic craft cord.	

VERY MERRY
Bears

Designs by Nancy Dorman

Warm your heart with this pair of darling, diminutive teddy bears! They're sure to get you in the Christmas spirit!

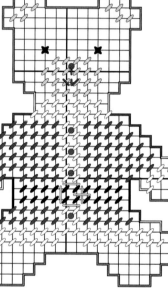

Skill Level: Beginner

Finished Sizes

Teddy Bear: 3¾ inches W x 4 inches H

Santa Bear: 3¼ inches W x 4¾ inches H

Materials

- ½ sheet 7-count plastic canvas
- Worsted weight yarn as listed in color key
- ¹⁄₁₆-inch-wide metallic yarn as listed in color key
- 6-strand embroidery floss as listed in color key
- #16 tapestry needle
- 6 inches ⅛-inch-wide green satin ribbon
- 6 inches ⅛-inch-wide red satin ribbon
- 6 inches ¹⁄₁₆-inch-wide green satin ribbon
- 6mm gold jingle bell
- 4 inches 8mm red and white twist chenille stem
- Hot-glue gun

Instructions

1. Cut plastic canvas according to graphs.

2. Stitch and Overcast pieces following graphs, working uncoded areas with light brown Continental Stitches.

3. Work embroidery when background stitching is completed.

4. Use photo as a guide through step 6. Tie red ribbon in a bow and glue to

teddy bear where indicated on graph. Glue jingle bell under bow.

5. Bend chenille stem into candy cane shape and glue to left side of teddy bear. Tie ¹⁄₁₆-inch-wide green ribbon in a bow and glue to candy cane.

6. For Santa bear, stitch hat to head at an angle with matching yarn. Tie ⅛-inch-wide green satin ribbon in a bow and glue to neck.

7. Hang as desired. ✂

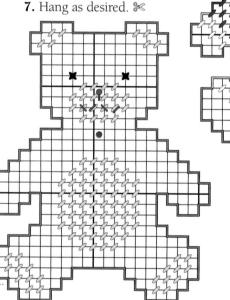

Teddy Bear
21 holes x 26 holes
Cut 1

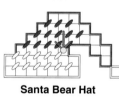

Santa Bear
21 holes x 27 holes
Cut 1

Santa Bear Hat
11 holes x 6 holes
Cut 1

COLOR KEY	
TEDDY BEAR	
Worsted Weight Yarn	**Yards**
☐ Tan	2
■ Black	1
Uncoded areas are light brown Continental Stitches	6
╱ Light brown Overcasting	
6-Strand Embroidery Floss	
╱ Black Backstitch	1
● Black French Knot	
■ Attach red bow	

COLOR KEY	
SANTA BEAR	
Worsted Weight Yarn	**Yards**
■ Red	6
☐ White	3
■ Black	1
☐ Tan	1
Uncoded areas are light brown Continental Stitches	4
╱ Light brown Overcasting	
╱ Green Straight Stitch	1
6-Strand Embroidery Floss	
╱ Black Backstitch	
● Black French Knot	
¹⁄₁₆-Wide Metallic Yarn	
╱ Gold Backstitch and Straight Stitch	1
○ Gold French Knot	

December December December December December December December

Skill Level: Beginner

Finished Size

3 inches W x 3½ inches H

Materials

- Small amount green 7-count plastic canvas
- Darice 4½-inch plastic canvas radial circle
- Darice metallic cord as listed in color key
- Darice Bright Pearls pearlized metallic cord as listed in color key
- #16 tapestry needle
- 6 (½-inch) Christmas presents in assorted colors
- 6 inches fine gold metallic braid or cord
- Hot-glue gun

Instructions

1. Cut plastic canvas according to graphs, cutting away gray area on base.

2. Overcast trees; stitch and Overcast base following graphs.

3. Slide tree A down over tree B until bottom edges are even; glue in place. Center and glue tree to stitched base.

PRESENTS UNDER
The Tree

Design by Robin Petrina

With green plastic canvas and a radial circle, this ornament can be stitched from start to finish in about an hour!

4. Using photo as a guide, glue presents to base around tree.

5. Thread gold braid or cord through top hole of tree. Tie ends together in a knot to form a loop for hanging. ✄

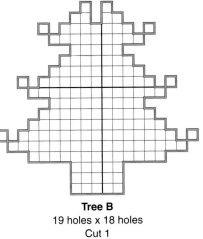

Tree B
19 holes x 18 holes
Cut 1

Tree A
19 holes x 20 holes
Cut 1

COLOR KEY	
Metallic Cord	**Yards**
✎ Christmas green/silver #34021-407 Overcasting	5
Pearlized Metallic Cord	
☐ White #340-01	6
Color numbers given are for Darice metallic cord and pearlized metallic cord.	

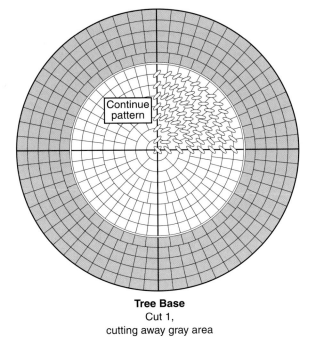

Tree Base
Cut 1,
cutting away gray area

OLD WORLD
St. Nicholas

Design by Janelle Giese

Bundled up against the winter elements, this old-world-style Santa holds a golden staff and toy-filled sack!

Skill Level: Beginner

Finished Size

5⅛ inches W x 4¾ inches H

Materials

- ¼ sheet Uniek Needloft 7-count plastic canvas
- Honeysuckle rayon chenille yarn by Elmore-Pisgah Inc. as listed in color key
- Uniek Needloft plastic canvas yarn as listed in color key
- Kreinik Medium (#16) Braid as listed in color key
- DMC #5 pearl cotton as listed in color key
- DMC 6-strand embroidery floss as listed in color key
- #16 tapestry needle
- 8 (6mm) gold jingle bells

Project Note

Use a double strand when stitching with rayon chenille yarn.

Instructions

1. Cut plastic canvas according to graph.

2. Leaving staff unworked at this time, stitch and Overcast remainder of piece with rayon chenille yarn and plastic canvas yarn following graph, working uncoded areas on Santa's bag with bright purple Continental Stitches and uncoded areas on face with flesh tone Continental Stitches.

3. Stitch staff using a double strand gold medium (#16) braid.

Begin by Overcasting edges. Work one long Straight Stitch, passing over two times to make four strands deep.

4. Using a single strand gold and beginning just above hand, Straight Stitch two times over intersections indicated. With same braid, attach a cluster of three gold jingle bells at top of staff; secure braid on back of staff.

COLOR KEY	
Rayon Chenille Yarn	**Yards**
□ White #1	4
■ Baked apple #24	7
Plastic Canvas Yarn	
■ Black #00	3
▨ Holly #27	1
■ Forest #29	3
■ Purple #46	3
Uncoded area on face is flesh tone #56 Continental Stitches	1
Uncoded areas on bag are bright purple #64 Continental Stitches	2
Medium (#16) Braid	
⁄ Gold #002 Straight Stitch and Overcasting	5
#5 Pearl Cotton	
⁄ Black #310 Backstitch and Straight Stitch	3
6-Strand Embroidery Floss	
✕ Salmon #760 Cross Stitch	1
● Attach gold jingle bell	
○ Attach hanger	
Color numbers given are for Elmore-Pisgah Honeysuckle rayon chenille yarn, Kreinik Medium (#16) Braid and DMC #5 pearl cotton and 6-strand embroidery floss.	

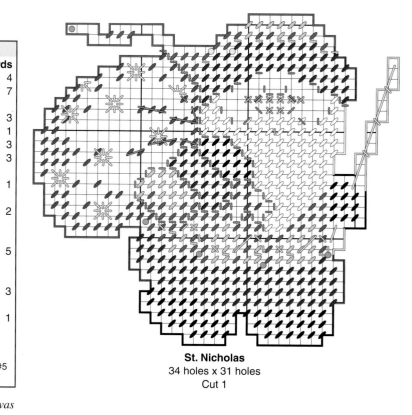

St. Nicholas
34 holes x 31 holes
Cut 1

December   December   December   December   December   December

Skill Level: Beginner

Finished Size

2⅛ inches W x 4¾ inches H x 1 inch D

Materials

- ¼ sheet 7-count plastic canvas
- Worsted weight yarn as listed in color key
- #16 tapestry needle
- Approximately 60 small beads in various colors
- 15 inches ⅛-inch-wide silver ribbon
- 1-inch terra-cotta pot
- Small stone to fit in pot
- Sewing needle and green sewing thread to match yarn
- Small amount fiberfill
- Hot-glue gun

Instructions

1. Cut plastic canvas according to graph.

2. Stitch trees following graph. Overcast bottom portion of trees from dot to dot.

3. Using photo as a guide, attach beads to trees as desired with sewing needle and green sewing thread.

4. Whipstitch wrong sides of trees together along unstitched edges. Stuff tree with fiberfill.

5. Glue stone in bottom of pot; cover with fiberfill. Glue tree in pot.

CHRISTMAS
Tree Favor

Design by Lee Lindeman

Tiny blue, pink and gold beads give this Christmas tree sparkle and life! Delight your Christmas dinner guests with a tiny tree to take home as a favor!

6. Using photo as a guide, wrap and glue silver ribbon around top of pot, so seam is in front; cut excess. Cut remaining ribbon in half. Tie each half in a bow. Glue one bow to top of tree; glue remaining bow to pot over ribbon seam. ✂

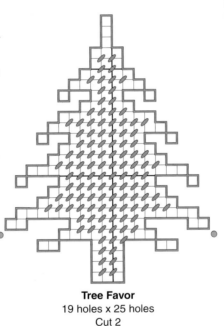

Tree Favor
19 holes x 25 holes
Cut 2

COLOR KEY	
Worsted Weight Yarn	**Yards**
■ Green	10

OLD WORLD
St. Nicholas

5. Using salmon floss, Cross Stitch cheeks with 2 strands and Straight Stitch mouth with 4 strands. Work remaining embroidery with gold medium (#16) braid and black pearl cotton, passing over eyes four times.

6. Attach remaining gold jingle bells with black pearl cotton where indicated on graph.

7. For hanger, cut a 7-inch length of gold medium (#16) braid. Thread ends from front to back through holes indicated on graph. Knot ends together on backside so loop extends 3 inches above top of ornament; trim excess. ✂

December   December   December   December   December   December

OLD-WORLD
Santas

Designs by Kathleen Hurley

Four different Santa ornaments reflect how people from times past pictured Santa Claus! Stitch them today for old-fashioned charm!

Skill Level: Intermediate

Finished Sizes

Santa A: 2½ inches W x 4¾ inches H

Santa B: 2¾ inches W x 4¾ inches H

Santa C: 2 inches W x 4¾ inches H

Santa D: 3¼ inches W x 4⅞ inches H

Materials

- 1 sheet 10-count plastic canvas
- Coats & Clark Red Heart Sport sport weight yarn Art. E289 as listed in color key
- Coats & Clark Red Heart Super Sport sport weight yarn Art. E327 as listed in color key
- DMC 6-strand embroidery floss as listed in color key
- 2 yards fine gold braid
- #22 tapestry needle
- #26 tapestry needle

Instructions

1. Cut plastic canvas according to graphs.

2. Using #22 tapestry needle, stitch and Overcast Santas following graphs, working uncoded areas with white Continental Stitches.

3. When background stitching and Overcasting are completed, work French Knots for tree ornaments on Santa D with 4 plies yarn. Using #26 tapestry needle, work Backstitches on all Santas

with 3 strands black embroidery floss.

4. For hanger, cut gold braid into 9-inch lengths. Attach one length with a Lark's Head Knot to center top of each Santa's head; tie ends together in a knot and trim close to knot. ✂

Santa A
24 holes x 47 holes
Cut 2

Santa C
20 holes x 46 holes
Cut 2

Santa B
26 holes x 47 holes
Cut 2

148 • *201 All-Occasion Ornaments in Plastic Canvas*

COLOR KEY

Sport Weight Yarn	Yards
■ Black #12	11
□ Yellow #230	4
□ Peach #247	10
■ Wood brown #361	4
□ Paddy green #687	19
■ Hunter green #689	15
□ Light raspberry #774	7
□ Blue jewel #819	1
□ Skipper blue #846	14
■ Soft navy #853	6
■ Jockey red #904	15
■ Cherry red #912	15
Uncoded areas are white #1	
Continental Stitches	34
⁄ White #1 Overcasting	
○ Yellow #230 French Knot	
○ Light raspberry #774 French Knot	
○ Skipper blue #846 French Knot	
● Cherry red #912 French Knot	
6-Strand Embroidery Floss	
⁄ Black #310 Backstitch and Straight Stitch	1

Color numbers given are for Coats & Clark Red Heart Sport
sport weight yarn Art. E289 and Super Sport sport weight yarn
Art. E327, and DMC 6-strand embroidery floss.

Santa D
32 holes x 48 holes
Cut 2

QUICK & EASY
Wreaths

Design by Nancy Barrett

Every Christmas tree needs a pretty wreath! With this easy pattern, you can stitch one or a dozen in no time at all!

Skill Level: Intermediate

Finished Size

3¾ inches W x 3¾ inches H

Materials

- ½ sheet 7-count plastic canvas
- Worsted weight yarn as listed in color key
- #16 tapestry needle
- 2 (12-inch) lengths ⅜-inch-wide red plaid Christmas ribbon
- 2 (12-inch) lengths red metallic craft cord
- Hot-glue gun

Instructions

1. Cut one wreath front, one wreath back and three berries from plastic canvas according to graphs, cutting out center opening for wreath front only, leaving wreath back intact. Wreath back will remain unstitched.

2. Using pine through step 4 and referring to Fig. 1 for Rug Stitch, work wreath front.

3. On front, Overcast opening and top edges between arrows. Whipstitch front to back along remaining edges.

4. Clip loops of Rug Stitch; fluff yarn with needle as desired.

5. Stitch and Overcast berries following graph. Using photo as a guide, glue to center top and to sides of wreath.

6. Tie one length of plaid ribbon in a bow; trim ends at an angle.

Glue bow to center bottom of wreath as in photo.

7. Thread one length red craft cord through top center hole of wreath front. Tie ends together in a knot to form a loop for hanging. Insert photo into opening at top.

8. Repeat steps 1–7 for remaining wreath. ✂

Berry
3 holes x 3 holes
Cut 3 for each

Wreath Front & Back
25 holes x 25 holes
Cut 2 for each
Stitch front only

Cut out for front only

COLOR KEY	
Worsted Weight Yarn	**Yards**
■ Cranberry red	36
✖ Pine green Rug Stitch	2

Fig. 1
Rug Stitch

Skill Level: Beginner

Finished Size

2¾ inches W x 3⅛ inches H

Materials

- 2 Uniek QuickShape plastic canvas hexagons
- Uniek Needloft plastic canvas yarn as listed in color key
- Caron International Christmas Glitter worsted weight yarn Article 1285 as listed in color key
- Lamé thread as listed in color key
- #16 tapestry needle

Designs by Ruby Thacker

Whether you are of Jewish heritage or not, this pair of pretty stars will add a festive touch to your winter home!

Instructions

1. Cut stars from plastic canvas hexagons according to graphs, cutting away gray areas.

2. Stitch and Overcast pieces following graphs, working silver lamé Backstitches when back-

ground stitching and Overcasting are completed.

3. For each ornament, cut a 6-inch length of silver lamé thread and thread through hole on one point of star. Tie ends together in a knot to form a loop for hanging. ✄

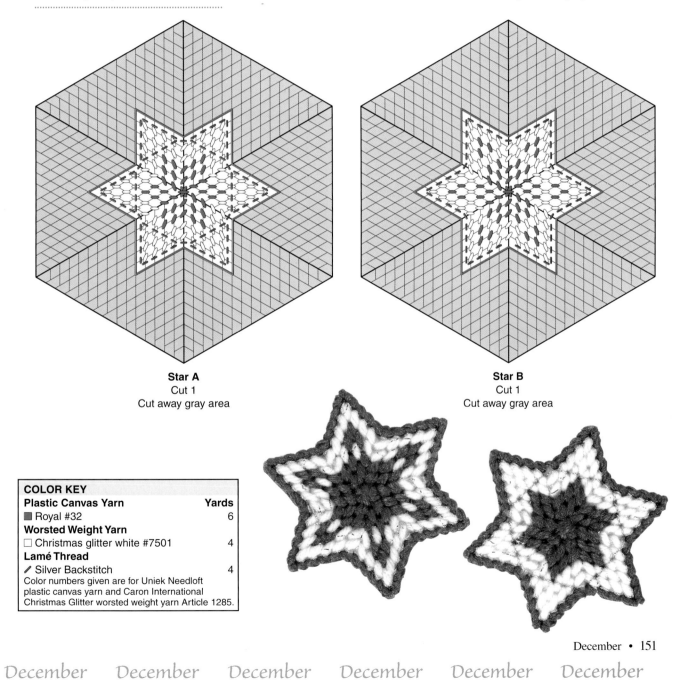

Star A
Cut 1
Cut away gray area

Star B
Cut 1
Cut away gray area

COLOR KEY

Plastic Canvas Yarn	Yards
■ Royal #32	6
Worsted Weight Yarn	
□ Christmas glitter white #7501	4
Lamé Thread	
╱ Silver Backstitch	4

Color numbers given are for Uniek Needloft plastic canvas yarn and Caron International Christmas Glitter worsted weight yarn Article 1285.

TASSELED
Treasures

Designs by Ruby Thacker

Golden beads, cord, cabochons and tassels add a rich and elegant look to this set of three classy ornaments!

Skill Level: Intermediate

Finished Sizes

Green ornament: 7¼ inches H x 4¼ inches in diameter, including tassel

Burgundy ornament: 8 inches H x 4 inches in diameter, including tassel

Blue ornament: 3 inches W x 6¾ inches H, including tassel

Materials

Each Ornament
- Uniek Needloft plastic canvas yarn as listed in color key
- Uniek Needloft solid metallic craft cord as listed in color key
- Lamé thread as listed in color key
- #16 tapestry needle
- 3-inch gold tassel

Green Ornament
- 3 Uniek QuickShape plastic canvas stars
- 4 (18mm x 13mm) oval gold cabochons
- Jewel glue

Burgundy Ornament
- ⅛ sheet Uniek QuickCount stiff 7-count plastic canvas
- 2 Uniek QuickShape plastic canvas hexagons
- 24 (5mm) round gold beads

Blue Ornament
- 2 (3-inch) Uniek QuickShape plastic canvas radial circles
- 18mm x 6mm sun pendant from The Beadery
- 16 (3mm) round gold beads

Project Note

Remove string from center of solid gold craft cord before stitching.

Green Ornament

1. Cut apart three stars along seams where indicated with arrows so there are 12 diamond-shaped segments (page 154).

2. Stitch eight diamond shapes with green and four with solid gold following graphs.

3. Using photo as a guide through step 8 and using forest for all Whipstitching through step 7, Whipstitch four green diamonds together along sides A and B, then work Backstitches with a double strand gold lamé thread. Repeat with remaining four green diamonds, so there are two sets.

4. Whipstitch sides 1 and 2 of four gold diamonds to sides C and D of one set of green diamonds.

5. Cut a 10-inch length gold cord and thread through loop on tassel; tie ends of cord together. Insert loop of cord from right side to wrong side through point of one set of green diamonds.

6. Continue by inserting loop from wrong side of remaining set up through point to right side (or outside) of remaining set. Place a drop of glue on top of tassel and pull cord up snugly.

7. Whipstitch sides 3 and 4 of gold diamonds to remaining set of green diamonds.

8. Glue gold cabochons to centers of gold diamonds.

Burgundy Ornament

1. Cut four center pieces from 7-count plastic canvas; cut apart two hexagons along seams where indicated with arrows so there are eight triangular segments (page 154).

2. Stitch triangles with burgundy; stitch middle part of center pieces with burgundy, then work solid gold stitches following Fig. 1.

3. Whipstitch sides of center pieces together with solid gold, forming a square.

4. Using photo as a guide and

using burgundy for all Whipstitching through step 7, Whipstitch four triangles together along sides A and B, then work Backstitches with a double strand gold lamé thread. Attach gold beads with gold lamé thread where indicated on graph.

5. Repeat with remaining four triangles, so there are two sets.

6. Whipstitch the square center section to sides C of one set of assembled triangles.

7. To attach tassel and hanging loop, follow steps 5 and 6 of green ornament, then Whipstitch remaining set of assembled triangles to center section.

Blue Ornament

1. Stitch circles with dark royal following graph.

2. Following Fig. 2, work gold lamé thread embroidery using a double strand. Using solid gold, work shorter Straight Stitches first, then longer Straight Stitches; work Cross Stitch over center last.

3. Attach beads where indicated using gold lamé thread.

4. Thread hanging cord of tassel through sun pendant. Cut a 12-inch length gold cord and thread through loop of tassel at top of bead; tie ends of cord together.

5. Place assembled cord, bead and tassel between wrong sides of stitched circles, making sure top of bead is next to bottom edge and loop of gold cord is extending above top edge; Whipstitch circles together with dark royal. ✂

TASSELED
Treasures

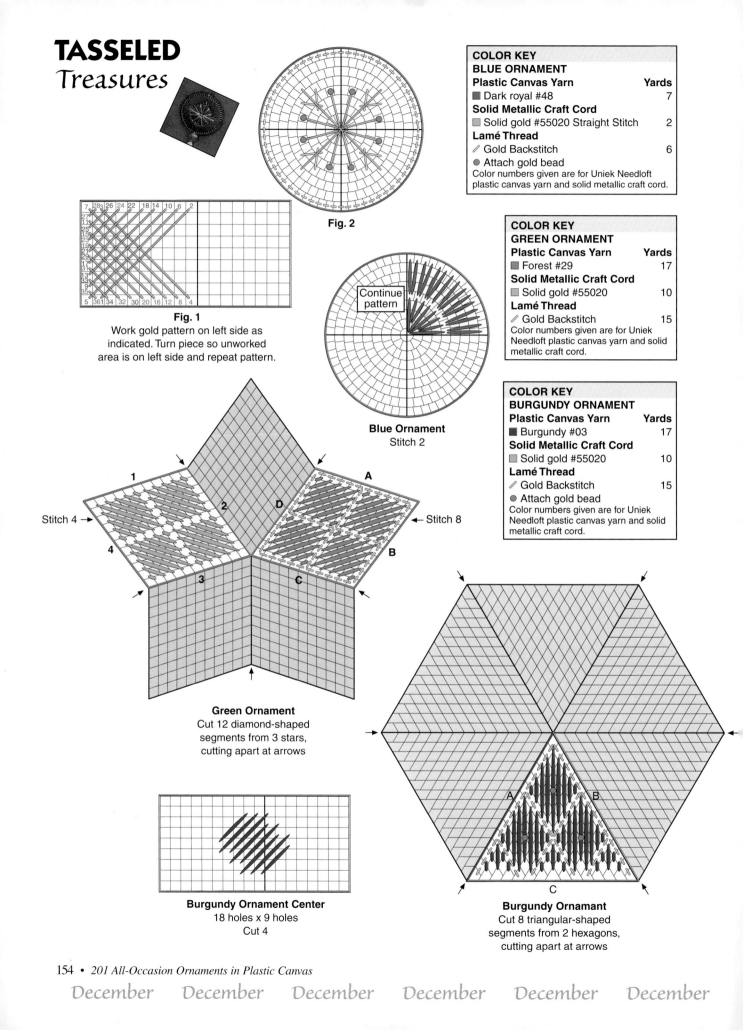

Fig. 2

Fig. 1
Work gold pattern on left side as
indicated. Turn piece so unworked
area is on left side and repeat pattern.

Continue
pattern

Blue Ornament
Stitch 2

Stitch 4 →

← Stitch 8

Green Ornament
Cut 12 diamond-shaped
segments from 3 stars,
cutting apart at arrows

Burgundy Ornament Center
18 holes x 9 holes
Cut 4

Burgundy Ornamant
Cut 8 triangular-shaped
segments from 2 hexagons,
cutting apart at arrows

December   December   December   December   December   December

Skill Level: Beginner

Finished Size

3 inches W x 2¼ inches H x 2¼ inches D

Materials

- ¼ sheet 7-count plastic canvas
- 2 (3-inch) plastic canvas radial circles
- Uniek Needloft plastic canvas yarn as listed in color key
- Uniek Needloft metallic craft cord as listed in color key
- Uniek Needloft iridescent craft cord as listed in color key
- #16 tapestry needle
- 16 (5mm) white pompoms
- Sewing needle
- Green and white sewing thread

Instructions

1. Cut plastic canvas according to graphs. Cut three outermost rows of holes from one plastic canvas radial circle for mug bottom. Cut four outermost rows of holes from remaining plastic canvas radial circle for hot chocolate.

2. Stitch mug and handle following graphs, working uncoded areas with white iridescent craft cord Continental Stitches.

3. Whipstitch short edges of mug together with white iridescent craft cord. Overcast handle and top edge of mug with gold metallic craft cord.

4. Continental Stitch and Overcast hot chocolate with brown yarn, working Cross Stitch in center of circle. Continental Stitch mug bottom with white iridescent craft cord, working Cross Stitch in center of circle.

5. Whipstitch bottom edge of mug to mug bottom with white iridescent craft cord.

6. Using sewing needle and white

HOT
Chocolate

Design by Ronda Bryce

Nothing hits the spot like a mug of hot chocolate after an hour of sled riding! Stitch this cute ornament to bring back fond memories of childhood!

sewing thread throughout, Whipstitch handle to top and bottom edges of mug at mug seam. Stitch pompoms to right side of hot chocolate.

7. Place hot chocolate in top of mug about ¼ inch from top edge. Attach to mug with sewing needle and green sewing thread.

8. Thread desired length of gold craft cord through top hole of mug near handle. Tie ends together in a knot to form a loop for hanging. ✂

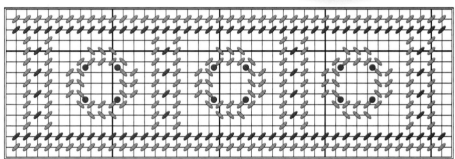

Mug
42 holes x 14 holes
Cut 1

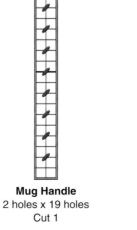

Mug Handle
2 holes x 19 holes
Cut 1

COLOR KEY

Plastic Canvas Yarn	Yards
■ Red #01	4
Brown #15	3
■ Christmas green #28	6
● Red #01 French Knot	
Metallic Craft Cord	
⁄ Gold #55001 Overcasting	3
Iridescent Craft Cord	
Uncoded areas are white #55033 Continental Stitches	9
⁄ White #55033 Whipstitching	

Color numbers given are for Uniek Needloft plastic canvas yarn, metallic craft cord, and iridescent craft cord.

LION & Lamb

Designs by Mary K. Perry

The Bible promises a time of peace on earth for both mankind and the animals. Look forward to this time with this inspiring ornament!

Skill Level: Beginner

Finished Size

4⅛ inches W x 2¾ inches H

Materials

- ¼ sheet 7-count plastic canvas
- Worsted weight yarn as listed in color key
- DMC #5 pearl cotton as listed in color key
- #16 tapestry needle

Instructions

1. Cut plastic canvas according to graphs. Instructions and graphs are for stitching three ornaments.

2. Following graphs through step 7, stitch pieces, working uncoded areas with light golden brown Continental Stitches.

3. When background stitching is completed, work Backstitches and Straight Stitches with black yarn and pearl cotton.

4. For ornament, Whipstitch wrong sides of one front and one back together around all edges.

5. Cut desired length of golden brown yarn and thread through hole indicated with blue dot on lion front graph. Tie ends together in a knot to form a loop for hanging.

6. For sitting piece, Whipstitch wrong sides of one front and one back together around sides and top, then Whipstitch base to bottom edges of front and back with green, easing around ends of base as needed.

7. For favor, Overcast bottom edges from dot to dot on remaining front and back, then Whipstitch wrong sides together along remaining edges. ✂

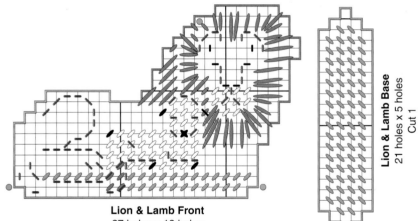

Lion & Lamb Front
27 holes x 18 holes
Cut 3

Lion & Lamb Base
21 holes x 5 holes
Cut 1

COLOR KEY	
Worsted Weight Yarn	**Yards**
■ Green	10
■ Golden brown	9
☐ White	3
■ Black	1
☐ Off-white	1
Uncoded areas are light golden brown Continental Stitches	15
╱ Light golden brown Whipstitching	
╱ Black Backstitch and Straight Stitch	
#5 Pearl Cotton	
╱ Black #310 Backstitch and Straight Stitch	5
Color number given is for DMC #5 pearl cotton.	

Lion & Lamb Back
27 holes x 18 holes
Cut 3

Designs by Joan Green

Skill Level: Beginner

Finished Sizes
Ski boot: 3 inches W x 3⅜ inches H

Cowboy boot: 3 inches W x 3¾ inches H

Materials
- ¼ sheet Uniek Needloft 7-count plastic canvas
- Coats & Clark Red Heart Classic worsted weight yarn Art. E267 as listed in color key
- ⅛-inch-wide Plastic Canvas 7 Metallic Needlepoint Yarn by Rainbow Gallery as listed in color key
- #16 tapestry needle
- Fabric glue

Instructions
1. Cut plastic canvas according to graphs.

2. Stitch and Overcast pieces following graphs, working uncoded areas on ski boot with jockey red Continental Stitches and uncoded areas on cowboy boot with warm brown Continental Stitches.

Here's a pair of ornaments sure to bring a smile to your face! If you have a family of skiers, they're sure to enjoy the ski boot ornament. Or, if you have cowboys at heart in your midst, stitch up a dozen cowboy boots in assorted colors!

3. When background stitching and Overcasting are completed, work gold Backstitches on ski boot. On cowboy boot, work French Knot with full strand jockey red and Backstitches with two plies coffee.

4. For each ornament, cut a 7-inch length of gold metallic yarn. Glue ends to top backside with fabric glue to form a loop for hanging. ✄

COLOR KEY
SKI BOOT

Worsted Weight Yarn	Yards
■ Paddy green #686	1
Uncoded areas are jockey red #902 Continental Stitches	6
╱ Jockey red #902 Overcasting	
⅛-Inch Metallic Needlepoint Yarn	
■ Gold #PM51	2
╱ Gold #PM51 Backstitch	

Color numbers given are for Coats & Clark Red Heart Classic worsted weight yarn Art. E267 and Rainbow Gallery Plastic Canvas 7 Metallic Needlepoint Yarn.

COLOR KEY
COWBOY BOOT

Worsted Weight Yarn	Yards
■ Coffee #365	3
Uncoded areas are warm brown #336 Continental Stitches	3
╱ Warm brown #336 Overcasting	
╱ Paddy green #686 Overcasting	1
╱ Jockey red #902 Overcasting	1
╱ Coffee #365 Backstitch	
● Jockey red #902 French Knot	

Color numbers given are for Coats & Clark Red Heart Classic worsted weight yarn Art. E267.

Ski Boot
19 holes x 22 holes
Cut 1

Cowboy Boot
19 holes x 24 holes
Cut 1

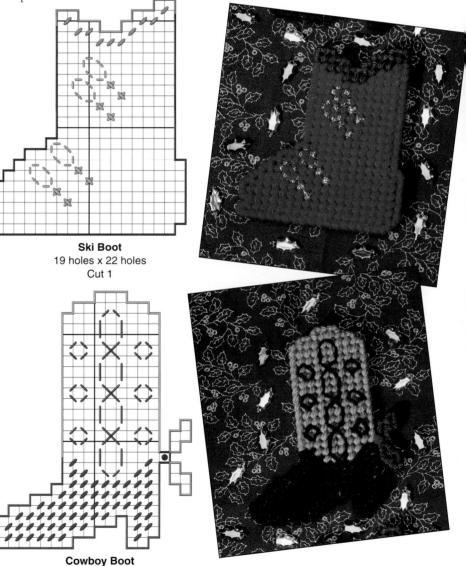

STOCKING
& Sled Accents

Designs by Lee Lindeman

A stocking filled with peppermint sticks and a heart-accented sled make a merry pair of holiday treasures!

Skill Level: Beginner

Finished Sizes

Stocking: 2½ inches W x 4 inches H x 1⅛ inch D, excluding peppermint sticks

Sled: 2 inches W x 5 inches H x 1 inch D

Stocking

Materials

- ½ sheet 7-count plastic canvas
- Coats & Clark Red Heart Classic worsted weight yarn Art. E267 as listed in color key
- #16 tapestry needle
- 6 (9mm) jingle bells
- Sewing needle and white sewing thread
- Small amount fiberfill
- 3 small rocks
- Tacky craft glue

Instructions

1. Cut plastic canvas according to graphs.

2. Stitch pieces following graphs, reversing one stocking before stitching.

3. Using white, Overcast top and bottom edges of cuffs, then Whipstitch wrong sides together along side edges.

4. Using cherry red, Overcast top edges of stocking sides. Whipstitch wrong sides together along front and back seams. Whipstitch sides to bottom.

5. Slip cuff over top of stocking until top edges are even; glue to secure. Allow to dry. Using sewing needle and white sewing thread, attach jingle bells to bottom points of cuff.

6. Glue three small rocks in base of stocking; cover with fiberfill. Fill with candy as desired.

Sled

Materials

- ½ sheet 7-count plastic canvas
- Coats & Clark Red Heart Classic worsted weight yarn Art. E267 as listed in color key
- 1/16-inch-wide Plastic Canvas 10 Metallic Needlepoint Yarn by Rainbow Gallery as listed in color key
- #16 tapestry needle
- Hot-glue gun

Instructions

1. Cut plastic canvas according to graphs.

2. Stitch top pieces following graph, working uncoded areas with tan Continental Stitches. Whipstitch wrong sides together with cherry red.

3. Stitch and Overcast sled runners, reversing one runner before stitching.

4. Glue runners to top where indicated with blue lines on graph.

5. For hanger, cut desired length of gold metallic yarn and thread through holes indicated with blue dots at top graph. Knot yarn on backside. ✂

COLOR KEY	
STOCKING	
Worsted Weight Yarn	**Yards**
□ White #1	6
■ Cherry red #912	15
Color numbers given are for Coats & Clark Red Heart Classic worsted weight yarn Art. E267.	

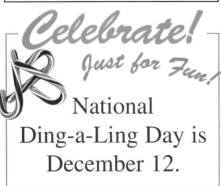

Celebrate!

Just for Fun!

National Ding-a-Ling Day is December 12.

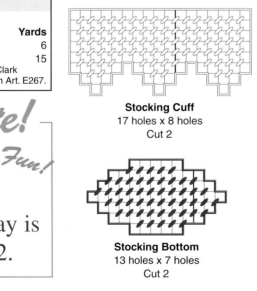

Stocking Cuff
17 holes x 8 holes
Cut 2

Stocking Bottom
13 holes x 7 holes
Cut 2

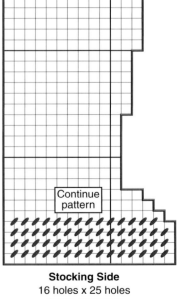

Continue pattern

Stocking Side
16 holes x 25 holes
Cut 2, reverse 1

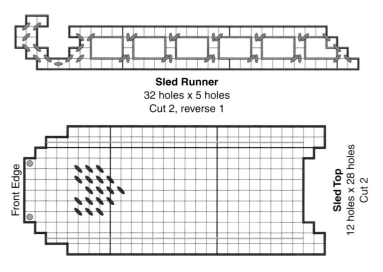

Sled Runner
32 holes x 5 holes
Cut 2, reverse 1

Front Edge

Sled Top
12 holes x 28 holes
Cut 2

COLOR KEY	
SLED	
Worsted Weight Yarn	**Yards**
■ Cherry red #912	8
Uncoded area is tan #334	
Continental Stitches	8
1/16-Inch Metallic Needlepoint Yarn	
■ Gold #PM51	5
Color numbers given are for Coats & Clark Red Heart Classic worsted weight yarn Art. E267 and Rainbow Gallery Plastic Canvas 10 Metallic Needlepoint Yarn.	

SNOW Kitties

Designs by Janelle Giese

Bundled up with their bright and colorful winter garb, this trio of kittens is ready for some winter fun and adventure!

Skill Level: Beginner

Finished Sizes

Shuffling Kitty: 4¼ inches W x 3¾ inches H

Sledding Kitty: 4¼ inches W x 3¾ inches H

Snowball Kitty: 2⅜ inches W x 4⅛ inches H

Materials

- ½ sheet 7-count plastic canvas
- Coats & Clark Red Heart Classic worsted weight yarn Art. E267 as listed in color key
- DMC #5 pearl cotton as listed in color key
- #16 tapestry needle
- 3 (½-inch) white pompoms
- 3 (¾-inch) button magnets
- Thick tacky glue

Instructions

1. Cut plastic canvas according to graphs.

2. Stitch and Overcast pieces following graphs, working uncoded areas with Continental Stitches in colors as follows: cornmeal on sledding kitty, tan on snowball kitty and silver on shuffling kitty.

3. When background stitching and Overcasting are completed, work pearl cotton embroidery, stitching over each eye and nose four times and wrapping pearl cotton around needle two times for French Knots.

4. Glue pompoms to tips of hats. Glue magnets to backsides.

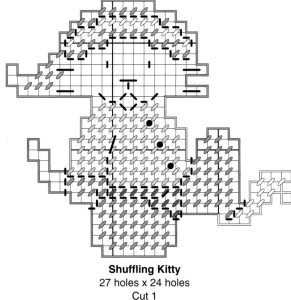

Shuffling Kitty
27 holes x 24 holes
Cut 1

Snowball Kitty
15 holes x 27 holes
Cut 1

December   December   December   December   December   December

Skill Level: Beginner

Finished Size

1¾ inches W x 2¾ inches H x 1¾ inches D

Materials

- ¼ sheet Uniek QuickCount pastel blue 7-count plastic canvas
- Uniek Needloft plastic canvas yarn as listed in color key
- Uniek Needloft metallic craft cord as listed in color key
- #16 tapestry needle
- White pony bead
- 8 inches 15 pound clear nylon cord
- Hot-glue gun

HANUKKAH
Dreidel

Design by Janna Britton

Jewish children will love this charming ornament fashioned after a favorite game!

Instructions

1. Cut plastic canvas according to graphs.

2. Stitch pieces following graphs, working uncoded areas with baby blue Continental Stitches.

3. When background stitching is completed, Straight Stitch gold metallic cord star on each side.

4. Using baby blue yarn, stitch pony bead to top where indicated on graph.

5. Using bright blue, Whipstitch sides together, then Whipstitch sides to top.

6. Thread nylon cord through pony bead. Tie ends together in a knot to form a loop for hanging. ✄

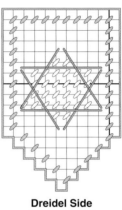

Dreidel Side
11 holes x 17 holes
Cut 4

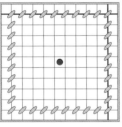

Dreidel Top
11 holes x 11 holes
Cut 1

COLOR KEY	
Plastic Canvas Yarn	**Yards**
☐ White #41	4
▨ Bright blue #60	12
Uncoded areas are baby blue #36	
Continental Stitches	10
Metallic Craft Cord	
╱ Gold #55001 Straight Stitch	4
● Attach pony bead	
Color numbers given are for Uniek Needloft plastic canvas yarn and metallic craft cord.	

COLOR KEY	
Worsted Weight Yarn	**Yards**
☐ White #1	2
▨ Yellow #230	3
▨ Emerald green #676	4
▨ Skipper blue #848	4
▨ Jockey red #902	3
Uncoded areas on sledding kitty are cornmeal #220 Continental Stitches	2
Uncoded areas on snowball kitty are tan #334 Continental Stitches	2
Uncoded areas on shuffling kitty are silver #412 Continental Stitches	2
╱ Cornmeal #220 Overcasting	
╱ Tan #334 Overcasting	
╱ Silver #412 Overcasting	
#5 Pearl Cotton	
╱ Black #310 Backstitch and Straight Stitch	7
● Black #310 French Knot	
Color numbers given are for Coats & Clark Red Heart Classic worsted weight yarn Art. E267 and DMC #5 pearl cotton.	

SNOW
Kitties

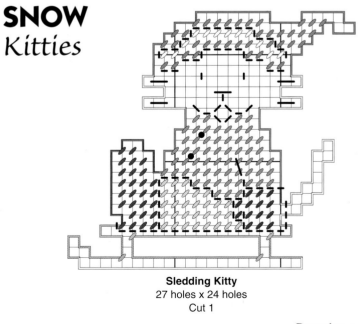

Sledding Kitty
27 holes x 24 holes
Cut 1

CHRISTMAS
Wind Chimes

Designs by Christina Laws

Hang this pair of festive wind chimes by a door or on the fireplace mantel to add a tinkling touch to your holiday season!

Skill Level: Intermediate

Finished Sizes

Snowman: 5 inches W x 5½ inches H x 2⅝ inches D

Santa: 5⅛ inches W x 5 inches H x 2½ inches D

Snowman

Materials

- 1 sheet 7-count plastic canvas
- Worsted weight yarn as listed in color key
- #16 tapestry needle
- 25mm steel split ring
- 4 (6mm) aluminum wind chimes
- Fishing line
- Hot-glue gun

Cutting & Stitching

1. Cut plastic canvas according to graphs (pages 163 and 164), cutting holes in base top only, leaving base bottom intact. Cut one 13-hole x 1-hole piece for hat brim and one 88-hole x 2-hole piece for base side.

2. Stitch hat brim with black Continental Stitches and base side with green Continental Stitches. Work uncoded base top and bottom with white Continental Stitches. Overcast hat brim with black.

3. Stitch one tree and one set of tree branches as graphed. Stitch remaining tree and remaining set of tree branches with Reverse Continental Stitches.

4. Stitch snowman front and back following graphs, working uncoded areas above yellow line on snowman front with white Continental Stitches and uncoded areas above yellow line on snowman back with white Reverse Continental Stitches.

5. When background stitching is completed, work black and orange embroidery on face and dark blue Backstitches on vest.

Assembly

1. Using photo as a guide and following graphs throughout assembly, Whipstitch wrong sides of snowman front and back together around sides and top where indicated. Bottom part of snowman will remain unstitched. Glue hat brim to snowman front between hatband and eyes.

2. Whipstitch wrong sides of tree together around sides and top where indicated. Bottom part of tree will remain unstitched.

3. For tree branches, matching edges, Whipstitch together wrong sides of one tree branch with Continental Stitches and one with Reverse Continental Stitches, leaving straight edge along one side unstitched. Repeat with remaining tree branches.

4. Whipstitch straight edges of tree branches to tree front and back down center of tree, where indicated with arrow.

5. Using white throughout, insert snowman in larger hole of base top, then Whipstitch snowman where indicated with yellow line to inside edges of base. Repeat with assembled tree, placing tree in smaller hole.

6. Using green throughout, Whipstitch short ends of base side together. Center seam along long back edge of base top, then Whipstitch together, easing around corners as necessary.

7. Using fishing line, attach four wind chimes to base bottom where indicated on graph, allowing chimes to hang approximately 1½ inches from bottom; knot on wrong side. Glue knots to secure.

8. Glue unworked bottom edges of snowman and tree to wrong side of base bottom, making sure to align edges of side and bottom. Using green, Whipstitch base bottom to side.

9. For hanger, thread desired length of fishing line through hole on arm where indicated on graph, then tie to steel ring.

Santa

Materials

- 1 sheet 7-count plastic canvas
- Worsted weight yarn as listed in color key
- #16 tapestry needle
- 25mm steel split ring
- 4 (6mm) aluminum wind chimes
- Fishing line
- Hot-glue gun

Cutting & Stitching

1. Cut plastic canvas according to graphs (pages 163 and 164), cutting holes in base top only, leaving base bottom intact. Cut one 29-hole x 2-hole piece and one 64-hole x 2-hole piece for base sides.

2. Continental Stitch base sides with red, then Whipstitch short ends together, forming one piece. Overcast mustache with white.

3. Stitch one reindeer as graphed. Reverse one reindeer and work with Reverse Continental Stitches and Reverse Slanted Gobelin Stitches.

4. Stitch Santa front and back following graphs, working uncoded areas above blue line on front with red Continental Stitches and uncoded areas above blue line on Santa back with red Reverse Continental Stitches.

5. For hands, work two peach stitches per hole for center stitches as indicated. For hair on Santa back, work two Long Stitches per hole as indicated.

6. When background stitching is completed, work red Straight Stitch on Santa front for mouth. Work black French Knots for eyes on Santa and reindeer.

Assembly

1. Using photo as a guide and following graphs throughout assembly, Whipstitch wrong sides of Santa front and back together around sides and top where indicated. Bottom part of Santa will remain unstitched. Glue mustache to Santa front.

2. Whipstitch wrong sides of reindeer together, leaving part below hooves unstitched. Straight Stitch red halter on deer, tying in a knot on back.

3. Using green throughout, insert Santa in larger hole of base top, then Whipstitch where indicated

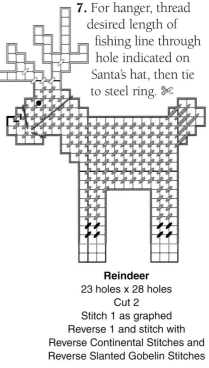

with blue line to inside edges of hole. Repeat with assembled reindeer, placing hooves in smaller holes.

4. Place longer piece of base side around front and sides of base top and shorter piece along back edge, then Whipstitch together with red, easing around corners as necessary.

5. Using fishing line, attach four wind chimes to base bottom where indicated on graph, allowing chimes to hang approximately 1½ inches from bottom; knot on wrong side. Glue knots to secure.

6. Glue unworked bottom edges of Santa and reindeer to wrong side of base bottom, making sure to align edges of side and bottom. Using red, Whipstitch base bottom to base sides.

7. For hanger, thread desired length of fishing line through hole indicated on Santa's hat, then tie to steel ring. ✂

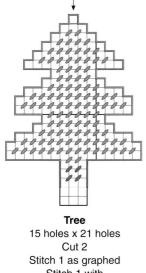

Tree
15 holes x 21 holes
Cut 2
Stitch 1 as graphed
Stitch 1 with
Reverse Continental Stitches

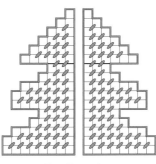

Tree Branches
8 holes x 16 holes
Cut 2 sets
Stitch 1 set as graphed
Stitch 1 set with
Reverse Continental Stitches

Reindeer
23 holes x 28 holes
Cut 2
Stitch 1 as graphed
Reverse 1 and stitch with
Reverse Continental Stitches and
Reverse Slanted Gobelin Stitches

CHRISTMAS
Wind Chimes

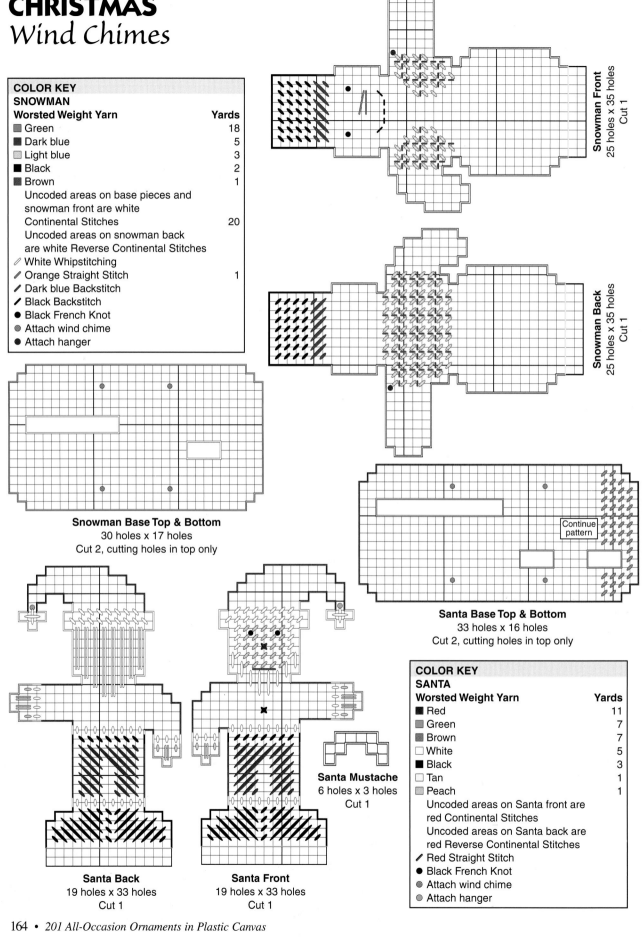

COLOR KEY
SNOWMAN

Worsted Weight Yarn	Yards
■ Green	18
■ Dark blue	5
□ Light blue	3
■ Black	2
■ Brown	1
Uncoded areas on base pieces and snowman front are white Continental Stitches	20
Uncoded areas on snowman back are white Reverse Continental Stitches	
⁄ White Whipstitching	
⁄ Orange Straight Stitch	1
⁄ Dark blue Backstitch	
⁄ Black Backstitch	
● Black French Knot	
● Attach wind chime	
● Attach hanger	

Snowman Front
25 holes x 35 holes
Cut 1

Snowman Back
25 holes x 35 holes
Cut 1

Snowman Base Top & Bottom
30 holes x 17 holes
Cut 2, cutting holes in top only

Continue pattern

Santa Base Top & Bottom
33 holes x 16 holes
Cut 2, cutting holes in top only

Santa Back
19 holes x 33 holes
Cut 1

Santa Front
19 holes x 33 holes
Cut 1

Santa Mustache
6 holes x 3 holes
Cut 1

COLOR KEY
SANTA

Worsted Weight Yarn	Yards
■ Red	11
■ Green	7
■ Brown	7
□ White	5
■ Black	3
□ Tan	1
■ Peach	1
Uncoded areas on Santa front are red Continental Stitches	
Uncoded areas on Santa back are red Reverse Continental Stitches	
⁄ Red Straight Stitch	
● Black French Knot	
● Attach wind chime	
● Attach hanger	

PONY CANDY
Cane Toppers

Designs by Amanda Putman

Delight little boys and girls with this set of colorful pony candy cane toppers! Let each child pick his or her pony's colors for extra fun!

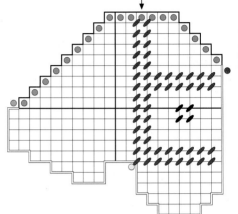

Pony Head
20 holes x 19 holes
Cut 2, reverse 1, for each ornament
Stitch 1 ornament as graphed
Stitch second ornament
reversing red and green
Stitch third ornament replacing
red with dark turquoise
and green with purple
Stitch fourth ornament replacing
red with purple and
green with dark turquoise

Skill Level: Beginner

Finished Size

4¼ inches W x 4 inches H

Materials

- 1 sheet 7-count plastic canvas
- Worsted weight yarn as listed in color key
- #16 tapestry needle
- 1 yard gold metallic cord

Instructions

1. Cut two pony heads for each topper from plastic canvas according to graph.

2. For first ornament, stitch two pony pieces following graph, reversing one head before stitch-

ing and working uncoded areas with Aran Continental Stitches.

3. Using Aran, Overcast neck edges from blue dot to yellow dot, then Whipstitch wrong sides together around front of head from yellow dot to red dot.

4. For mane, cut 38 (2½-inch) lengths green yarn. For each hole indicated, place two lengths together and attach with a Lark's Head Knot through both thicknesses; fray ends.

5. Work second ornament following steps 2–4, reversing red and green yarn.

6. Work third ornament following steps 2–4, replacing red with dark turquoise and green with purple.

7. Work fourth ornament following steps 2–4, replacing red with purple and green with dark turquoise.

8. Cut gold metallic cord into four 9-inch lengths. For each ornament, thread one length through hole indicated with arrow at top of head. Tie ends together in a knot to form a loop for hanging. ✄

SKATING
Snowmen

Designs by Janelle Giese

In your mind's eye, watch these snowmen skate and slide across a frozen pond on a clear, winter day! Use them to decorate a wreath as shown, or as gift-package ornaments!

Skill Level: Beginner

Finished Sizes

Right-Facing Snowman: 4¼ inches W x 5¼ inches H

Front-Facing Snowman: 5 inches W x 5½ inches H

Left-Facing Snowman: 5 inches W x 5⅝ inches H

Materials

- ¾ sheet Uniek Needloft 7-count plastic canvas
- Uniek Needloft plastic canvas yarn as listed in color key
- Kreinik ⅛-inch-wide Ribbon as listed in color key
- DMC #5 pearl cotton as listed in color key
- #16 tapestry needle
- 1⅓ yards 1-inch-wide dusty pale green satin ribbon
- 6 (6-inch) lengths 24-gauge florist wire
- 10-inch eucalyptus wreath
- 12 inches 24-gauge florist wire
- Needle-nose pliers
- Tacky craft glue

Instructions

1. Cut plastic canvas according to graphs.

2. Stitch pieces following graphs, working uncoded areas with white Continental Stitches. Overcast all edges except ends of scarves as indicated.

3. When background stitching and Overcasting are completed, work silver Straight Stitches on skates. Straight Stitch noses with red yarn, passing over each nose three times.

4. Work remaining embroidery with black pearl cotton, passing over diagonal eyes four times and vertical eyes six times.

5. For scarf fringe, attach 4-inch lengths of white yarn where indicated on graphs with a Lark's Head Knot. Trim fringe to ¾ inch.

6. Using photo as a guide through step 8, twist and intertwine ribbon over and under branches around front of wreath, gluing ends together where one snowman will be placed.

7. For each snowman, thread two 6-inch lengths of florist wire through back of a few stitches at top and bottom of motif, pulling wire through to midpoint.

8. Bend each length into a "U" shape and attach snowmen as desired by twisting wires onto wreath, making sure to place one snowman over ribbon seam. Secure ribbon with a few dabs of glue.

9. For hanger, bend 12-inch length of wire in half and twist together. Bend in half again and insert ends through wire frame on wreath back. Bend ends up and twist to form a secure loop. ✂

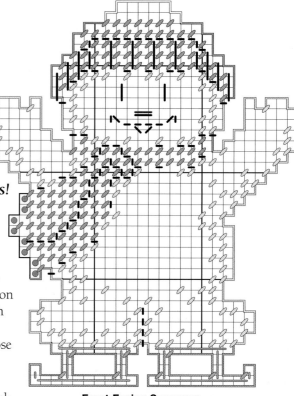

Front-Facing Snowman
29 holes x 36 holes
Cut 1

COLOR KEY	
Plastic Canvas Yarn	**Yards**
■ Red #01	4
□ Gold #17	3
□ Baby blue #36	12
■ Turquoise #54	4
Uncoded areas are white #41 Continental Stitches	17
⁄ White #41 Overcasting	
⁄ Red #01 Straight Stitch	
⅛-Inch-Wide Ribbon	
▨ Silver #001	6
⁄ Silver #001 Straight Stitch	
#5 Pearl Cotton	
⁄ Black #310 Backstitch and Straight Stitch	7
● Attach scarf fringe	
Color numbers given are for Uniek Needloft plastic canvas yarn, Kreinik ⅛-inch-wide Ribbon and DMC #5 pearl cotton.	

Left-Facing Snowman
32 holes x 37 holes
Cut 1

Right-Facing Snowman
28 holes x 34 holes
Cut 1

December   December   December   December   December   December

FRIENDLY
Faces

Designs by Lee Lindeman

Given individually or as a set, this trio of ornaments is sure to please all!

Skill Level: Intermediate

Finished Sizes
Indian: 3½ inches W x 7 inches H
Clown: 4¼ inches W x 6¾ inches H
Dog: 3½ inches W x 5 inches H

Indian

Materials
- ½ sheet 7-count plastic canvas
- Worsted weight yarn as listed in color key
- Metallic craft cord as listed in color key
- 6-strand embroidery floss as listed in color key
- #16 tapestry needle
- 2 (8mm) brown crystal eyes from Westrim Crafts
- 3-inch circle tan synthetic suede or felt
- Pinking shears
- Small amount fiberfill
- Hot-glue gun

Instructions
1. Cut plastic canvas according to graphs. For collar, trim around edges of tan synthetic suede or felt circle with pinking shears.

2. Stitch plastic canvas following graphs, working uncoded areas with black Continental Stitches.

3. When background stitching is completed, work black floss Backstitches and Straight Stitch. Work five light pink Straight Stitches for nose.

4. Following graphs, Whipstitch wrong sides of head front and back together, stuffing with fiber-fill before closing.

5. Using photo as a guide through step 8, glue eyes to face front.

6. For each braid, cut nine 14-inch lengths of black yarn. Place all nine lengths together; tie another length of black yarn around center.

7. Divide yarn into three groups of six strands and braid, making braid 3 inches long. Wrap red yarn around bottom of braid; secure end. Trim ends to measure 1 inch. Trim tails of center tie.

8. Glue one braid to each side of head front where indicated on graph. Fold collar in half; center and glue to bottom edge of Indian.

9. Thread an 8-inch length of gold craft cord through top hole of feather. Tie ends together in a knot to form a loop for hanging.

Clown

Materials
- ½ sheet 7-count plastic canvas
- Worsted weight yarn as listed in color key
- Metallic craft cord as listed in color key
- 6-strand embroidery floss as listed in color key
- #16 tapestry needle
- 2 (8mm) brown crystal eyes from Westrim Crafts
- 18mm red button
- 8mm round gold bead
- 10 inches ⅝-inch-wide dark green ribbon
- 1½-inch-long red tassel
- Small amount fiberfill
- Hot-glue gun

Instructions
1. Cut plastic canvas according to graphs.

2. Stitch pieces following graphs, working uncoded areas with white Continental Stitches.

3. When background stitching is completed, work black floss Straight Stitches on face. Fill in bronze hair area on both front and back with bronze Turkey Loop Stitches, making loops approximately ¼-inch long.

4. Using adjacent colors throughout, Whipstitch wrong sides of head front and back together, stuffing with fiberfill before closing.

5. For each ear, Whipstitch wrong sides of two ear pieces together, then Whipstitch ears to head sides where indicated on graph.

6. Using photo as a guide through step 8, glue eyes and red button for nose to face.

7. Thread bead onto hanger of tassel, then attach tassel to center bottom hole with Lark's Head Knot.

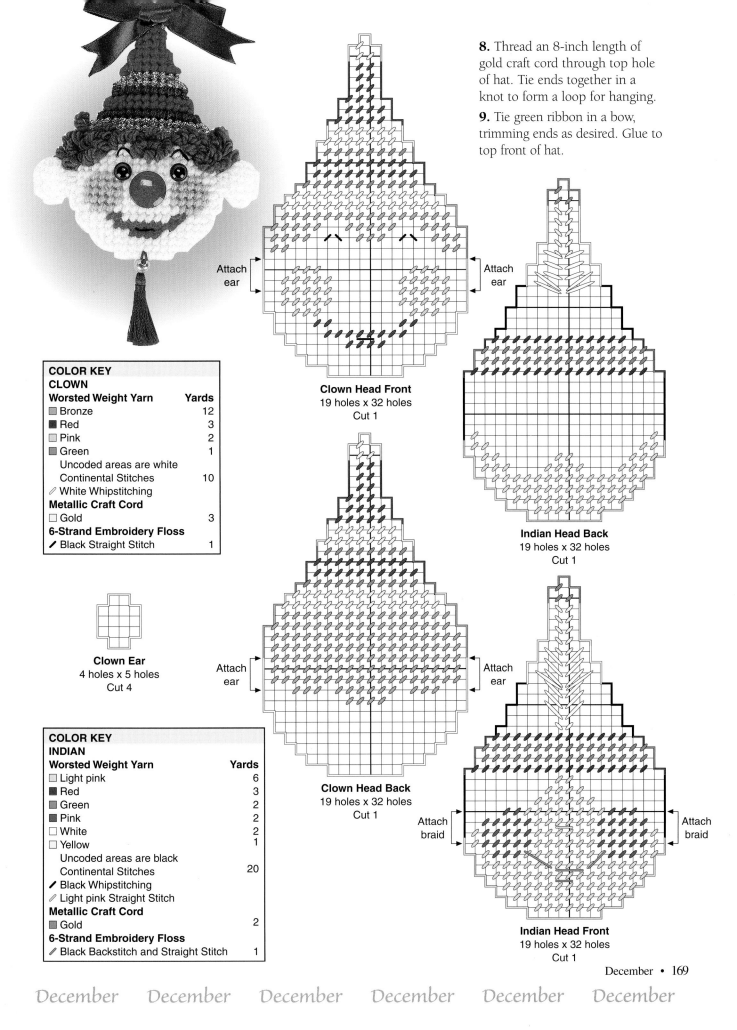

8. Thread an 8-inch length of gold craft cord through top hole of hat. Tie ends together in a knot to form a loop for hanging.

9. Tie green ribbon in a bow, trimming ends as desired. Glue to top front of hat.

Clown Head Front
19 holes x 32 holes
Cut 1

Attach ear

Attach ear

Indian Head Back
19 holes x 32 holes
Cut 1

Clown Ear
4 holes x 5 holes
Cut 4

Attach ear

Attach ear

Clown Head Back
19 holes x 32 holes
Cut 1

Attach braid

Attach braid

Indian Head Front
19 holes x 32 holes
Cut 1

COLOR KEY
CLOWN
Worsted Weight Yarn	Yards
Bronze	12
Red	3
Pink	2
Green	1
Uncoded areas are white Continental Stitches	10
White Whipstitching	
Metallic Craft Cord	
Gold	3
6-Strand Embroidery Floss	
Black Straight Stitch	1

COLOR KEY
INDIAN
Worsted Weight Yarn	Yards
Light pink	6
Red	3
Green	2
Pink	2
White	2
Yellow	1
Uncoded areas are black Continental Stitches	20
Black Whipstitching	
Light pink Straight Stitch	
Metallic Craft Cord	
Gold	2
6-Strand Embroidery Floss	
Black Backstitch and Straight Stitch	1

FRIENDLY
Faces

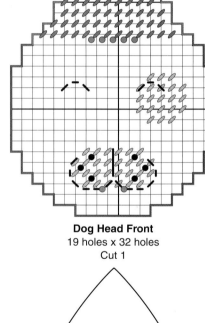

Dog

Materials

- ½ sheet 7-count plastic canvas
- Worsted weight yarn: small amount pink, 1 yard black and as listed in color key
- Metallic craft cord as listed in color key
- 6-strand embroidery floss as listed in color key
- #16 tapestry needle
- 2 (8mm) brown crystal eyes from Westrim Crafts
- ⅝-inch shiny flat black button
- Multi-colored beads in various sizes
- Small amount black Rainbow Plush felt from Kunin
- Sewing needle and lavender sewing thread
- Small amount fiberfill
- Hot-glue gun

Instructions

1. Cut plastic canvas according to graphs.

2. Cut two ears from black plush felt using pattern given.

3. Stitch plastic canvas following graphs, working uncoded areas with medium brown Continental Stitches.

4. When background stitching is completed, work black floss Backstitches, Straight Stitches and French Knots.

5. Using a double strand black yarn, make five loops approximately ½-inch long where indicated with green dots on face front. For tongue, make a short loop with pink yarn from pink dot to pink dot.

6. Using photo as a guide, attach beads to lavender hat area on front and back with sewing needle and lavender yarn.

7. Using adjacent colors, Whipstitch wrong sides of head front and back together, stuffing with fiberfill before closing.

8. Using photo as a guide, glue eyes and black button for nose to face front. Glue ears with plush side out to sides of head.

9. Thread an 8-inch length of gold craft cord through top hole of hat. Tie ends together in a knot to form a loop for hanging. ✄

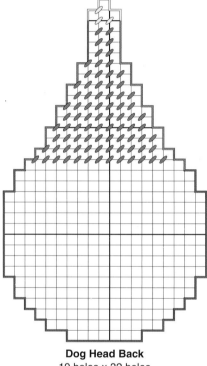

Dog Head Back
19 holes x 32 holes
Cut 1

Dog Head Front
19 holes x 32 holes
Cut 1

COLOR KEY	
DOG	
Worsted Weight Yarn	**Yards**
■ Lavender	6
▧ Tan	1½
Uncoded areas are medium brown Continental Stitches	12
╱ Medium brown Whipstitching	
Metallic Craft Cord	
☐ Gold	2
6-Strand Embroidery Floss	
╱ Black Backstitch and Straight Stitch	1
● Black French Knot	

Dog Ear
Cut 2 from
black plush felt

Skill Level: Beginner

Finished Sizes

Harp: 2½ inches W x 3⅝ inches H

Mandolin: 2¼ inches W x 4⅝ inches H

Horn: 4⅝ inches W x 2½ inches H

Materials

- ½ sheet 7-count plastic canvas
- Uniek Needloft metallic craft cord as listed in color key
- Rayon metallic RibbonFloss from Rhode Island Textile Co.: 3 yards green #144F-6 and as listed in color key
- #16 tapestry needle
- Nylon thread

Instructions

1. Cut plastic canvas according to graphs, carefully cutting away gray areas in centers of mandolin and harp, leaving bars shown for "strings."

2. Stitch pieces following graphs, working red/red Backstitches on mandolin when background stitching is completed.

3. Overcast inside and outside edges of each instrument with white/silver. Using red/red ribbon floss, Overcast approximately every other hole of outside edges on each instrument and inside edges on harp and horn.

4. Wrap red/red ribbon floss around center bars on harp and mandolin, threading ribbon floss under stitches on backside to secure.

5. For each instrument, cut three 12-inch lengths of green ribbon floss. Place the three lengths together. For mandolin and harp, thread ends from back to front

MERRY
Musical Trio

Designs by Mary T. Cosgrove

Add a touch of sparkle to your tree with this set of three metallic instruments—a harp, mandolin and horn!

through holes indicated on instrument; tie in a knot, then in a small bow.

6. For horn, wrap lengths around horn where indicated at arrow; tie in a knot in front, then in a small bow.

7. Thread desired length of nylon thread through cord or ribbon floss at top center backside of each instrument. Tie ends together in a knot to form a loop for hanging. ✂

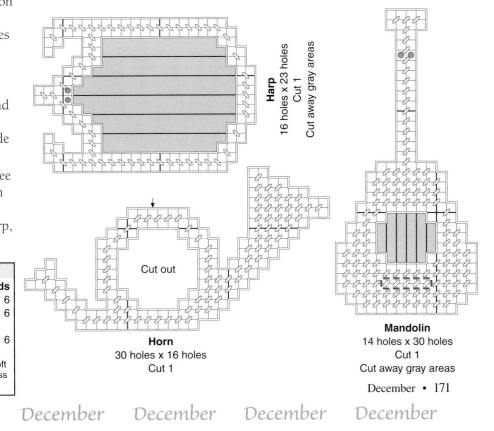

Harp
16 holes x 23 holes
Cut 1
Cut away gray areas

Horn
30 holes x 16 holes
Cut 1

Cut out

Mandolin
14 holes x 30 holes
Cut 1
Cut away gray areas

COLOR KEY	
Metallic Craft Cord	**Yards**
☐ Gold #55001	6
☐ White/silver #55008	6
Rayon Metallic Ribbon Floss	
╱ Red/red #148F-19 Backstitch	6
● Attach green ribbon floss	
Color numbers given are for Uniek Needloft metallic craft cord and metallic RibbonFloss from Rhode Island Textile Co.	

MINIATURE
Toys

Designs by Nancy Barrett

Reminiscent of antique wooden toys, this set of three ornaments including a wagon, drum and sled, is sure to add good, old-fashioned country Christmas cheer!

Skill Level: Beginner

Finished Sizes

Wagon: 2 inches W x 4¼ inches L x 3 inches H

Drum: 2 inches H x 2¼ inches in diameter

Sled: 2⅜ inches W x 4⅛ inches L x ¾ inches H

Materials

- 1 sheet 7-count plastic canvas
- Worsted weight yarn as listed in color key
- #16 tapestry needle
- 2 (2⅛-inch-long) wooden craft sticks
- Blue acrylic paing
- Clear thread
- Hot-glue gun

Instructions

1. Cut plastic canvas according to graphs. Cut two 22-hole x 7-hole pieces for wagon sides, one 10-hole x 7-hole piece each for wagon front and back and one 22-hole x 10-hole piece for wagon bottom. Wagon bottom will remain unstitched.

COLOR KEY	
Worsted Weight Yarn	**Yards**
■ Red	13
▨ Tan	4
■ Blue	3
□ Off-white	3
Uncoded area on drum side is red Continental Stitches	13
⁄ Yellow Straight Stitch	1
⁄ Forest Backstitch	½
● Red French Knot	

2. Using black throughout, Overcast wagon tongue. Stitch and Overcast wagon handle.

3. Using red throughout, Continental Stitch wagon front, back and sides. Stitch and Overcast sled runners, reversing one runner before stitching and leaving tan edge from dot to dot unworked at this time.

4. Stitch remaining pieces following graphs, overlapping drum side as indicated before stitching and working uncoded area with red Continental Stitches.

5. When background stitching is completed, work yellow Straight Stitches on drum side and forest Backstitches and red French Knots on sled top.

6. Using tan, Whipstitch sled top sides to unstitched edges on sled runners; Overcast remaining sled top edges.

7. Overcast wagon wheels with black. Using red, Whipstitch wagon front and back to wagon sides, then Whipstitch front, back and sides to unstitched bottom; Overcast top edges.

8. Using blue, Overcast drum top and top and bottom edges of drum side.

Finishing

1. Using photo as a guide through step 4, glue ends of wagon tongue to wagon bottom at front corners. Where indicated on graph, glue bottom end of handle to wagon tongue, also gluing handle to wagon front.

2. Glue wheels to wagon sides, making sure bottom edges of wheels are even.

3. Glue drum top to top edge of drum side. For drumsticks, paint tips of craft sticks blue; allow to dry.

4. Cut desired length of clear thread for each ornament. Thread one length through center top holes on wagon sides. Tie ends together in a knot to form a loop for hanging. Thread remaining lengths as desired through sled and drum; tie ends together in a knot. ✄

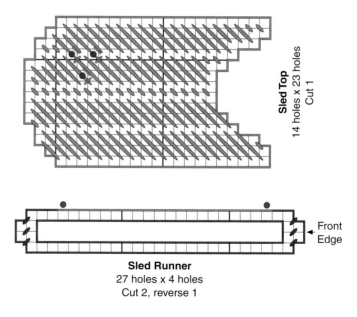

Sled Top
14 holes x 23 holes
Cut 1

Front Edge

Sled Runner
27 holes x 4 holes
Cut 2, reverse 1

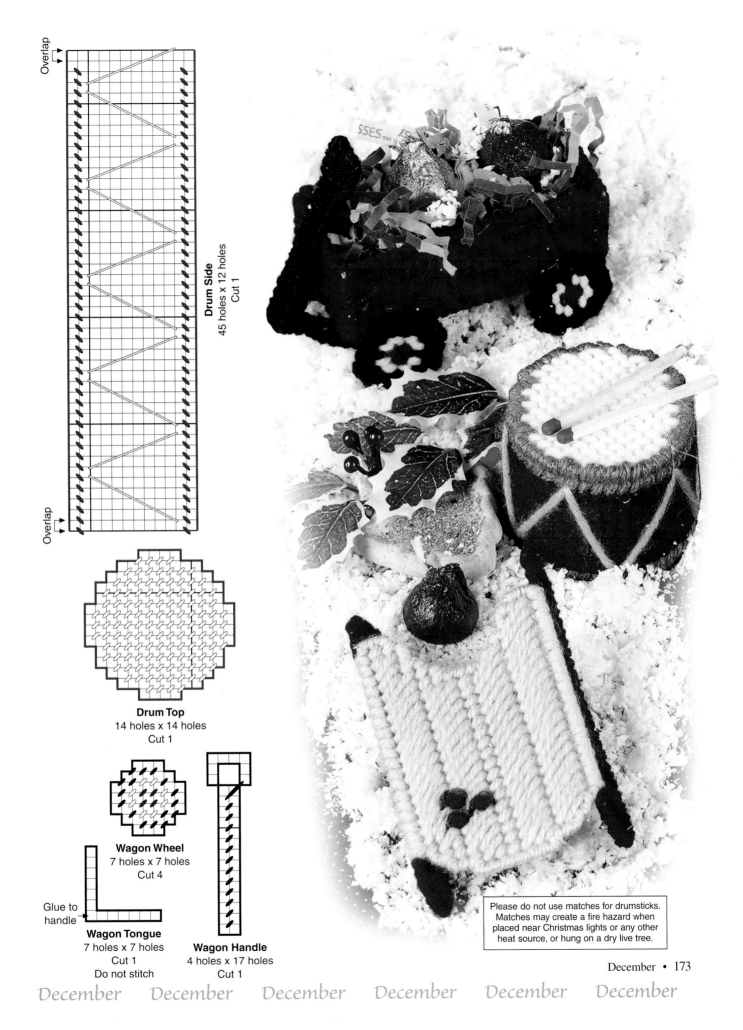

Drum Side
45 holes x 12 holes
Cut 1

Overlap

Overlap

Drum Top
14 holes x 14 holes
Cut 1

Wagon Wheel
7 holes x 7 holes
Cut 4

Glue to
handle

Wagon Tongue
7 holes x 7 holes
Cut 1
Do not stitch

Wagon Handle
4 holes x 17 holes
Cut 1

Please do not use matches for drumsticks.
Matches may create a fire hazard when
placed near Christmas lights or any other
heat source, or hung on a dry live tree.

TEDDY BEAR
Christmas Trio

Designs by Angie Arickx

Give this set of three adorable ornaments to a friend or family member who collects teddy bears! She's sure to love it!

Skill Level: Beginner

Finished Sizes

Stocking bear: 2¾ inches W x 3⅜ inches H

Candy cane bear: 3½ inches W x 3½ inches H

Wreath bear: 3⅜ inches W x 3⅜ inches H

Materials

- ½ sheet Uniek QuickCount 7-count plastic canvas
- Uniek Needloft plastic canvas yarn as listed in color key
- #16 tapestry needle
- Hot-glue gun

Instructions

1. Cut plastic canvas according to graphs.

2. Stitch and Overcast plastic canvas following graphs, working uncoded areas with maple Continental Stitches.

3. Using black, work Straight Stitches for eyes and French Knots for noses.

4. Place one holly leaf each on stocking and candy cane where indicated on graphs, then work Christmas red French Knots through both layers of canvas.

5. For hangers, cut one 8-inch length Christmas green yarn for wreath and one 8-inch length each maple yarn for stocking and candy cane. Thread lengths through holes indicated on graphs. Tie ends together in a knot to form a loop for hanging.

6. Using photo as a guide throughout, glue bow to wreath under hanger. Glue wreath bear to wreath. Glue paws to stocking cuff. ✂

Holly Leaf
8 holes x 8 holes
Cut 1 for candy cane bear
Cut 1 for stocking bear

Bear Paw
4 holes x 3 holes
Cut 2

COLOR KEY

Plastic Canvas Yarn	Yards
■ Christmas red #02	6
▨ Christmas green #28	7
▨ Beige #40	2
☐ White #41	3
Uncoded areas are maple #13 Continental Stitches	7
╱ Maple #13 Overcasting	
╱ Black #00 Straight Stitch	1
● Black #00 French Knot	
● Christmas red #02 French Knot	
○ Attach holly leaf	
○ Attach hanger	
Color numbers given are for Uniek Needloft plastic canvas yarn.	

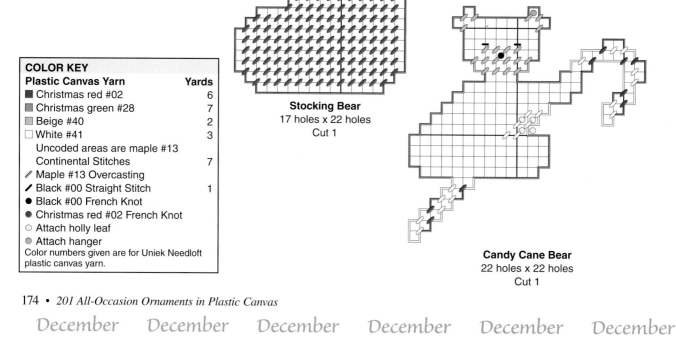

Stocking Bear
17 holes x 22 holes
Cut 1

Candy Cane Bear
22 holes x 22 holes
Cut 1

December December December December December December

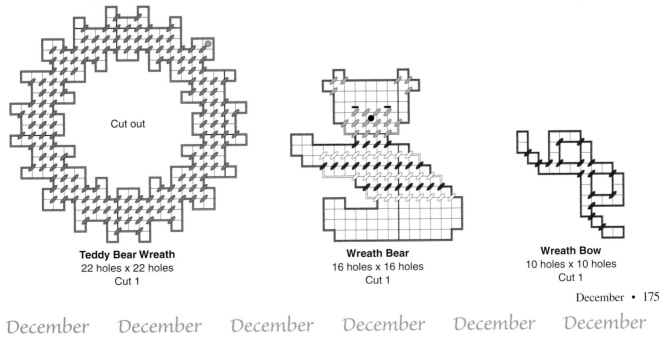

Teddy Bear Wreath
22 holes x 22 holes
Cut 1

Wreath Bear
16 holes x 16 holes
Cut 1

Wreath Bow
10 holes x 10 holes
Cut 1

December   December   December   December   December   December

DAINTY
Snowflakes

Designs by Nancy Dorman

This set of six enchanting snowflakes will add seasonal beauty to your home! Hang them in a window, on a pine wreath or on your Christmas tree.

Skill Level: Intermediate

Finished Sizes

Snowflake A: $2^3/8$ inches W x $2^3/8$ inches H

Snowflake B: $2^7/8$ inches W x $2^7/8$ inches H

Snowflake C: $2^7/8$ inches W x $2^7/8$ inches H

Snowflake D: 3 inches W x 3 inches H

Snowflake E: $3^1/4$ inches W x $3^1/4$ inches H

Snowflake F: $3^1/4$ inches W x $3^1/4$ inches H

Materials

- $^1/2$ sheet 7-count plastic canvas
- Worsted weight yarn as listed in color key
- Narrow metallic braid as listed in color key
- #16 tapestry needle
- Nylon cord

Instructions

1. Cut plastic canvas according to graphs, cutting away gray areas.

2. Backstitch and Overcast snowflakes with white following graphs.

3. When white yarn stitching is completed, work silver braid Backstitches over each white Backstitch.

4. Thread desired length of nylon cord through hole at any tip of each snowflake. Tie ends together in a knot to form a loop for hanging. ✄

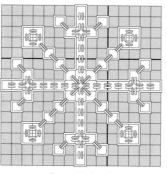

Snowflake A
15 holes x 15 holes
Cut 1
Cut away gray areas

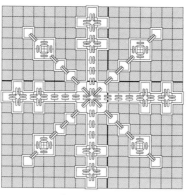

Snowflake B
17 holes x 17 holes
Cut 1
Cut away gray areas

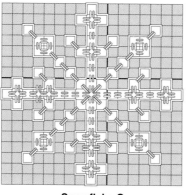

Snowflake C
17 holes x 17 holes
Cut 1
Cut away gray areas

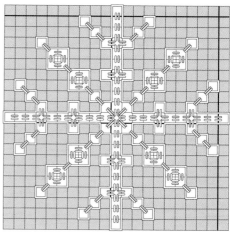

Snowflake D
19 holes x 19 holes
Cut 1
Cut away gray areas

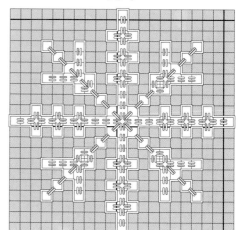

Snowflake E
21 holes x 21 holes
Cut 1
Cut away gray areas

Snowflake F
21 holes x 21 holes
Cut 1
Cut away gray areas

COLOR KEY

Worsted Weight Yarn	Yards
⁄ White Backstitch and Overcasting	48
Narrow Metallic Braid	
⁄ Silver Backstitch	18

TOUCH OF GOLD
Treasures

Designs by Lee Lindeman

Gold metallic yarn and gold wire add the perfect finishing touches to this set of three unique ornaments!

Skill Level: Beginner

Finished Sizes

Tree: $3\frac{5}{8}$ inches W x $4\frac{7}{8}$ inches H

Ball: $4\frac{1}{4}$ inches W x $4\frac{1}{4}$ inches H

Diamond: $5\frac{1}{4}$ inches W x $5\frac{1}{4}$ inches H

Materials

- 1 sheet 7-count plastic canvas
- Coats & Clark Red Heart Super Saver worsted weight yarn Art. E300 as listed in color key
- ⅛-inch-wide Plastic Canvas 7 Metallic Needlepoint Yarn by Rainbow Gallery as listed in color key
- #16 tapestry needle
- 2 yards 19-gauge gold wire
- Wire cutters
- Round-nose pliers
- Thin gold metallic cord
- Hot-glue gun

Instructions

1. Cut plastic canvas according to graphs. Instructions and graphs are for two of each Santa ornament.

2. Stitch pieces following graphs, working uncoded areas with green Continental Stitches.

3. Using patterns given and round-nose pliers through step 4, bend 19-gauge wire into one star and eight hearts; cut wire with wire cutters.

4. Shape 14 curlicues following pattern given. Make remaining eight curlicues, cutting straight ends gradually shorter to fit tree going to top.

5. Following photo, glue wire hearts to wrong side of one ball, eight curlicues to wrong side of one diamond, and star and remaining curlicues to wrong side of one tree.

6. Whipstitch wrong sides of ornaments together with gold yarn, stitching around wire.

7. Cut desired length of gold cord for each ornament. Thread one length each through holes indicated on ball and diamond and through top of wire star on tree. Tie ends of each length together in a knot to form a loop for hanging. ✂

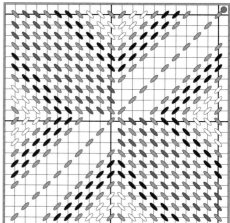

Diamond
21 holes x 21 holes
Cut 2

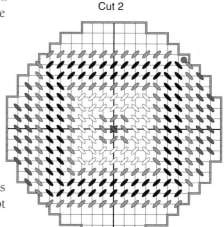

Ball
20 holes x 20 holes
Cut 2

Star
Make 1 from gold wire

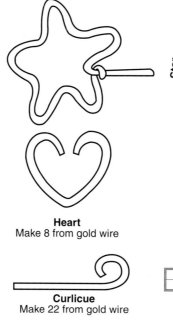

Heart
Make 8 from gold wire

Curlicue
Make 22 from gold wire

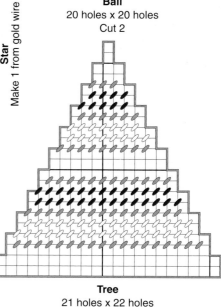

Tree
21 holes x 22 holes
Cut 2

COLOR KEY	
Worsted Weight Yarn	**Yards**
☐ White #311	16
■ Hot red #390	18
■ Grass green #687	20
Uncoded areas are grass green #687 Continental Stitches	
⅛-Inch Metallic Needlepoint Yarn	
▨ Gold #PC1	10
● Attach hanger	
Color numbers given are for Coats & Clark Red Heart Super Saver worsted weight yarn Art. E300 and Rainbow Gallery Plastic Canvas 7 Metallic Needlepoint Yarn.	

SANTA & Friends

Designs by Lee Lindeman

You'll love hanging Santa, Mrs. Claus, an elf and reindeer on your tree year after year to add hand-stitched charm!

Skill Level: Intermediate

Finished Sizes

Santa: 4 inches W x 8 inches H

Mrs. Claus: 3⅝ inches W x 7¾ inches H

Elf: 4⅜ inches W x 7¼ inches H

Reindeer: 5 inches W x 8⅝ inches H

Santa

Materials

- 1 sheet 7-count plastic canvas
- Coats & Clark Red Heart Classic worsted weight yarn Art. E267 as listed in color key
- Coats & Clark Red Heart Super Saver worsted weight yarn Art. E301 as listed in color key
- 6-strand embroidery floss as listed in color key
- #16 tapestry needle
- 2 (3mm) round black beads
- ⅜-inch white dome button
- ¾-inch x ⅜-inch silver buckle
- 1⅜-inch x ¼-inch piece black synthetic suede or felt
- Small amount white Rainbow Plush Felt from Kunin Felt
- Small amount polyester fiberfill
- 12 inches gold metallic braid
- Hot-glue gun

Cutting & Stitching

1. Cut plastic canvas according to graphs.

2. From white felt, cut one piece each for mustache, beard and collar using patterns given. Also cut two ½-inch circles for pompom and one 4-inch x ⅜-inch piece for hair from white felt. Using photo as a guide, cut a craggy-looking edge along 4-inch bottom edge of hair.

3. Working uncoded areas with cherry red Continental Stitches through step 4, stitch head front as graphed. Reverse head back and stitch hat as graphed and head area with lily pink Continental Stitches only.

4. Stitch body pieces, arms and legs following graphs, reversing two arms and two legs before stitching. Overcast top and bottom edges of body pieces.

5. When background stitching is completed, work mouth with black embroidery floss. Work lily pink French Knot for nose.

6. Attach beads for eyes with black floss. Sew white button to body front where indicated on graph.

Assembly

1. Use photo as a guide throughout assembly. Following graphs through step 2, Whipstitch wrong sides of head front and back together, stuffing with a small amount of fiberfill before closing.

2. Whipstitch body front and back together along side edges. Matching edges, Whipstitch wrong sides of two arms and two legs together. Repeat with remaining arms and legs.

3. Place neck of head in top opening of body; glue to secure. Stuff a little fiberfill into body, then glue in legs. At shoulders, glue one arm to body back on right side and one arm to body front on left side.

4. Glue pompom pieces together over tip of hat. Glue hair around head just under hat cuff, trimming craggy edges as necessary to see face. Glue mustache between nose and mouth, collar around neck and beard to head front, trimming as necessary to fit.

5. Cut a small slit in center of black synthetic suede or felt, then thread through buckle. Center and glue buckle to body front over black belt.

6. For hanger, thread gold metallic braid through hole indicated on Santa's hat. Tie ends together in a knot to form a loop for hanging.

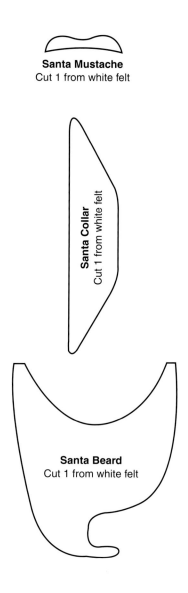

Santa Mustache
Cut 1 from white felt

Santa Collar
Cut 1 from white felt

Santa Beard
Cut 1 from white felt

SANTA & Friends

Mrs. Claus

Materials

- 1 sheet 7-count plastic canvas
- Coats & Clark Red Heart Classic worsted weight yarn Art. E267 as listed in color key
- Coats & Clark Red Heart Super Saver worsted weight yarn Art. E301 as listed in color key
- 6-strand embroidery floss as listed in color key
- #16 tapestry needle
- 2 black seed beads
- 12 inches ¼-inch-wide white satin ribbon
- 2-inch x 3½-inch piece flat white eyelet
- 10 inches ½-inch-wide white lace
- ¾-inch white pompom
- Sewing needle and white sewing thread
- Small amount white Rainbow Plush Felt from Kunin Felt
- Small amount polyester fiberfill
- 22 inches thin gold metallic cord
- Thin wire
- Needle-nose pliers
- Pencil
- Mini scallop paper edger or rotary cutter with mini scallop blade
- Fabric glue
- Hot-glue gun

Cutting & Stitching

1. Cut plastic canvas according to graphs (page 184).

2. For hair, from white felt cut one ⅜-inch x 4½-inch strip, cutting 4½-inch bottom edge with mini scallop paper edger or rotary cutter with mini scallop blade.

3. From eyelet, cut a 2½-inch-wide piece for apron skirt. Fold sides under about ¼ inch and glue in place with fabric glue. For apron top, cut a 1¼-inch-wide x ⅞-inch-long piece from eyelet, measuring length from bottom of eyelet. Fold sides under ⅛ inch and glue in place.

4. Stitch pieces following graphs, working uncoded areas with cherry red Continental Stitches and reversing two arms and two legs before stitching.

5. When background stitching is completed, work mouth with black embroidery floss. Work lily pink French Knot for nose. Attach beads for eyes with black floss.

6. Overcast top and bottom edges of body pieces.

Assembly

1. Following steps 1–3 for Santa assembly (page 180), Whipstitch and assemble Mrs. Claus, gluing arms to sides at shoulders.

2. Use photo as a guide throughout assembly. Cut white lace in half. Using sewing needle and white sewing thread, work a running stitch along top edge of each length. Gather and wrap one length around each wrist and tie in place; trim ends.

3. Using needle-nose pliers, shape wire into eyeglasses by wrapping wire around pencil to form each eyeglass. Glue to face, resting center piece on top of nose.

4. With scallops at bottom, wrap and glue hair around head along bottom of white hairline; trim excess on backside. For bun, cut a ½-inch-wide strip from white felt and tightly roll and glue until ⅜ inch in diameter. Glue to center bottom of head back over white felt hair.

5. Center apron top and skirt on body front, gluing cut edge of top under top edge of skirt.

6. For neck strap, cut needed length of white ribbon; wrap around neck and glue ends under top edge of apron top. Center and glue remaining ribbon over top of skirt; wrap around waist and tie in a bow on backside.

7. For shoe laces, cut two 5-inch lengths of gold metallic cord. Lace cord through holes on shoes where indicated on graph with yellow dots. Tie each in a bow at top of shoe.

8. For hanger, thread remaining length gold metallic cord through top center hole of cap; tie ends together in a knot along top edge. Thread looped end of cord through center of white pompom. Glue pompom to top of hat and to cord.

Elf

Materials

- 1 sheet 7-count plastic canvas
- Coats & Clark Red Heart Classic worsted weight yarn Art. E267 as listed in color key
- Coats & Clark Red Heart Super Saver worsted weight yarn Art. E301 as listed in color key
- Acrylic worsted weight yarn as listed in color key
- 6-strand embroidery floss as listed in color key
- #16 tapestry needle
- 2 (3mm) round black beads
- 5 (6mm) gold jingle bells
- 8mm round gold metallic bead
- 6 inches gold metallic yarn
- Sheet green felt
- ⅜-inch x 4½-inch piece black synthetic suede or felt
- Mini jute hair
- Sewing needle
- Medium green and medium brown sewing thread
- Small amount polyester fiberfill
- 8 inches thin gold metallic cord
- Pinking shears
- Hot-glue gun

Cutting & Stitching

1. Cut plastic canvas according to graphs (pages 184 and 185).

2. Using patterns given, cut one collar, one hat brim, two wrist cuffs and two ankle cuffs from green felt, cutting outside edges of hat brim, wrist cuffs and ankle cuffs with pinking shears and all other edges with regular scissors.

3. Stitch pieces following graphs, working uncoded areas with medium green Continental Stitches and reversing two arms and two legs before stitching.

4. Overcast top and bottom edges of body pieces.

5. When background stitching is completed, work mouth with black embroidery floss. Work lily pink French Knot for nose. Attach beads for eyes with black floss.

6. Using sewing needle and medium green sewing thread, attach jingle bells to body front where indicated on graph.

Assembly

1. Use photo as a guide throughout assembly. Whipstitch head, body, arms and legs together following steps 1 and 2 of Santa assembly (page 180).

2. Slip neck of head into collar; slip ankle cuffs down over legs to top of boots and wrist cuffs down over arms to wrists. Using sewing needle and medium brown sewing thread, attach one jingle bell to tip of each boot.

3. Assemble elf following step 3 of Santa assembly.

4. Slip hat brim over top of hat to bottom of green area; glue to secure. Glue short lengths of jute mini curls all around head under hat brim.

5. Sew gold bead to tip of hat with sewing needle and medium green sewing thread. Tie gold metallic yarn in a small bow, trimming ends to desired length; glue to collar front.

6. For hanger, thread gold metallic cord through hole indicated on hat; tie ends together in a knot to form a loop for hanging.

Reindeer

Materials

- 1 sheet 7-count plastic canvas
- Coats & Clark Red Heart Classic worsted weight yarn Art. E267 as listed in color key
- Coats & Clark Red Heart Super Saver worsted weight yarn Art. E301 as listed in color key
- 6-strand embroidery floss as listed in color key
- #16 tapestry needle
- 3 (1/4-inch) white buttons
- 2 (6mm) brown animal eyes
- 6mm round black cabochon
- 1-inch off-white or tan pompom
- 8 inches 1/8-inch-wide gold ribbon
- 2 twigs with shoots
- Small amount polyester fiberfill
- Sewing needle and tan sewing thread
- 13 inches thin gold metallic cord
- Hot-glue gun

Cutting & Stitching

1. Cut plastic canvas according to graphs (page 185).

2. Following graphs and working uncoded areas with warm brown Continental Stitches through step 3, stitch head front, body front and ear front pieces as graphed; stitch head back, body back and ear back pieces entirely with warm brown Continental Stitches.

3. Stitch remaining pieces following graphs, reversing one arm front, one arm back and two legs before stitching.

4. Overcast top and bottom edges of body front and back. Overcast head front and back between arrows on both sides of head.

5. When background stitching is completed, work mouth with black embroidery floss. Work eggshell Lark's Head Knots where indicated at top of head front. Fray edges and trim to about 1/2 inch.

6. Using sewing needle and tan sewing thread, attach buttons to body front where indicated on graph.

Assembly

1. Use photo as a guide throughout assembly. Following graphs through step 4, Whipstitch wrong sides of head front and back together along unstitched edges, stuffing with a small amount of fiberfill before closing.

2. Whipstitch wrong sides of body front and back together along side edges. For each ear, Whipstitch wrong sides of one front and one back together.

3. Matching edges, Whipstitch wrong sides of two legs together and wrong sides of one arm front and one arm back together. Repeat with remaining arms and legs.

4. Assemble reindeer following step 3 of Santa assembly (on page 180), gluing ears in openings of head and arms on backside of body at shoulders.

5. For hanger, thread gold metallic cord through top center hole of head. Tie ends together in a knot to form a loop for hanging.

6. Glue cabochon to face for nose. Glue pompom just above center bottom edge of body back.

7. Wrap gold ribbon around neck and tie in a bow. Glue twigs to head back for antlers. ✂

SANTA & Friends

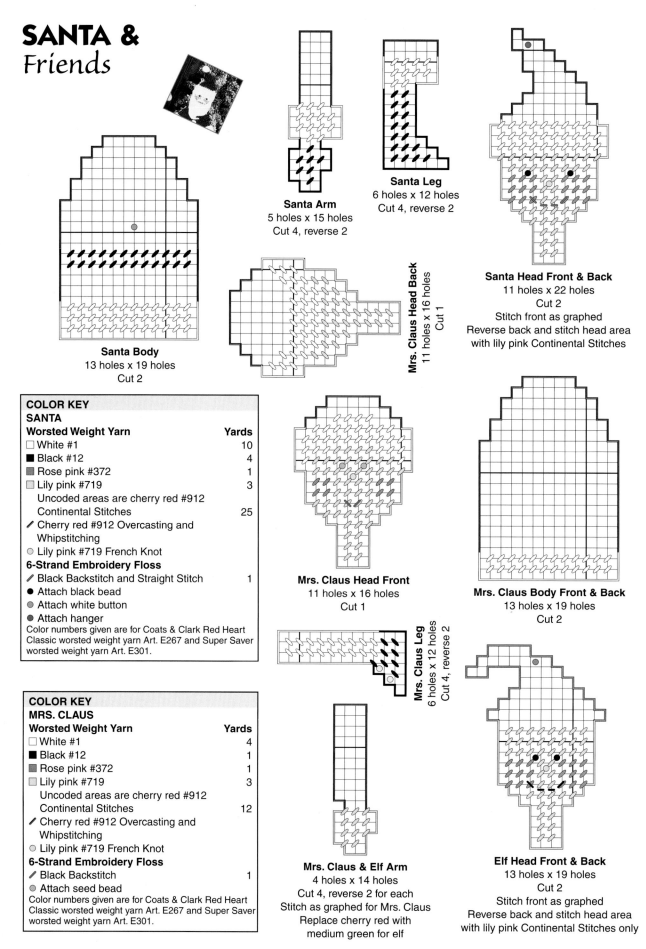

Santa Arm
5 holes x 15 holes
Cut 4, reverse 2

Santa Leg
6 holes x 12 holes
Cut 4, reverse 2

Santa Body
13 holes x 19 holes
Cut 2

Mrs. Claus Head Back
11 holes x 16 holes
Cut 1

Santa Head Front & Back
11 holes x 22 holes
Cut 2
Stitch front as graphed
Reverse back and stitch head area
with lily pink Continental Stitches

Mrs. Claus Head Front
11 holes x 16 holes
Cut 1

Mrs. Claus Body Front & Back
13 holes x 19 holes
Cut 2

Mrs. Claus Leg
6 holes x 12 holes
Cut 4, reverse 2

Mrs. Claus & Elf Arm
4 holes x 14 holes
Cut 4, reverse 2 for each
Stitch as graphed for Mrs. Claus
Replace cherry red with
medium green for elf

Elf Head Front & Back
13 holes x 19 holes
Cut 2
Stitch front as graphed
Reverse back and stitch head area
with lily pink Continental Stitches only

COLOR KEY
SANTA
Worsted Weight Yarn	Yards
□ White #1	10
■ Black #12	4
▨ Rose pink #372	1
▢ Lily pink #719	3
Uncoded areas are cherry red #912 Continental Stitches	25
⟋ Cherry red #912 Overcasting and Whipstitching	
○ Lily pink #719 French Knot	

6-Strand Embroidery Floss
⟋ Black Backstitch and Straight Stitch	1
● Attach black bead	
● Attach white button	
● Attach hanger	

Color numbers given are for Coats & Clark Red Heart Classic worsted weight yarn Art. E267 and Super Saver worsted weight yarn Art. E301.

COLOR KEY
MRS. CLAUS
Worsted Weight Yarn	Yards
□ White #1	4
■ Black #12	1
▨ Rose pink #372	1
▢ Lily pink #719	3
Uncoded areas are cherry red #912 Continental Stitches	12
⟋ Cherry red #912 Overcasting and Whipstitching	
○ Lily pink #719 French Knot	

6-Strand Embroidery Floss
⟋ Black Backstitch	1
● Attach seed bead	

Color numbers given are for Coats & Clark Red Heart Classic worsted weight yarn Art. E267 and Super Saver worsted weight yarn Art. E301.

December December December December December December December

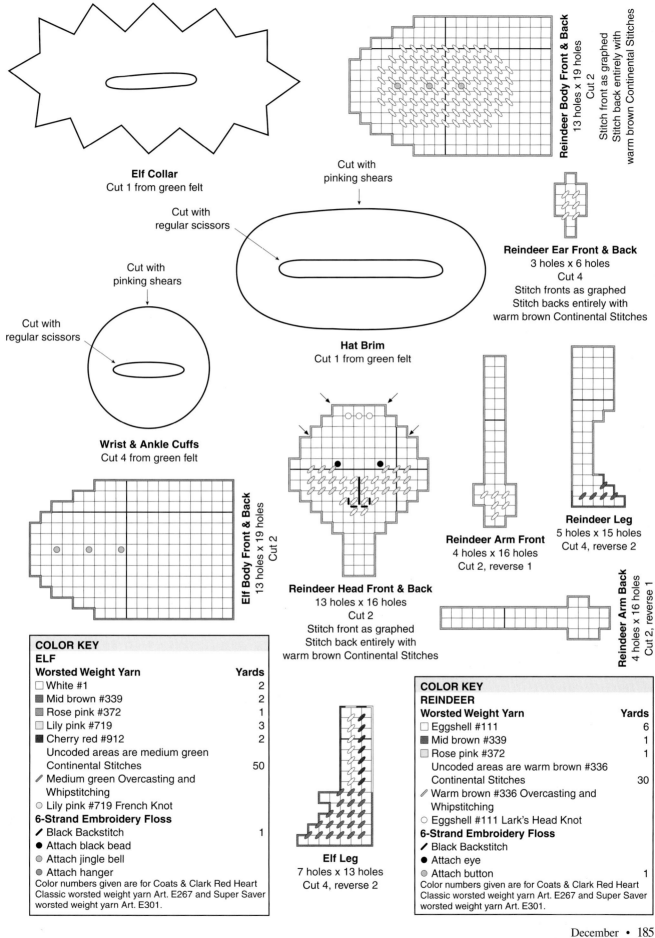

Elf Collar
Cut 1 from green felt

Cut with
pinking shears

Cut with
regular scissors

Hat Brim
Cut 1 from green felt

Cut with
pinking shears

Cut with
regular scissors

Wrist & Ankle Cuffs
Cut 4 from green felt

Reindeer Body Front & Back
13 holes x 19 holes
Cut 2
Stitch front as graphed
Stitch back entirely with
warm brown Continental Stitches

Reindeer Ear Front & Back
3 holes x 6 holes
Cut 4
Stitch fronts as graphed
Stitch backs entirely with
warm brown Continental Stitches

Elf Body Front & Back
13 holes x 19 holes
Cut 2

Reindeer Head Front & Back
13 holes x 16 holes
Cut 2
Stitch front as graphed
Stitch back entirely with
warm brown Continental Stitches

Reindeer Arm Front
4 holes x 16 holes
Cut 2, reverse 1

Reindeer Leg
5 holes x 15 holes
Cut 4, reverse 2

Reindeer Arm Back
4 holes x 16 holes
Cut 2, reverse 1

Elf Leg
7 holes x 13 holes
Cut 4, reverse 2

COLOR KEY	
ELF	
Worsted Weight Yarn	**Yards**
☐ White #1	2
☐ Mid brown #339	2
☐ Rose pink #372	1
☐ Lily pink #719	3
☐ Cherry red #912	2
Uncoded areas are medium green Continental Stitches	50
⁄ Medium green Overcasting and Whipstitching	
○ Lily pink #719 French Knot	
6-Strand Embroidery Floss	
⁄ Black Backstitch	1
● Attach black bead	
○ Attach jingle bell	
● Attach hanger	
Color numbers given are for Coats & Clark Red Heart Classic worsted weight yarn Art. E267 and Super Saver worsted weight yarn Art. E301.	

COLOR KEY	
REINDEER	
Worsted Weight Yarn	**Yards**
☐ Eggshell #111	6
☐ Mid brown #339	1
☐ Rose pink #372	1
Uncoded areas are warm brown #336 Continental Stitches	30
⁄ Warm brown #336 Overcasting and Whipstitching	
○ Eggshell #111 Lark's Head Knot	
6-Strand Embroidery Floss	
⁄ Black Backstitch	
● Attach eye	
● Attach button	1
Color numbers given are for Coats & Clark Red Heart Classic worsted weight yarn Art. E267 and Super Saver worsted weight yarn Art. E301.	

GINGERBREAD
Cottage

Design by Ronda Bryce

Stitch a cottage of fun and fantasy with this sweet ornament decorated with candy canes, gumdrops and frosting!

Skill Level: Beginner

Finished Size

5 inches W x 5 inches H

Materials

- ½ sheet 7-count plastic canvas
- Uniek Needloft plastic canvas yarn as listed in color key
- Uniek Needloft iridescent craft cord as listed in color key
- #16 tapestry needle
- 5 gumdrop Dress It Up buttons in assorted colors from Jesse James & Co.
- 3 candy cane Dress It Up buttons from Jesse James & Co.
- Green wrapped candy Dress It Up button from Jesse James & Co.
- 8 (10mm) white pompoms
- 21 (3mm) white pearl beads
- 3 (½-inch) red ribbon roses
- 8 inches ½-inch-wide white pearl trim
- Sewing needle
- White, green and red sewing thread

Instructions

1. Cut plastic canvas according to graphs. Cut four 3-hole x 7-hole pieces from plastic canvas for shutters.

2. Continental Stitch shutters with brown; Overcast with cinnamon. Stitch tree and cottage following graphs, working uncoded areas with brown Continental Stitches. Do not stitch lines on cottage highlighted with blue at this time.

3. Work red French Knot for doorknob and holly French Knots around door frame following graph.

4. Use photo as a guide through step 9. Using cinnamon, tack shutters to cottage along lines highlighted with blue. Sew tree to cottage with sewing needle and green sewing thread.

5. Using sewing needle and white sewing thread through step 7, attach pearl beads to tree and to top of windows where indicated on graphs.

6. Stitch white pearl trim to roof edges, cutting trim to fit and tacking ends to backside.

7. Sew one candy cane for chimney to backside of roof edge. Sew two pompoms to right side of roof edge in front of candy cane. Sew gumdrops and remaining candy canes and pompoms as desired to cottage on both sides of door. Center and sew green wrapped candy to cottage above shutters.

8. Using sewing needle and red sewing thread, attach one ribbon rose to door and one to Christmas tree.

9. Thread desired length of red yarn through top hole of cottage. Tie ends together in a knot to form a loop for hanging. Sew remaining ribbon rose to apex of roof. ✂

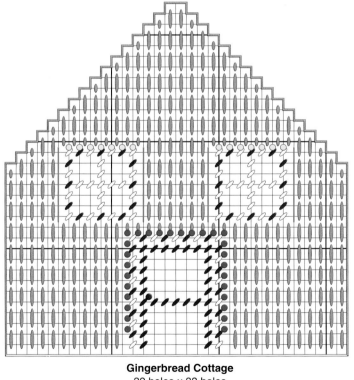

Gingerbread Cottage
32 holes x 33 holes
Cut 1

COLOR KEY

Plastic Canvas Yarn	Yards
■ Red #01	2
▨ Maple #14	7
■ Cinnamon #14	3
▨ Holly #27	5
Uncoded areas are brown #15 Continental Stitches	3
● Red #01 French Knot	
● Holly #27 French Knot	
Iridescent Craft Cord	
☐ White #55033	3
○ Attach pearl bead	

Color numbers given are for Uniek Needloft plastic canvas yarn and iridescent craft cord.

Cottage Tree
9 holes x 11 holes
Cut 1

Celebrate!
Just for Fun

National Egg Nog
Day is
Dec. 24

STITCH Guide

Use the following diagrams to expand your plastic canvas stitching skills. For each diagram, bring needle up through canvas at the red number one and go back down through the canvas at the red number two. The second stitch is numbered in green. Always bring needle up through the canvas at odd numbers and take it back down through the canvas at the even numbers.

Background Stitches

The following stitches are used for filling in large areas of canvas. The Continental Stitch is the most commonly used stitch. Other stitches, such as the Condensed Mosaic and Scotch Stitch, fill in large areas of canvas more quickly than the Continental Stitch because their stitches cover a larger area of canvas.

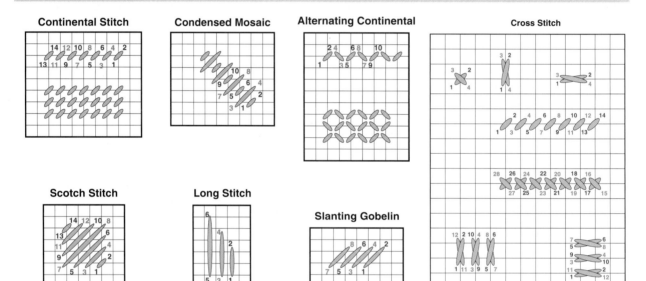

Embroidery Stitches

These stitches are worked on top of a stitched area to add detail to the project. Embroidery stitches are usually worked with one strand of yarn, several strands of pearl cotton or several strands of embroidery floss.

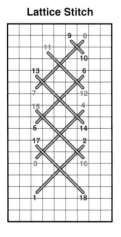

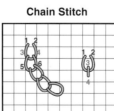

Embroidery Stitches

French Knot

Bring needle up through canvas.

Wrap yarn around needle 1 to 3 times, depending on desired size of knot; take needle back through canvas through same hole.

Lazy Daisy

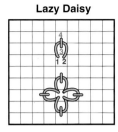

Bring yarn needle up through canvas, then back down in same hole, leaving a small loop.

Then, bring needle up inside loop; take needle back down through canvas on other side of loop.

Loop Stitch or Turkey Loop Stitch

The top diagram shows this stitch left intact. This is an effective stitch for giving a project dimensional hair. The bottom diagram demonstrates the cut loop stitch. Because each stitch is anchored, cutting it will not cause the stitches to come out. A group of cut loop stitches gives a fluffy, soft look and feel to your project.

Specialty Stitches

The following stitches can be worked either on top of a previously stitched area or directly onto the canvas. Like the embroidery stitches, these too add wonderful detail and give your stitching additional interest and texture.

Diamond Eyelet

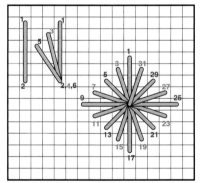

For each stitch, bring needle up at odd numbers and down through canvas at center hole.

Smyrna Cross

Satin Stitches

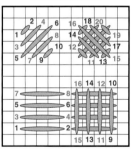

This stitch gives a "padded" look to your work.

Finishing Stitches

Overcast/Whipstitch

Overcasting and Whipstitching are used to finish the outer edges of the canvas. Overcasting is done to finish one edge at a time. Whipstitching is used to stitch two or more pieces of canvas together along on edge. For both Overcasting and Whipstitching, work one stitch in each hole along straight edges and inside corners, and two or three stitches in outside corners.

Lark's Head Knot

The Lark's Head Knot is used for a fringe edge or for attaching a hanging loop.

BUYER'S
Guide

When looking for a specific material, first check your local craft and retail stores. If you are unable to locate a product locally, contact the manufacturers listed below for the closest retail source in your area or a mail-order source.

Annie's Attic
1 Annie Ln.
Big Sandy, TX 75755
(800) 582-6643
www.anniesattic.com

The Beadery
P.O. Box 178
Hope Valley, RI 02832
(401) 539-2432

Blumenthal Lansing Co.
1929 Main St.
Lansing, IA 52151
(800) 553-4158

Bucilla
1 Oak Ridge Rd.
Humboldt Industrial Park
Hazelton, PA 18201-9764
(800) 233-3239

Caron International
Customer Service
P.O. Box 222
Washington, NC 27889
www.caron.com

Coats & Clark
Consumer Service
P.O. Box 12229
Greenville, SC 29612-0229
(800) 648-1479
www.coatsandclark.com

Creative Beginnings
P.O. Box 1330
Morro Bay, CA 93442
(800) 367-1739

Creative Crystals Co.
P.O. Box 1476
Middletown, CT 06457
(800) 578-0716
www.creativecrystals.com

Darice
Mail-order source:
Schrock's International
P.O. Box 538
Bolivar, OH 44612
(330) 874-3700

DecoArt
P.O. Box 386
Stanford, KY 40484
(800) 367-3047
www.decoart.com

Designs by Joan Green
P.O. Box 715
Oxford, OH 45056
(513) 523-0437
(Mon.–Fri., 9 a.m.–5 p.m.)

DMC Corp.
Hackensack Ave. Bldg. 10A
South Kearny, NJ 07032-4688
(800) 275-4117
www.dmc-usa.com

Duncan Enterprises
5673 E. Shields Ave.
Fresno, CA 93727
(559) 291-4444
www.duncan-enterprises.com

Elmore-Pisgah Inc.
P.O. Box 187
Spindale, NC 28160
(828) 286-3665

Fiskars Inc.
781 W. Stewart Ave.
Wausau, WI 54402-8027
(800) 950-0203

James Button and Trim
615 N. New St.
Allentown, PA 18102
(610) 435-7899

Kreinik Mfg. Co. Inc.
3106 Timanus Ln., #101
Baltimore, MD 21244-2871
(800) 537-2166

Kunin Felt Co./
Foss Mfg. Co. Inc.
P.O. Box 5000
Hampton, NH 03842-5000
(800) 292-7900
www.kuninfelt.com

Lion Brand Yarn Co.
34 W. 15th St.
New York, NY 10011
(800) 795-5466

C.M. Offray & Son Inc./
Lion Ribbon Co. Inc.
Rte. 24, Box 601
Chester, NJ 07930
(800) 551-LION
www.offray.com

One & Only Creations
P.O. Box 2730
Napa, CA 94558
(800) 262-6768

Rainbow Gallery
Mail-order source:
Designs by Joan Green
P.O. Box 715
Oxford, OH 45056
(513) 523-0437
(Mon.–Fri., 9 a.m.–5 p.m.)

Uniek
Mail-order source:
Annie's Attic
1 Annie Ln.
Big Sandy, TX 75755
(800) 582-6643
www.anniesattic.com

Westrim Crafts/
Western Trimming Corp.
9667 Canoga Ave.
P.O. Box 3879
Chatsworth, CA 91311
(818) 998-8550

SPECIAL
Thanks

We would like to acknowledge and thank the following designers whose original work has been published in this collection. We appreciate and value their creativity and dedication to designing quality plastic canvas projects!

Angie Arickx
All-American Bears, Bunny in a Basket, Little Indian Bear, Lullaby Baby Swings, Spooky Window Ornaments, Teddy Bear Christmas Trio, Wedding & Anniversary Globes

Nancy Barrett
Miniature Toys, Quick & Easy Wreaths

Vicki Blizzard
Conversation Cuties, Irish Welcome, Plaid Easter Eggs

Janna Britton
Bee Happy, Birthday Cake, Congratulations, Graduate! (Graduate), Bookworm Buddy, Boo to You!, Falling Leaves, Golden Notes, Hanukkah Dreidel, May Flowers Bouquet, Quilt Blocks, Spring Lamb, Sunny Days Kite, Tooth Fairy

Ronda Bryce
Chocolate Layer Cake, Floral Mirrors, Gingerbread Cottage, Holy Bible, Hot Chocolate, Juicy Strawberry, Rainbow Kites, School Bus, Vintage Car, Yellow Rose of Texas

Judy Collishaw
Golfing Buddies

Mary T. Cosgrove
Baby Rattle Frame, Happy Birthday Cake & Clown, Merry Musical Trio

Nancy Dorman
Cape Hatteras Lighthouse, Dainty Snowflakes, Scallop Seashells, Very Merry Bears

Kathleen J. Fischer
Button Turkey, Firecracker & Flag, Ghostly Pumpkin, Lucky Shamrock

Susan D. Fisher
Cuddly Koalas

Janelle Giese
Bears in Love, Celebration Balloons, Cherub Valentine, Christmas Friends, Count Your Blessings, Friendly Leprechaun, Friends Forever, Friendship Blooms, Happy Spring, Halloween Friends, Old World St. Nicolas, Patriotic Trio, Skating Snowmen, Snow Kitties, Summertime Sue & Bill, Thankful Sampler, Thanksgiving Friends

Joan Green
Autumn Leaves, Birthstone Heart, Boot Ornaments, Congratulations, Graduate! (Mortar Board), Grandma's Tree of Life, Nautical Trio, Rippling Flags, Shamrock Suncatcher, Star Ornaments

Kathleen Hurley
Old-World Santas, Pastel Egg Frames, Springtime Sunshine

Christina Laws
Butterfly Trio, Christmas Wind Chimes, Hearts & Flowers Frames

Lynne L. Langer
Elegant Crosses, Ski Sweater

Susan Leinberger
#1 Teacher, Bunny Buddy, First Mate Frame, Welcome Little Star

Lee Lindeman
Christmas Tree Favor, Clowning Around, Friendly Faces, Little Leprechaun, Pumpkin Minimobile, Santa & Friends, Squirrel's Harvest, Stocking & Sled Accents, Swinging Witch, Three in the Family, Touch of Gold Treasures

Alida Macor
Bluebell & Rosebud Angels, Lucky Dice

Nancy Marshall
Babes in Blankets, Balloon Trio, Fourth of July Rockets, Lattice Heart, Midnight Bat, Pumpkin Pals, Snowman With Lights, Valentine Angel

Sue Penrod
Sunflower Doorknob Ornament

Mary K. Perry
Lion & Lamb

Robin Petrina
Presents Under the Tree

Amanda Putman
Pony Candy Cane Toppers

Terry Ricioli
Teddy's Heart

Ruby Thacker
Dream Catchers, Festive Gift Packages, Hexagon Turkey, Jolly Jack-o'-Lanterns, Simple Stars, Sparkling Snowflakes, Spot & Ginger, Star Ornaments Tasseled Treasures, Touch-of-Gold Crosses

Michele Wilcox
Birds & the Bees, Fish Family, Ghost & Pumpkin, Kitty in the Window, Mini Valentine Basket

Special Thanks   Special Thanks   Special Thanks   Special Thanks